Ba...

D0446013

You Have Forgiven And Covered Up My Past Sins,

blessing me in you and changing my soul by faith and by your sacrament; yet when the confessions of these past sins are read and heard, they rouse up the heart and prevent it from sinking into the sleep of despair and saying "I cannot." Instead they encourage it to be wakeful in the love of your mercy and the sweetness of your grace. . . .

(The Confessions of St. Augustine, X, 3)

St. Augustine's *Confessions* have for fifteen centuries inspired and encouraged devoted readers. In his epic journey—at once exceptional and profoundly human—every man finds a mirror for perfection and the consolation of great hope.

In this new translation of the immortal classic, scholar, poet, and novelist Rex Warner renders faithfully Augustine's vision and with consummate skill transposes into modern, readable English all the beauty, power and drive which have made the *Confessions* a classic of Western culture.

MENTOR Books of Interest

The Confessions of St. Augustine

A NEW TRANSLATION BY

REX WARNER

A MENTOR BOOK from
NEW AMERICAN LIBRARY
TIMES MIRROR
New York and Scarborough, Ontario
The New English Library Limited, London

Contents

Introduction

IN EVERY ERA there are certain great personalities who leave their mark on the history and culture of mankind—men who personally influence the ways in which their contemporaries think, act, live, and die. Perhaps Gandhi and Schweitzer are such in the twentieth century. How long their fame and example will last, no one knows. We do know a man who lived more than fifteen hundred years ago, the Catholic bishop of a small town in North Africa, who set an inspiring example for his period and who in every subsequent century has continued to spark the fire of Christian culture and indeed of Western civilization. This man is Saint Augustine of Hippo. He has told the moving story of his early life in this classic autobiography, the *Confessions*.

This introduction will not attempt to retell his story but merely to suggest certain details of time and place which may help the reader to enjoy more fully Augustine's own account. When he wrote the *Confessions*, A.D. 397–401, Augustine had just started his career as a bishop in Hippo: we will note briefly what his life was in the ensuing thirty years. Since the *Confessions* has been read in every century after his death, we shall also sketch something of the effect that his personality and thought have had in the medieval and modern world.

Of course, the *Confessions* is more than a simple autobiography: it is a vast hymn of praise to the goodness and grace of God. What Augustine confesses is not only his own faults but also the greatness of divine providence. In this, as in all his writing, he found inspiration in the Bible. Psalm 66:6 reads, "Let the people, O God, confess to thee: let all the people give praise to thee." Commenting on this passage, Augustine says: "This song of praise is the confession of thy sins and of the power of God. To confess thy iniquity, to confess to the grace of God: accuse thyself, glorify Him." Hence the meaning of "confession" in the title is perhaps near to what we would call today a "profession" of faith. Basic to the development of his epic theme and to the structure of this work is the view of time that we find in the eleventh book. We live and think only in the present; the past is gone and the future is yet to come. But from the fleeting present we may look back in memory (*memoria*) to the past, we may directly observe (*contuitus*) our experience of the present instant, and we may look forward (*exspectatio*) to the future. (For this terminology, see also Book XII, Chapter 15.) Time, for Augustine, is not so much a physical dimension as a psychological extension of consciousness. Since all our psychic experiences, all awarenesses, are stored in memory, there is a remembrance not only of the past but of the present and even of the future.

So there are three parts in the dynamic structure of the *Confessions*. The first nine books recount the memory of his own past and of God's forbearance and assistance to a more than typical sinner. Book X is the second division; it depicts the present state of his soul; it is a bishop's examination of conscience at the time of writing these confessions. The last three books look forward to the ultimate meaning of human life in the divine plan for creation. Thus, the last part is actually a meditation on the opening verses of the Book of Genesis. On first reading, most people are immediately attracted by the frank revelations of the first part, puzzled by the intimate personal reflections of the second, and perhaps somewhat repelled by the lengthy speculations of the last section. The work merits more than one quick scanning. Eventually, one comes to see the unity in the whole: that Augustine's personal life and his tribulations and successes (for it is a success story) constitute but a minor though instructive incident in the Christian epic of mankind's life under God.

Augustine was born on November 13, A.D. 354, in Tagaste, a small town situated about fifty miles inland from the port of Hippo, which is on the northern coast of Africa. This was in the Roman province of Numidia Proconsularis. He was the son of African natives, ethnically related to the present Berbers. His parents, Monica and Patricius, owned a house and a few acres of land but were not considered wealthy. Monica was a fervent Christian, Patricius a pagan until shortly before his death in 370. There were two children younger than Augustine, a brother named Navigius and a sister who is traditionally known as Perpetua, although this name is never mentioned by Augustine. After elementary schooling in Tagaste, Augustine was sent, at about the age of ten, to study grammar and classical literature in Madaura, a nearby town. Approximately in the year 370, the young Augustine returned home to spend a year in idleness. At the end of the first and the beginning of the second book of the *Confessions* he speaks of the youthful sins of this period.

Romanianus, a wealthy Tagastan, provided the money for Augustine to go to Carthage for advanced studies in rhetoric. This was in the autumn of 370. A brilliant student, Augustine soon became a teacher in his own right, opening a grammar school in Tagaste (373–374) and then teaching rhetoric at Carthage until 383.

His mother, recognized in Catholic tradition as a saint, had doubtless given Augustine some instructions in her faith, but she refrained from having him baptized as an infant. As a youth he was simply a catechumen and not a full-fledged member of the Catholic Church. In Carthage he occasionally visited churches but he was not a practicing Catholic. For many years he lived with a girl who bore him a son, in 372, named Adeodatus. The following year Augustine became a member of the Manichaean sect, and he remained an auditor in this religion for about nine years. Carthage was a cosmopolitan seaport, where people came from all parts of the Mediterranean world. Many strange religions had found a foothold there. Augustine speaks, both in the *Confessions* and in his *City of God*, of the sometimes obscene pagan ceremonies that he witnessed there. The Manichaeans believed in two great gods: one was the source of light and goodness, the other the ruler of darkness and evil. This dualism was embroidered with a fantastic set of myths about a "first man" (sometimes confused with Christ) and the perpetual struggle between the forces of good and evil. Though the name of Christ was used with respect, Manichaeism gave evidence of its eastern origins in its borrowings from Persian Zoroastrianism. What attracted Augustine to this sect was the claim that all their beliefs could be explained and proved by reasoning. His education had not included formal courses in philosophy, but he had acquired a love of philosophical wisdom from a private reading of Cicero's *Hortensius*. During his twenties he waited impatiently for a noted Manichaean bishop, Faustus, to come to Carthage and give a philosophical explanation of his religion. When Faustus did arrive (in 383; see the account in Book V), Augustine found him an able orator but comparatively unlearned. Faustus was obviously unable to answer Augustine's questions, and, ironically, the Manichaean bishop became a pupil under Augustine. Disillusionment with Manichaeism began with this encounter.

His teaching in Carthage was also not fully satisfactory and Augustine dreamed of going to Rome, the heart of the Empire, where he looked for better students and greater success as a master of rhetoric. Eluding his widowed mother, Monica, who wished to accompany him, he sailed for Rome in the fall of 383. Illness overtook him in Rome, where he probably lived in the unhealthy marshy area about the seaport of Ostia. A kind Manichaean gave him lodging and nursed him back to health. Augustine was not a remarkable success as a teacher in Rome, partly because he was in a disturbed frame of mind. He now broke his last ties with Manichaeism and momentarily dallied in skepticism. Late in 384 he heard of an opening for a municipal instructor in rhetoric at Milan, auditioned for this post before the Roman prefect Symmachus, and won the position. Two eventful years (384–386) were spent in Milan, where he met the people who were to be instrumental in his conversion to Christianity.

Now quite a success professionally and financially, Augustine found himself providing a home in Milan for more than a dozen relatives and friends from North Africa. Monica came with Navigius; Adeodatus and his mother arrived; two country cousins, Rusticus and Lastidianus, moved in. Romanianus brought his son, Nebridius, as a pupil. Evodius and Alypius (later to become well-known bishops in Africa) joined the household. Augustine made many friends in Milan. The Catholic bishop was the famous St. Ambrose, a leader in Milanese cultural life. Augustine met him, attended some of his sermons, but was not yet ready to accept the message of Christianity. An elderly priest, Simplicianus, became a closer friend and possibly a greater personal influence. Recent research (Courcelle, O'Meara) has revealed that Milan was at this time the center for a group of devotees of Neoplatonic philosophy and that Augustine was intellectually influenced by his contacts with these scholars. How he came to understand something of the reality of immaterial beings; how this freed his mind from the limitations of materialism; how his will was turned from sensual pleasures to the love of God—these stirring phases of his conversion are described in books V to VIII. The incident (in the summer of 386), when he heard a chanting voice telling him to "take up and read" the Scriptures is but the climax of a long personal struggle.

The fall of the year 386 found Augustine ready to resign his teaching position and to begin his preparation for baptism in the Catholic Church. He retired to a country villa (Cassiciacum) with his relatives and friends and there held the discussions on philosophy and religion which provided much of the content of his first writings in dialogue form. St. Ambrose baptized him, with Adeodatus and Alypius, on the Saturday evening before Easter, 387. On their way back to Africa, Augustine and Monica were delayed in Rome. The touching account of the death of his mother, in the late spring of 387, is found in the ninth book. Archaeological discoveries at Ostia in 1946 of portions of an inscribed stone tablet have confirmed the historicity of the Roman burial of St. Monica. With this event we reach the end of Augustine's story in the *Confessions*.

Other writings of Augustine (notably the *City of God* and certain sermons and letters), combined with early chronicles and a contemporary biography by his pupil Possidius, provide rather full information on the remainder of his life. With Adeodatus, Alypius, and Euodius, he returned by way of Carthage to Tagaste. There he established a sort of lay monastery. In 391, while on a visit, he was ordained priest at Hippo (now Bône, in Algeria) and began a very active career as a cleric. Four years later he became auxiliary bishop of Hippo, succeeding to the see in 396.

His years were now filled with the activities of his diocese, with almost annual participation in the Councils of Carthage, with the writing of many books, and with polemics against various heresies. He traveled a great deal. Wherever he went, he preached. His fame and stature as a churchman extended throughout the Christian world. The first decade of the fifth century found him frequently speaking and writing in criticism of Manichaeism and Donatism. The latter was in essence an effort to set up a schismatic national church in North Africa. Donatists were quite numerous in the early part of the century. At a conference of Donatist and Catholic bishops, in 411, Augustine was the leading figure. This meeting practically brought the Donatist schism to an end. Later religious controversies in which he engaged produced numerous writings: against Pelagianism (on the role of divine grace); against Aryanism (on the doctrine of the Holy Trinity); and against a resurgent neopaganism.

Most of Augustine's important treatises appeared in the first quarter of the fifth century. We have noted that the *Confessions* was written in the years about 400. Between 400 and 416 he wrote, in fifteen books, *On the Trinity*, long recognized as the major Patristic treatise on this subject. In almost the same period (401–416), his most important Biblical work was composed, the

Literal Commentary on Genesis. Responding to a growing attack on Christianity within the Roman Empire,
Augustine began his famous *City of God* in 413 and did
not complete its twenty-two books before 426. His
numerous letters and sermons were carefully preserved
and now provide precious information about the course
of his life and thought. Four years before his death
Augustine undertook to review his many writings, in
chronological order. These *Retractations* (426) give a
solid basis for determining the dates and authenticity of
the more than 1,000 books that came from his pen.

Though he achieved much personal fame in his own
lifetime, life was never easy for Augustine. In 423 he
offered to resign his bishopric, as a result of difficulties
with a fellow bishop, Antoninus. Three years later he
was much disturbed to find that one of his priests, Janu-
arius, died a wealthy man, though he was supposed to
be living (as Augustine did) a life of poverty. In the
same year (426) Bishop Severus of Milevis died, and
there ensued a bitter quarrel as to his successor. Though
advanced in years, Augustine undertook the journey to
Milevis, settled this dispute—and it is a mark of his stature
in Christendom that his decision was accepted without
question. On returning to Hippo, Augustine named the
priest Heraclius to succeed him in the diocese of Hippo.

Meanwhile, political and military events were shaking
the Roman Empire to its foundations. Corruption and
dissension from within left Rome prey to attack from
without. The people of the Caesars were no longer able
or willing to defend their lives and institutions. In 410
Alaric and his Goths sacked the city of Rome. Later the
northern invaders swept down through Spain and ravaged
their way across North Africa. Rumor had it that the
end of the world was at hand. Then, as we do today,
people worried whether it was better to die than to live
under conquerors with foreign ideologies. Augustine was
asked by correspondents to tell them when the world
would end. He assured them (*Letters* 197–199, of A.D.
418–419) that no man knows the date of the final cata-
clysm, and he reminded them that Christians should be
ever-ready for their personal ends. By 429 Roman leaders

in Africa were vainly seeking an armistice with the Vandals. Count Boniface's army was defeated, and he took refuge in Hippo. The Vandals laid siege to the city in May of 430. The elderly bishop became ill during the rigors of this siege. He died on August 28, A.D. 430.

One cannot read the *Confessions* without feeling the living appeal of a great Christian personality. Literary figures of our day—Rebecca West, Giovanni Papini, and Louis Bertrand—have written biographies of the saintly bishop in which they quite obviously identify their own personal and religious struggles with his. Augustine's introspective analyses of his thoughts and feelings have provided much of the groundwork for later Christian psychologies. The theologians and philosophers of the Middle Ages acknowledge their debt to Augustinian wisdom. Anselm of Canterbury, Bonaventure, Thomas Aquinas, and Duns Scotus drew heavily upon Augustine's thought. Much the same could be said for the thinkers of the Renaissance, men such as Nicholas of Cusa and Erasmus. Augustine's phrase "faith seeking understanding" became the slogan of Christian intellectualism. Many twentieth-century theologians, both Protestant and Catholic, look to Augustine as an interpreter of authentic Christianity. In contemporary philosophy, theistic existentialism stemming from Kierkegaard finds some of its roots in Augustinism.

In the practical realm, Augustine's social and political views have had a varied history and impact. Doubtless Charlemagne misinterpreted the *City of God*, when he thought to find there a charter for his Holy Roman Empire. But even this erroneous interpretation had important consequences. Some readers of the *City of God* think that Augustine's views offer the only basis on which world peace might be achieved today.

Augustine is known as the father of Western monasticism. The monasteries of medieval Europe ensured the preservation of learning and classical culture through ages that had few other claims to scholarly distinction. Yet his interests were not confined to life within a monastery. Augustine's views on marriage and family life have been cited in all recent papal encyclicals on these topics.

Today is the period of a resurgent Africa. There is much discussion as to the ability of the peoples of this huge continent to assimilate Western culture and to enter fully into the life of the world community. Racist writers have claimed that people with dark skins are inferior to others. Perhaps not the least lesson that Augustine can teach us is that many of the seeds of our civilization were planted in Europe by an African native—Augustine of Hippo.

VERNON J. BOURKE

Book I

1   *Great art thou, O Lord, and greatly to be praised;*
great is thy power, and thy wisdom is infinite.
And man wants to praise you, man who is only a small
portion of what you have created and who goes about
carrying with him his own mortality, the evidence of his
own sin and evidence that *Thou resistest the proud.* Yet
still man, this small portion of creation, wants to praise
you. You stimulate him to take pleasure in praising you,
because you have made us for yourself, and our hearts are
restless until they can find peace in you. Grant me, O
Lord, to know and understand which should come first,
prayer or praise; or, indeed, whether knowledge should
precede prayer. For how can one pray to you unless one
knows you? If one does not know you, one may pray
not to you, but to something else. Or is it rather the case
that we should pray to you in order that we may come to
know you? But *how shall they call on him in whom they
have not believed? Or how shall they believe without a
preacher?* And again, *they that seek the Lord shall praise
Him;* for *they that seek shall find Him,* and they that find
Him shall praise Him. Let me seek you, Lord, by praying
to you and let me pray believing in you; since to us you
have been preached. My faith prays to you, Lord, this
faith which you gave me and with which you inspired
me through the Incarnation of your Son and through the
ministry of the Preacher.

17

2 AND HOW SHALL I pray to my God, my God and
my Lord? When I pray to Him, I call Him into
myself. And in me what place or room is there into which
my God should come? How should God come into me,
God who made heaven and earth? Can it really be so, my
Lord God? Can there be in me anything capable of containing you? Can heaven and earth contain you, heaven
and earth which you made and in which you made me?
Or, since nothing in existence could exist without you,
does it therefore follow that everything that exists must
contain you? I too exist. Why then do I ask you to enter
into me? For unless you were in me, I could not exist.
For after all I am not in Hell—and yet you are there too.
For *if I go down into Hell, Thou art there*. I could not
exist therefore, my God, were it not for your existence
in me. Or would it be truer to say that I could not exist
unless I existed in you, *of whom are all things, by whom
are all things, in whom are all things?* So it is, Lord, so
it is. How can I call you when I am already in you? Or
where can you come from to enter into me? Can I find
a place outside heaven and earth so that there my God
may come to me? My God who has said: *I fill the heaven
and I fill the earth.*

3 YOU FILL the heaven and the earth. Do they therefore contain you? Or after you have filled them,
is there still something of you left over, since they are
unable to contain you? If so, when heaven and earth are
filled with you, into what do you pour that surplus of
yourself which remains over? Or is it not rather the case
that you have no need to be contained by anything? You
yourself contain all things and it is by containing things
that you fill them. For those vessels which are full of you
do not, as it were, keep you in a fixed condition; since, if
they were broken, you would not be dispersed. And when
you are poured out over us, it is not you who are brought
low but us who are raised up, not you who are scattered
but us who are brought together. You who fill everything
are wholly present in everything which you fill. Or can
we say that, because all things together are unable to

contain you wholly, therefore each thing contains only a part of you? Does every thing contain the same part? Or are there different parts for different things in accordance with the varying sizes of the things? That would mean that some parts of you could be greater and some smaller than others. Shall we not rather say this: everywhere you are present in your entirety, and no single thing can contain you in your entirety?

4   WHAT, THEN, is my God? What, I ask, except the Lord *God? For who is Lord but the Lord? Or who is God save our God?* O highest and best, most powerful, most all-powerful, most merciful and most just, most deeply hidden and most nearly present, most beautiful and most strong, constant yet incomprehensible, changeless, yet changing all things, never new, never old, making all things new; *bringing the proud to decay and they know it not;* always acting and always at rest, still gathering yet never wanting; upholding, filling and protecting, creating, nourishing and bringing to perfection; seeking, although in need of nothing. You love, but with no storm of passion; you are jealous, but with no anxious fear; you repent, but do not grieve; in your anger calm; you change your works, but never change your plan; you take back what you find and yet have never lost; never in need, you are yet glad of gain; never greedy, yet still demanding profit on your loans; to be paid in excess, so that you may be the debtor, and yet who has anything which is not yours? You pay back debts which you never owed and cancel debts without losing anything. And in all this what have I said, my God, my Life, my holy sweetness? What does any man succeed in saying when he attempts to speak of you? Yet woe to those who do not speak of you at all, when those who speak most say nothing.

5   OH THAT I might find my rest and peace in you! Oh, that you would come into my heart and so inebriate it that I would forget my own evils and embrace

my one and only good, which is you! What are you to
me? Have mercy on me that I may speak. What am I to
you, that you should demand to be loved by me? That
you should be angry with me, if I fail to love you, and
should threaten me with the utmost misery? And not
to love you, is not this in itself misery enough? Oh, in
the name of all your mercies, O Lord my God, tell me
what you are to me! *Say unto my soul; I am thy salvation.* Speak so that I can hear. See, Lord, the ears of my
heart are in front of you. Open them and *say unto my
soul: I am thy salvation.* At these words I shall run and I
shall take hold of you. Do not hide your face from me.
Let me die, lest I should die indeed; only let me see your
face.

My soul's house is narrow for you to enter; will you
not make it broader? It is in a state of collapse; will you
not rebuild it? It contains things which must offend your
eyes; this I know and I admit. But who will make it clean?
To whom, except you, shall I cry: *Lord, cleanse me from
my secret faults, and spare Thy servant from the power
of the enemy. I believe, and therefore do I speak.* Lord,
you know this. *Have I not confessed against myself my
transgressions unto Thee, and Thou, O God, has forgiven
the iniquity of my heart? I contend not in judgment with
Thee,* for you are Truth. And I will not deceive myself:
lest my iniquity lie unto itself. Therefore I do not contend
in judgment with you; *for if Thou should'st mark what is
done amiss, O Lord, Lord, who shall abide it?*

6   YET NEVERTHELESS allow me to speak in front of
your mercy. I am only dust and ashes, but allow
me to speak, since, see, it is to your mercy that I am
speaking and not to man, my mocker. You too may smile
at me, but you will turn and have compassion on me. For
what do I want to say, O Lord, except that I do not know
where I came from into this mortal life or (should I say?)
into this vital death. Then it was the comforts of your
mercy which upheld me, as I have heard from the parents
of my flesh, from where and in whom you fashioned me
in time; for I myself do not remember. I was welcomed

then with the comfort of woman's milk; but neither my mother nor my nurses filled their own breasts with milk; it was you who, through them, gave me the food of my infancy, according to your own ordinance and according to the way in which your riches are spread throughout the length and depth of things. You also granted me not to desire more than you supplied; and on those who suckled me you bestowed a desire to give to me what you gave to them. Their feelings were so ordered that they wanted to give me something of that abundance which they received from you. For the good that I got from them was good for them—not that this good came to me from them, but rather it came to me by means of them. Since in truth all good things, God, come from you, and *from my God is all my health*. This I came to know later, when you were crying out to me by means of all those senses and faculties, internal and external, which you bestow on us. Then all I knew was how to suck, to be content with bodily pleasure, and to be discontented with bodily pain; that was all.

Afterward I began to smile; first when I was asleep and later when awake. So, at least, I have been told and I can easily believe it, since we see the same thing in other babies. I cannot of course remember what happened in my own case. And now little by little I began to become conscious of where I was, and I wanted to express my desires to those who could satisfy them; but this was impossible, since my desires were inside me and those to whom I wished to express them were outside and could not by any sense perception of their own enter into my spirit. And so I used to jerk my limbs about and make various noises by way of indicating what I wanted, using the limited forms of communication which were within my capacity and which, indeed, were not very like the real thing. And when people did not do what I wanted, either because I could not make myself understood or because what I wanted was bad for me, then I would become angry with my elders for not being subservient to me, and with responsible people for not acting as though they were my slaves; and I would avenge myself on them by bursting into tears. This, I have learned, is what babies are like, so far as I have been able to observe them; and they in their ignorance have shown me that I myself was like this better than my nurses who knew that I was.

And now my infancy has been long dead, while I still live. But you, O Lord, who are always alive and in whom nothing dies—since before the beginning of the worlds, before anything that can be called "before," you are and are God and Lord of all that you have created; and in you stand the causes of all things that are unstable; in you remain the unchanging sources of all that changes; in you live the eternal reasons of all that is temporal and will not submit to reason—answer my prayer, God, and tell me, pitiable as I am, be pitiful to me and tell me this: did I have another period of life, which died and was succeeded by my infancy? Was this the period which I spent inside my mother's womb? I have heard something of this too, and of course have seen women who were pregnant. And what about the time even before then, O God, my sweetness? Was I anywhere, or anybody? For I have no one to tell me this. My father and mother could not tell me, nor could the experience of others or my own memory. Or do you smile at me for asking such questions? Is it your will that I should simply praise you and acknowledge you for what I do know? Indeed I acknowledge you, Lord of heaven and earth, and I give praise to you for my first beginnings and for that infancy of mine which I do not remember, for on this subject you have granted man to guess from others about himself and to believe many things about himself merely on the evidence of weak women. So even then I had life and being, and by the end of my infancy I was already trying to find signs by which I could make my feelings intelligible to others. From what source, O Lord, except from you could such a living creature come into existence? Can anyone design his own creation? Or can there be tapped elsewhere any other vein or source from which life and being can stream into us, except from you, Lord, in whom life and being are not two different things, since for you it is one and the same thing fully to be and fully to live? *For Thou art most high and art not changed*, and this Today does not come to an end in you; and yet it does come to an end in you, since all times are in you; for they would have no way of succeeding each other, if they were not all contained in you. And since *Thy years do not fail*, your years are Today. And how many of our years and of our fathers' years have passed through this Today of yours, receiving from it the pattern and form of the existence which they had; and more still will pass through it, also receiving their pattern and degree of existence. But *Thou art still the same*, and all things of tomorrow and after tomorrow, all things of yesterday and before yesterday, you will accomplish today and you have accomplished today. What does it matter to me if someone finds this incomprehensible? I should like him too to rejoice as he says: "What does this mean?" Yes; this is the way I should like him to rejoice, preferring to find you in his uncertainty rather than in his certainty to miss you.

7   Hear me, God. Alas for man's sin. So says man and you pity him; for you made him, but you did not make sin in him. Who can recall to me the sin I did in my infancy? *For in thy sight no one is clean of sin, not even the infant whose life is but one day upon earth.* Who can recall those sins to me? Surely this is done by every little child I see, since in him I can see what I do not remember in myself. What, then, was my sin? Was it that I cried for more as I hung upon the breast? If I were to do this now (not, of course, crying for the breast but for the sort of food which is suitable to me at my age), I should very rightly be laughed at and blamed. Even in my infancy, therefore, I was doing something that deserved blame, but because I could not understand anyone who blamed me, custom and reason did not allow me to be blamed. For as we grow up we root out and get rid of such childish ways, and certainly I have never seen anyone knowingly throw away what is good when he is clearing his ground. But can we say that, just for the time being, even such things as these were good: to at-

tempt by crying to get what would do one harm if it was given? To get into a bad temper when people who are responsible and who are one's elders do not do exactly as one wants? To get angry even with one's own parents? And with many others too who were wiser than oneself, when they failed to give in to one's least whim? To strike out and do one's best to hurt when one's commands which, if they had been obeyed would have done one harm, were not obeyed? It is clear, indeed, that infants are harmless because of physical weakness, not because of any innocence of mind. I myself have seen and known a baby who was envious; it could not yet speak, but it turned pale and looked bitterly at another baby sharing its milk. All this is well known, and mothers and nurses say that they have various ways and means of dealing satisfactorily with these things. But can one really describe as "innocence" the conduct of one who, when there is a fountain of milk flowing richly and abundantly, will not allow another child to have his share of it, even though this other child is in the greatest need and indeed at this stage depends entirely on this nourishment to keep alive? As it is we put up kindly enough with this behavior, not because there is nothing wrong with it or nothing much wrong, but because it will disappear as the child grows older. This can be proved by the fact that these same faults, if found in an older person, are considered quite intolerable.

You, therefore, my Lord God, who gave me when an infant life and a body which, as we see, you have equipped with senses, fitted with limbs, adorned with its due proportion and, for its general good and safety, have implanted in it all the impulses of a living creature—you command me to praise you in these things, *to confess to Thee and to sing unto Thy name, O Thou most Highest.* For you are God, Almighty and good, even if you had done nothing else but only this, which no one else could do except you, the one alone from whom is every manner of form, you, most beautiful, the creator of beauty in all things, you who by your law lay down for all things the rule.

So then, Lord, as to this period of my life, which I

cannot remember having lived, which I take on the word
of others, and which, however reliable the evidence may
be, is still a matter of conjecture from the behavior of
other infants, I am reluctant to count it as part of this
present life of mine which I live in the world; for, so far
as the darkness of forgetfulness is concerned, it is just
the same as the period of life which I spent in my
mother's womb. But if *I was shapen in iniquity, and in sin
did my mother conceive me,* where I beseech you, my
God, where Lord, or when was I, your servant, ever
innocent? But, see, I will pass over that time; for what
have I to do now with it, considering that there is not a
trace of it that I can recall?

8   EVIDENTLY I grew out of this state of infancy and
reached boyhood. Or should I say that boyhood
grew in me, replacing infancy? For infancy did not go
away. Where could it have gone to? Nevertheless it was
no longer my state. For I was no longer an infant, incapable of speech; I was now a speaking boy. This I can
remember, and since then I have observed how I learned
to speak. It was not that my elders provided me with
words by some set method of teaching, as they did later
on when it came to learning my lessons. No, I learned to
speak myself by the use of that mind which you, God,
gave me. By making all sorts of cries and noises, all sorts
of movements of my limbs, I desired to express my inner
feelings, so that people would do what I wanted; but I was
incapable of expressing everything I desired to express
and I was incapable of making everyone understand. Then
I turned things over in my memory. When other people
gave a particular name to some object and, as they spoke,
turned toward this object, I saw and grasped the fact that
the sound they uttered was the name given by them to the
object which they wished to indicate. That they meant
this object and no other one was clear from the movements of their bodies, a kind of universal language, expressed by the face, the direction of the eye, gestures of
the limbs and tones of the voice, all indicating the state
of feeling in the mind as it seeks, enjoys, rejects, or avoids

various objects. So, by constantly hearing words placed in their proper order in various sentences, I gradually acquired the knowledge of what they meant. Then, having broken in my mouth to the pronunciation of these signs, I was at last able to use them to say what I wanted to say. So I was able to share with those about me in this language for the communication of our desires; and in this way I launched out further into the stormy intercourse of human life, though still dependent on the authority of my parents and subject to the commands of my elders.

9   O GOD, MY GOD, what misery did I experience in my boyhood, and how foolish I was made to look! I was told that, at my age, the proper thing to do was to pay due attention to those who taught me how to get on in the world, and to excel in the kind of literary and rhetorical learning which would provide me with a reputation among men and with deceitful riches. I was then sent to school to become learned, though I, poor boy, had no idea of what was the use of learning. Nevertheless if I failed to work hard at my studies, I was beaten. This kind of discipline was considered very good by our ancestors, and many people before us, who had gone through this way of life, had already organized wearisome courses of study along which we were compelled to go; the trouble was multiplied and so was the sorrow upon the sons of Adam.

But we saw, God, how men prayed to you and, with our limited capacities, we formed an impression of you as of someone great, who was able, even when not present to our senses, to hear us and to help us. For when still a boy I began to call upon you, my Help and my Refuge, and in praying to you I broke through the knots of language; I was small, but it was with no small earnestness that I prayed to you that I should not be beaten at school. And when you did not answer my prayer (thus not encouraging my foolishness), the beatings I had, which were then the great misery of my days, became subjects for merriment among my elders and even among my parents who, of course, wished me no evil at all.

When I think, Lord, of how our parents used to laugh at the torments with which we boys were afflicted by our masters, I wonder whether anyone exists with so great a spirit, with so deep and fast an affection for you (for the same result can be produced by a kind of stupidity) —can there be anyone, I say, so devoutly and closely united to you in feeling who can look at the racks and hooks and different forms of torture, in terror of which people pray to you all over the world that they may be spared the anguish, and can consider these things so unimportant that he can just be amused by those who are so keenly terrified of them, as our parents were by us in our schooldays? For we were just as frightened of our torments and prayed just as earnestly that we might escape them. Yet still we sinned by doing less than was demanded of us in writing or reading or studying literature. It was not, Lord, that we were deficient in memory or intelligence: you were pleased to grant us, considering our age, enough of these. But what we liked to do was to play, and for this we were punished by those who were themselves behaving in just the same way. But the amusements of older people are called "business," and when children indulge in their own amusements, these older people punish them for it. And no one is sorry for the children; no one is sorry for the older people; no one is sorry for both of them. I doubt whether any good judge of things would say that it was a good thing for me, as a boy, to be beaten for playing some ball game simply on the grounds that by playing this game I was impeded in my studies, the point of which was that I should be able to perform, when I grew older, in some game more unbecoming still. For this was the behavior of the teacher who beat me. If he was defeated on some trifling point of argument by another schoolmaster, he was far more bitter and more tortured by envy than I was if I was defeated in a game of ball by one of my playfellows.

10   AND YET I sinned, my Lord God, you who are the controller and creator of all things in nature, though of sins only the controller. I sinned in acting con-

trary to the commands of my parents and of those school-masters. For whatever purpose these preceptors of mine may have had in mind when they wanted me to learn, I could still afterward have made good use of this learning. For I was not disobedient because I was making some better choice, but only because I loved playing; I loved feeling proud when I won and I loved having my ears tickled by false stories, so that they might itch all the more. The same or an even greater curiosity sparkled in my eyes, when I looked at the shows and the games of my elders. And those who organize and pay for these games are so very greatly honored and admired for it that nearly all the spectators would wish their own little children to be like them, which does not prevent them being quite pleased to have their children beaten if, by spectacles of this sort, they are kept away from those studies which, so the parents hope, will result in their being able to produce such spectacles themselves someday. Look mercifully, Lord, on these things, and deliver us who now call upon you. Deliver also those who do not yet call upon you, so that they may call upon you and you may deliver them.

11 WHILE I WAS still a boy, then, I had heard of an eternal life promised us through the humility of our Lord God stooping to our pride. My mother had great hope in you, O God, and as soon as I came out of her womb I was marked with the sign of the Lord's cross and was salted with His salt. You saw, Lord, how, when I was still a boy, I was suddenly taken ill with a pain in the stomach and seemed likely to die. You saw, my God, since you were already my Keeper, with what deep emo-tion and with what faith I turned to the goodness of my mother and of your church, the mother of us all, and begged for the baptism of your Christ, my God and Lord. And the mother of my flesh was greatly moved (since, with her heart pure in your faith, she more loving-ly still *travailed in the birth* of my eternal salvation) and she was already hastening on with the preparations for me to be initiated and cleansed in your health-giving sacraments, confessing you, Lord Jesus, for the remission

of sins; and so I would then have been baptized, if I had not suddenly recovered. As a result of my recovery my cleansing was deferred, the argument being that, if I went on living, I should become still more defiled, because the guilt incurred in the filth of sin would be greater and more perilous after that washing than before. At that time I already believed; so did my mother and our whole household, except for my father. Yet, though he did not yet believe in Christ, he did not break the hold over me of my mother's goodness and did not stop me believing. For she earnestly endeavored, my God, that you rather than he should be my father, and in this you aided her and helped her to overcome her husband, to whom, though she was the better of the two, she was still obedient because this is your command and in this she was obedient to you.

I ask you, my God (for I would like to know, if you would like to tell me), what was the reason that my baptism was put off at that time? Was it for my own good that I was given, as it were, more free rein to sin? Or was I not given more free rein? How is it that even now one is constantly and everywhere hearing it said of one person or another: "Leave him alone; let him do as he likes; he is not baptized yet?" But when it is a question of physical health, we do not say: "Let him have a few more wounds: he is not well yet." How much better, therefore, would it have been, if I had been made well at once and then, by my own care and that of my friends, had managed to bring it about that the recovered health of my soul had been preserved in your keeping, who gave it to me! Surely this would have been better. Yet wave after great wave of temptation seemed to be hanging over me after my boyhood. My mother could see them coming and she preferred to expose to them the mere clay out of which I might afterward be reshaped, rather than the express image itself.

12 LESS APPREHENSION, then, was felt about me in boyhood than in adolescence. Yet in this period of boyhood I did not enjoy my lessons, and I hated being forced to do them. However I was forced to do them, and this was a good thing for me, though it was not I who did the good for myself; for I would never learn, unless under compulsion; and no one can act well against his will, even if what he does happens to be good. Nor were those who forced me to learn acting well; the good that was done to me was from you, my God. For my teachers had no idea of how I was to use the education which they forced upon me except for satisfying the insatiable desires of that wealth which is poverty and of that glory which is shame. But you, *by whom the very hairs of our head are numbered*, used for my good the errors of all those who kept forcing me to learn, and as to me, who was so unwilling to learn, you made use of my error in order to punish me, and I richly deserved it, I, so small a boy and so great a sinner. Thus by means of people who were not themselves acting well, you acted well toward me, and for my own sin you punished me as I deserved. For you have commanded it to be so, and so it is, that every inordinate affection should be its own punishment.

13   BUT I STILL cannot quite understand why I hated the Greek which I had to study as a boy. For I was very fond of Latin, not the elementary grammar but the literature. As to the rudiments—reading, writing, and arithmetic—I found these just as boring and troublesome as all my Greek studies. And how can this be explained except from the sin and vanity of life, because I *was flesh, and a breath that passeth away and cometh not again?* For by means of these rudiments I acquired and still retain the power to read what I find written and to write what I want to write myself; they are therefore undoubtedly better, because more reliable, than those other studies in which I was forced to learn all about the wanderings of a man called Aeneas, while quite oblivious of my own wanderings, and to weep for the death of Dido, because she killed herself for love, while all the time I could bear with dry eyes, O God my life, the fact that I myself, poor wretch, was, among these things, dying far away from you.

What indeed can be more pitiful than a wretch with no pity for himself, weeping at the death of Dido, which was caused by love for Aeneas, and not weeping at his own death, caused by lack of love for you, God, light of my heart, bread of the inner mouth of my soul, strength of my mind, and quickness of my thoughts? You I did not love. Against you I committed fornication, and in my fornication I heard all around me the words: "Well done! Well done!" *For the love of this world is fornication against Thee* and when one hears these words: "Well done! Well done!" they have the effect of making one ashamed not to be that sort of person. But this was not what I wept for; I wept for dead Dido "who by the sword pursued a way extreme," meanwhile myself following a more extreme way, that of the most extremely low of your creatures, having forsaken you, and being earth going back to earth. And if I were forbidden to read these things, I would be sad at not being allowed to read what would make me sad. And this sort of madness is considered a superior and richer form of learning than learning how to read and write!

But now let my God cry out in my soul; let your truth speak to me and say: "Not so, not so at all. Those first studies were very much better." For obviously I would rather forget about the wanderings of Aeneas and every-thing of that sort than how to read and write. True enough that curtains are hung at the doors of Schools of Literature. Why? Rather as a covering for error than as a mark of the distinction of some special knowledge. These professors of literature, of whom I am no longer afraid, need not cry out against me as I confess to you, my God, what my soul wishes to confess and as I find rest in the condemnation of my evil ways in order that I may love those good ways of yours. There is no need for either the buyers or sellers of literary knowledge to cry out against me. For suppose I were to ask them: "Is it really true that, as the poet says, Aeneas came at some time to Carthage?" the more ignorant ones will reply: "We don't know," and the more learned: "No, it is not true." But if I ask: "What is the correct spelling of the name 'Aeneas,'" all who have learned it will give me the correct answer, an answer in accordance with the general agreement which men have made among themselves for the use of these signs. And again if I were to ask: "Which would have the worse effect on man's life, to forget how to read and write, or to forget all these imaginary stories of the poets?" is it not obvious what everyone not quite out of his mind would reply? I sinned, therefore, in my boyhood when I showed greater affection for these empty studies than for the others that were more useful; or, it would be truer to say, I loved the former and I hated the latter. At that time "One and one make two; two and two make four" was a horrible kind of singsong to me. What really delighted me were spectacles of vanity—the Wooden Horse full of armed men, the Burning of Troy, and "there the very shade of dead Creüsa."

14   BUT WHY, THEN, did I hate Greek literature, which is full of such things? For Homer too is skillful at putting together this sort of story and there is great sweetness in his vanity; yet when I was a boy he was not to my taste. I think that Greek children must feel just the same about Vergil, when they are forced to study him as I was forced to study Homer. No doubt it was a question of difficulty; and this difficulty of mastering a foreign language was like bitter gall sprinkled over all the sweetness of Greek stories and fables. For I simply did not know the words, and strict measures were taken, punishments and cruel threats, to make me learn them. There had been a time too, of course, in my infancy, when I did not know any Latin words either; yet simply by paying attention I learned Latin without any fears or torments; I learned it in the caressing language of my nurses and in the laughter and play and kindness of those about me. In this learning I was under no pressure of punishment, and people did not have to urge me on; my own heart urged me on to give birth to the thoughts which it had conceived, and I could not do this unless I learned some words; these I learned not from instructors but from people who talked to me and in whose hearing I too was able to give birth to what I was feeling. It is clear enough

from this that free curiosity is a more powerful aid to the learning of languages than a forced discipline. Yet this discipline restrains the dissipation of that freedom: and this, God, is through your laws, your laws which, from the master's cane to the martyr's trials, have the power to make a blend of healthful bitterness, calling us back to you from these deadly pleasures in the enjoyment of which we become separated from you.

15 LORD, HEAR MY PRAYER: let my soul not faint under your discipline, and let me not faint in confessing to you those acts of mercy of yours by means of which you have drawn me from all those most evil ways of mine, so that you may become to me something sweeter than all these alluring pleasures that I used to follow, and so that I may love you with all my strength and clasp your hand with the fullest affection, and you may still draw me away from every temptation now and to the end. For see, Lord, my King and my God, I would wish everything useful which I learned as a boy to be used in your service—speaking, reading, writing, arithmetic, all. For you granted me your discipline when I was learning useless things, and you have forgiven me my sin in enjoying those things. Certainly in these studies I did learn a number of useful words: but I could have learned them just as well in studies that were not useless; and that is the safe path along which boys should go.

16 BUT HOW one must condemn the river of human custom! Who can stand firm against it? When will it ever dry up? How long will it continue to sweep the sons of Eve into that huge and fearful ocean which can scarcely be passed even by those who have the mark of the Cross upon their sails? Was it not here, in this stream of custom, that I read of Jupiter thundering at one moment and committing adultery the next? Undoubtedly he could not do both these things; but the idea was this: that a false notion of thunder should be used as a bawd to give countenance to real adultery. And which of our long-robed professors nowadays would listen seriously to one of his own school (like Cicero) who cried out: "These were Homer's fictions. He merely gave human qualities to the gods. How I wish he had given divine qualities to men!" Though in fact it is truer to say: "Certainly these were fictions of Homer, but his method was to give something of the divine to wicked men, so that crimes should not be called crimes and that whoever was guilty of such things might appear to be following in the footsteps, not of abandoned men, but of the heavenly gods."

Nevertheless into this hellish river of custom the sons of men are hurled, and much money is spent on acquiring this learning; a great thing is made of it when it is advertised in the forum and laws are there written down for men to see which fix extra salaries for the teachers in excess of the normal scholar's fees, and this river of custom dashes against the rocks and roars out: "This is where you can learn words. This is where you can learn that art of eloquence which is so essential for gaining your own ends and for expressing your own opinions." As though we should never have learned such words as "shower" and "golden" and "lap" and "beguile" and "temples of the sky" and the others which occur in the passage I am thinking of, if it had not been for the fact that Terence had put into one of his plays a worthless young man who regards Jupiter as an example to himself of how to seduce people. He is looking at a painted fresco

> Which told how Love descended in a golden shower
> to Danaë's lap and so a woman was beguiled.

And then observe how he excites himself to lust, as though he had an example for it among the gods.

> What God? Why, he who shakes the temples of the
> sky with his own thunder. Am not I, mere man, al-
> lowed to do the same? I did; and I enjoyed it too.

Most certainly this disgraceful sentiment does not make the words any easier to learn; it is rather the case that by means of such words disgraceful actions are committed with more confidence. Not that I blame the words themselves; they are like choice and valuable vessels. What I blame is the wine of error which is put into them; and then our drunken teachers raise their glasses to us and, if we do not drink to them too, we get beaten for it, without any chance of appealing to any sober judge. Yet, my God (in whose sight I may now safely recall all this), I myself (poor wretch) took easily to these studies and indeed was delighted with them and for that reason was considered a most promising boy.

17 ALLOW ME, my God, to say something of my intelligence, which was your gift to me, and of how I wasted it on mere stupidities. I remember how I was set some work, which was troublesome enough to my spirit, but it was a matter which would be rewarded either by praise or by disgrace, and indeed one might have to fear a beating too. The work set was that I should declaim a speech supposed to be made by Juno when she was sad and indignant at the fact that she was unable

From Italy to turn the Trojan King.

I had been told that Juno in fact had never uttered these words, but we were forced to go wandering ourselves in the tracks of these poetic fictions, and to turn into prose for declamation what the poet had expressed in verse. And the declaimer who won most applause was the one who, while preserving the dignity of the character he was representing, gave in his performance the best imitation of the passions of anger and grief and found the most appropriate words to express his meaning. What was all this to me, my God and my true life? What did it matter that when I declaimed I won more praise for it than so many others of my own age and class? Is not all this mere smoke and wind? And was there really no other subject on which I could have employed my tongue and exercised my intelligence? Indeed there was. I might have praised you, Lord, and your praises through your Scriptures could have supported the tender shoot of my spirit, so that it would not have draggled shamefully on the ground among these empty trifles, a prey to the birds of the air. For there is more than one way to sacrifice to the fallen angels.

18 HOWEVER, considering the kind of men who were set up as models for me to imitate, it is no wonder that I was swept away into vanities and that I went out of your presence, my God. These men would be thought little of and would be thoroughly abashed if, while relating some of their own actions which were not at all bad, they made use of some solecism or barbarism of speech; but if they told the story of their lusts in a neat, well-decorated style and with an apt use of words, they would be praised for it by others and would take pride in it themselves. You see these things, Lord, and you remain silent, *long-suffering, and plenteous in mercy and in truth*. But will you always be silent? And even now you will draw out of this horrible pit the soul that seeks for you and that thirsts for your pleasures, *whose heart saith unto Thee: I have sought Thy face; Thy face, Lord, will I seek*. For to be in a darkness of affection is to be far from you. We do not go from you or return to you on foot or by spatial measurement. Nor did that younger son in the Gospel get horses for himself or chariots or ships; he did not fly away on any visible wings or travel by any motion of the limbs in order that in a far country he might waste in riotous living what you gave him at his departure. A loving father you were to him by your gifts, and more loving still when he returned empty-handed. In lust, therefore, that is to say, in the darkness of affection, is the real distance from your face.

Look down, my Lord God, and, as you always do, look down with patience on how the sons of men most carefully observe the agreed rules of letters and syllables which they received from those who spoke before them and yet pay no attention to the eternal covenant of everlasting salvation which they received from you. Indeed it is true that a teacher and learner of these traditional rules of pronunciation would cause more offense if he were to break the grammarians' laws and say " 'uman being," without the aspirate, than if, being a human being himself, he were to break your laws and hate another human being. As if one could suffer more harm from any enemy than one suffers from the hatred which one feels against him; or as if one could do more harm to an enemy by any kind of persecution than one does to one's own soul by the mere act of hating. Certainly no kind of literary learning comes so close to one as does this verdict of conscience: "You are doing to someone else what you would not like to have done to you." How secret you are, dwelling silently in the Highest, God only great, whose never-flagging justice scatters the punishment of blindnesses over unlawful desires! A man who is trying to win a reputation as a good speaker will, in front of a human judge and surrounded by a crowd of human beings, attack his opponent with the utmost fury and hatred, and he will take great care to see that by some slip of the tongue he does not mispronounce the word "human"; but he will not be concerned as to whether his rage and fury may have the effect of utterly destroying a real human being.

19   IT WAS ON the verge of this sort of life that I, poor wretch, stayed dotingly in my boyhood; this was my field of exercise and ambition, one where I was more frightened of committing a barbarism than I was careful to avoid, once I had committed one, envying those who had not. I tell you these things, my God, in my confession, and these were the things for which I was praised by people whose good opinion then meant to me the same thing as living a good and proper life. For I could not see the foul abyss into which, far from your eyes, I had been cast out. And in your eyes what could be more disgusting than I was—I who was disapproved of even by people like myself, because of the innumerable lies I told to deceive my tutor and my masters and my parents: all for love of play, eagerness to watch worthless shows, and a restless hankering to imitate them?

I also was a thief, stealing things from my parents' larder or table, either out of sheer gluttony or in order to have something to give to the other boys, who liked being paid to play with me, though they enjoyed the play just as much as I did. In these games too I often used to try to overcome my rivals by cheating, all the time being overcome myself by the empty desire to be thought the best. But if I caught someone else cheating me, I simply could not abide it and would attack him in the most savage language for doing just what I had been doing to others. And if I was caught cheating myself and blamed for it in the same way, I preferred to get into a rage rather than to yield and submit.

Is this what is called "the innocence of boyhood"? Not so, Lord, not so. I beg your leave, my God. For it is just these same sins which, as the years pass by, become related no longer to tutors, schoolmasters, footballs, nuts, and pet sparrows, but to magistrates and kings, gold, estates, and slaves; just as in later years punishments are more severe than the schoolmaster's cane. It must, therefore, have been the low stature of children, O our King, which you used as a sign of humility and commended in the words: *of such is the Kingdom of Heaven.*

20 YET, LORD, even if it had been your will for me to have advanced no further than boyhood, my thanks would still be due to you, our God, most excellent and most good, Creator and Governor of the universe. For even then I had a being; I lived and I felt; I took care for my own security (which is a sign of that mysterious Unity from which I had my being); by my inward sense I watched over the integrity of my outer senses; even in these little things and in my thoughts about these little things truth delighted me. I hated to be deceived; I had a vigorous memory; I was educated in speech; and I was made tractable by kindness. I avoided pain, meanness, ignorance. How wonderful and how praiseworthy are all these things in such a little living creature! But all these things are the gifts of my God; it was not I who gave them to myself, and they are good and all of them together am I. Good, therefore, is He who made me, and He is my good, and in Him I rejoice for all those good things which even as a boy I had. For my sin was in this— that I looked for pleasures, exaltations, truths not in God Himself but in His creatures (myself and the rest), and so I fell straight into sorrows, confusions, and mistakes. I thank you, my sweetness and my glory and my confidence, my God, I thank you for your gifts. But I pray you to preserve them for me; so you will preserve me and those things which you gave me will be increased and brought to perfection, and I myself shall be with you; for my very being is your gift.

Book II

1 I WANT TO call back to mind my past impurities and the carnal corruptions of my soul, not because I love them, but so that I may love you, my God. It is for the love of your love that I do it, going back over those most wicked ways of mine in the bitterness of my recollection so that the bitterness may be replaced by the sweetness of you, O unfailing sweetness, happy sweetness and secure! And gathering myself together from the scattered fragments into which I was broken and dissipated during all that time when, being turned away from you, the One, I lost myself in the distractions of the Many.

For in that youth of mine I was on fire to take my fill of hell. Outrageously in all my shady loves I began to revert to a state of savagery: *my beauty consumed away* and I stank in your sight; pleasing myself and being anxious to please in the eyes of men.

2 AND WHAT was it that delighted me? Only this— to love and be loved. But I could not keep that true measure of love, from one mind to another mind, which marks the bright and glad area of friendship. Instead I was among the foggy exhalations which proceed from the muddy cravings of the flesh and the bubblings of first manhood. These so clouded over my heart and darkened it that I was unable to distinguish between the clear calm of love and the swirling mists of lust. I was storm-tossed by a confused mixture of the two and, in my weak unstable age, swept over the precipices of desire and thrust into the whirlpools of vice. Your wrath had gathered above me, and I was not aware of it. I had grown deaf through the clanking of the chain of my mortality. This was your punishment for my soul's pride. I was going further and further from you, and you let me be. I was tossed here and there, spilled on the ground, scattered abroad; I boiled over in my fornications. And still you were silent, O my joy so slow in coming! Then you were silent, and I went on going further from you and further, making my way into more and more of these sterile plantations of sorrow, arrogant in my dejection and still restless in my weariness.

How I wish that there had been someone at that time to put a measure on my disorder and to turn to good use the fleeting beauties of these new temptations and to put limits to their delights. Then the waves of my youth might at last have spent themselves on the shore of marriage, if tranquility could not be found simply in the purposeful begetting of children, as your law, Lord, prescribes; for you shape even the offspring of our mortality and are able with a gentle hand to blunt the thorns which were excluded from your paradise. And not far from us is your omnipotence, even when we are far from you. Or certainly I ought to have listened with greater heed to the voice from those clouds of yours: *Nevertheless such shall have trouble in the flesh, but I spare you.* And, *it is good for a man not to touch a woman.* And, *he that is without a wife thinketh of the things of God, how he may please God; but he that is married thinketh of the things of the world, how he may please his wife.* I should have listened more carefully to words such as these and should have become a *eunuch for the kingdom of heaven's sake,* so in greater happiness awaiting your embraces.

But I, poor wretch, boiled up and ran troubled along the course of my own stream, forsaking you. I broke through all the boundaries of your law but did not escape your chastisement. What mortal can? For you were always with me, angered against me in your mercy, scattering the most bitter discontent over all my illicit pleasures, so that thus I might seek for pleasure in which there was no discontent and be unable to find such a thing except in you, Lord, except in you, who shape sorrow to be an instructor, who give wounds in order to heal, who kill us lest we should die away from you. Where was I, and how far was I banished from the delights of your house in that sixteenth year of my flesh when the madness of lust (forbidden by your laws but too much countenanced by human shamelessness) held complete sway over me and to this madness I surrendered myself entirely! And those about me took no care to save me from falling by getting me married; their one aim was that I should learn how to make a good speech and become an orator capable of swaying his audience.

3   IN THIS YEAR there was a break in my studies. I came back home from Madaura, the nearby city to which I had gone to learn the beginnings of literature and rhetoric, and now money was being provided for me to go further afield, to Carthage. This was rather because my father had big ideas than because he was rich. He was only a poor citizen of Tagaste. But to whom am I relating this? Not to you, my God. But I am telling these things in your presence to my own kind, to that portion of mankind, however small it may be, which may chance to read these writings of mine. And my object in doing so is simply this: that both I myself and whoever reads what I have written may think *out of what depths we are to cry unto Thee*. For nothing comes nearer to your ears than a confessing heart and a life of faith.

At that time, then, people on all sides praised my father for spending more money than his means really allowed so that his son could be equipped with what was necessary for a long journey and be able to continue his studies. Many citizens much richer than my father did no such a thing for their children. And yet this father of mine was not at all interested in how I was growing up in relation to you, or how chaste I was. The only idea was that I should become "cultured," though this "culture" really meant a lack of cultivation from you, God, the one true and good landlord and farmer of this field of yours, my heart.

But in this sixteenth year of my age when, because of our straitened circumstances, I had a period of leisure, living at home with my parents and not doing any school-work at all, the brambles of lust grew up right over my head, and there was no hand to tear them up by the roots. In fact when my father saw me at the baths and noticed that I was growing toward manhood and showing the signs of the burgeoning of youth he told my mother of it with great pleasure, as though he were already confident of having grandchildren; but his pleasure proceeded from that kind of drunkenness in which the world forgets you, its creator, and falls in love with your creature instead of with you; so drugged it is with the invisible wine of a perverse self-will, bent upon the lowest objects. But in my mother's breast you had already begun to build your temple and had laid the foundation for your holy dwelling place. My father was still a catechumen, and had only been a catechumen for a short time. My mother, there-fore, was seized with a holy fear and trembling; even though I was not yet baptized, she was alarmed for me, fearing those crooked ways which are trodden by those who turn their backs to you and not their face.

How bitter this is to me! And do I dare to say that you, my God, kept silent while I was going further and further from you? Did you really say nothing to me then? Whose words were they except yours which, by the means of my mother, your devoted servant, you kept crying in my ears? Not that any of them sank down into my heart and made me act in accordance with them. For it was her wish, and I remember how privately and with what great anxiety she warned me not to commit fornication and especially not to commit adultery with another man's wife. And these warnings seemed to me merely the sort of things which one might expect from a woman and which it would be a shame for me to follow. But, though I did not know it, these warnings came from you. I thought that you were silent and that it was my mother who was speaking; but you were not silent; you spoke to

me through her, and in despising her I was despising you,
I, her son, the son of your handmaid, I, your servant. But
I did not know. I went headlong on my way, so blind that
among people of my own age I was ashamed to be more
modest than they were. I heard them boasting of their
acts of vice (and the worse these were, the more they
boasted), and so I enjoyed the pleasure not only of the
act but also of the praise one got for having committed it.

What deserves censure except vice? I, to avoid censure,
made myself more vicious than I was, and when, in fact, I
had not committed a sin that would put me on a level
with the worst sinners, I used to pretend that I had committed it, so that I might not be despised for my greater
degree of innocence or thought less of for a comparative
chastity. With what companions did I walk the streets
of Babylon and wallow in its mire as though I lay in a bed
of spices and precious ointments! And, so that I should
stick the closer to the very center of it, the invisible
enemy trod me underfoot and seduced me, since I was
easy to seduce. And as to the mother of my flesh (who
had herself already *fled out of the center of Babylon*, yet
still lingered in the outskirts), she had certainly advised
me to be chaste; but she did not give the attention she
might have given to what she heard about me from her
husband; she thought that if my desires could not be, as
it were, cut off at the root, it would be unhealthy for
the moment and dangerous for the future to restrain them
within the bounds of the affections of marriage. The reason why she was against my getting married was that
she feared that a wife would be a handicap to me in my
hopes for the future, and these hopes were not those
which my mother had of a future life in you; they were
merely hopes that I might attain proficiency in literature.
In these hopes both of my parents indulged too much—my
father, because he hardly thought of you at all and only
thought in the most trivial way about me; my mother,
because, in her view, these usual courses of learning
would be, not only no hindrance, but an actual help to
me in attaining you. So at least I conjecture when I
recollect to the best of my ability what the characters
of my parents were. Meanwhile, the reins were loosened;

I was given free play with no kind of severity to control me and was allowed to dissipate myself in all kinds of ways. In all of these was a mist cutting me off, my God, from the pure brightness of your truth, and *mine iniquity burst out as from my fatness.*

4   CERTAINLY, Lord, your law punishes theft; indeed there is a law written in men's hearts which not iniquity itself can erase; for no thief will submit to being robbed by another; even a rich thief will not tolerate another man who is forced to steal by poverty. Yet I both wanted to steal and did steal, and I was not forced to it by any kind of want; it was only that I lacked and despised proper feeling and was stuffed with iniquity. For I stole something of which I had plenty myself, and much better than what I stole. I had no wish to enjoy what I tried to get by theft; all my enjoyment was in the theft itself and in the sin.

Near our vineyard there was a pear tree, loaded with fruit, though the fruit was not particularly attractive either in color or taste. I and some other wretched youths conceived the idea of shaking the pears off this tree and carrying them away. We set out late at night (having, as we usually did in our depraved way, gone on playing in the streets till that hour) and stole all the fruit that we could carry. And this was not to feed ourselves; we may have tasted a few, but then we threw the rest to the pigs. Our real pleasure was simply in doing something that was not allowed. Such was my heart, God, such was my heart which you had pity on when it was at the very bottom of the abyss. And now let my heart tell you what it was looking for there, that I became evil for nothing, with no reason for wrongdoing except the wrongdoing itself. The evil was foul, and I loved it; I loved destroying myself; I loved my sin—not the thing for which I had committed the sin, but the sin itself. How base a soul, falling back from your firmament to sheer destruction, not seeking some object by shameful means, but seeking shame for itself!

5   CERTAINLY the eye is pleased by beautiful bodies, by gold, and silver and all such things, and in the sense of touch a great part is played by a kind of reciprocity. All the other senses too have their own proper modulations with regard to their particular objects. Worldly honor also has its own grace and the power to command and prevail over others (from which comes too the eagerness to assert one's own rights); yet in following all these things, we must not depart from you, Lord, or transgress your law. The life too, which we live here, has its own enchantment because of a certain measure in its own grace and a correspondence with all these beautiful things of this world. And human friendship, knotted in affection, is a sweet thing because of the unity between many different souls which it expresses. Yet for all these things and all things of this sort sin is committed. For there are goods of the lowest order, and we sin if, while following them with too great an affection, we neglect those goods which are better and higher—you, our Lord God, and your truth and your law. Certainly these lower things have their delights, but not like my God, who made all things, *for in Him doth the righteous delight, and He is the joy of the upright in heart.*

So, when we inquire into why any particular crime was committed, the only motives which, as a rule, we regard as credible are when it appears that there might have been either a desire for gaining or a fear of losing some of these goods which we have described as "lower." For they certainly are objects of beauty and worth, although they are low and mean enough when compared with those higher goods which confer real happiness. Suppose a man has committed murder. Why did he do it? Perhaps he was in love with the other man's wife, or with his estate; or he wanted to rob him of his money in order to live himself; or he was afraid that the other man might despoil him of one of these things; or he had been injured and was eager to revenge himself. Certainly a man does not commit murder for no reason at all, simply for the pleasure of doing the deed. No one could believe such a thing. Even in the case of that brutal and savage man of whom it was said that he was evil and cruel just for the sake of evil and cruelty, there is still a reason given for it. It was (says Sallust) "to prevent his hand and heart from growing slow through inactivity." And why was that? Why indeed? Obviously the point of this exercise in crime was that, after having seized Rome, he might obtain honors, commands, and riches and, in his poverty and guilty knowledge of his own evil deeds, might be freed from all fear of the law and all financial difficulties. Even Catiline, therefore, did not love his own crimes; what he loved was something else, for the sake of which he committed them.

9   AND WHAT DID I, wretched I, love in you, you theft of mine, you sin in the night committed by me in my sixteenth year? There was nothing beautiful about you, because you were merely theft. But are you in fact anything, for me to speak to you like this? Certainly the pears that we stole were beautiful since they were of your creation, yours, most beautiful of all, Creator of all, good God, God supremely good, and my true good. The pears certainly were beautiful, but it was not the pears that my miserable soul desired. I had plenty of better pears of my own; I only took these ones in order that I might be a thief. Once I had taken them I threw them away, and all I tasted in them was my own iniquity, which I enjoyed very much. For if I did put any of these pears into my mouth, what made it sweet to me was my sin. And now, my Lord God, I inquire what it was that delighted me in that act of theft. Clearly there is no beauty about it at all. I am not speaking about the beauty that is to be found in justice and wisdom; nor of that which is in the mind and memory and senses and animal life of man; nor of the stars, which, set in their places, are beautiful and glorious; nor the earth and the sea, which is full of new life constantly being born to replace what passes away; no, it has not even got that incomplete and shadowy beauty which we find in deceiving vices.

Pride too strives to appear as though it was high and lofty, whereas you alone are God high over all. Ambition's one aim is honor and glory, whereas you alone and before all else are to be honored and are glorious forever and ever. Great men in their anger wish to inspire fear; but who is to be feared except God alone? From His power what can be withdrawn or subtracted? And where, or when, or whither, or by whom? The tender endearments of passion aim at provoking love. But nothing can be more tender and more dear than your charity, and nothing can be loved more healthfully than your truth, that truth which is beautiful and brilliant above all things. Curiosity puts on the appearance of a zeal for knowledge, while you, in the highest degree, know everything. Even ignorance and mere foolishness go under the names of simplicity and innocence, because there is nothing more simple than you; and what can be more innocent than you, since what brings hurt to the wicked is their own actions? And laziness seems to be looking for rest; but what sure rest is there except in the Lord? Luxury would like to be called plenty and abundance; but you are the fullness and the unfailing supply of a sweetness that is incorruptible. Prodigality shows, as it were, the shadow of liberality; but you are the most supremely rich bestower of all good things. Avarice wishes to possess much: you possess everything. Envy disputes for the first place; what place is higher than yours? Anger seeks requital; what requital is more just than yours? Fear shows its agitation in the presence of what is unusual or sudden and endangering to things that are loved, and it tries to secure their safety. But to you nothing is unusual, nothing is sudden. No one can take away from you the thing which you love, and nowhere except with you is there real safety. Grief pines away at the loss of things in which the desire delighted; this is because it would like nothing to be taken away, just as nothing can be taken away from you.

So the soul commits fornication when she turns away from you and tries to find outside you things which, unless she returns to you, cannot be found in their true and pure state. So all men who put themselves far from you and set themselves up against you, are in fact attempting awkwardly to be like you. And even in this imitating

of you they declare you to be the creator of everything
in existence and that consequently there can be no place
in which one can in any way withdraw oneself from
you.

What then was it that I loved in that theft of mine?
In what way, awkwardly and perversely, did I imitate
my Lord? Did I find it pleasant to break your law and
prefer to break it by stealth, since I could not break it by
any real power? And was I thus, though a prisoner,
making a show of a kind of truncated liberty, doing un-
punished what I was not allowed to do and so producing
a darkened image of omnipotence? What a sight! A servant running away from his master and following a
shadow! What rottenness! What monstrosity of life and
what abyss of death! Could I enjoy what was forbidden
for no other reason except that it was forbidden?

7   *What shall I render unto the Lord* because, while
     my memory recalls these things, my soul is not
terrified at them? *I will love Thee, O Lord, and thank
Thee and confess unto Thy name,* because you have forgiven me these great sins and these evil doings of mine.
To your grace I owe it, and to your mercy, that you have
melted away my sins like ice. And to your grace too I
owe the not doing of whatever evil I have not done. For
what evil might I not have done, I who loved crime
simply for crime's sake? Yes, I own it: all these evils
have been forgiven me—both those which I committed of
my own will and those which, because of your guidance,
I did not commit.

No man who considers his own weakness can dare to
say that it is because of his own virtue that he is chaste
or innocent, and so love you less, as though he had less
need of your mercy, by which you remit the sins of those
that turn to you. And if a man has heard your voice
and followed it and not committed those sins which he
reads of in this recollection and confession of mine, he
ought not to laugh at me, who was sick and then cured
by the Physician owing to whose care he himself avoided
sickness or rather was not so sick; for this he should love

you just as much, or rather much more; he sees that I have recovered from the great weakness and depression of my sins, and he sees that my recovery was due to that same Physician who preserved him from being the victim of the same weakness and depression.

8   WHAT ADVANTAGE did I gain then, poor wretch, from these things which I now blush to remember? And in particular what advantage did I get from that act of theft, in which the only thing that I loved was just the act of theft itself, and it too was nothing, and I, therefore, who loved it, still more of a wretch. And yet I would not have done it by myself; for I can remember what I was like then; no, I would certainly never have done it by myself. Then in the act of theft I must have loved something else too, namely the company of those with whom I committed it. And so I did not love nothing except the theft itself; yet, no; indeed there was nothing else, since this fact of having accomplices is also nothing. What is the real truth of the matter? Who can teach me, except he who sheds his light into my heart and scatters the shadows that are within it? And what is it which makes me indulge in all this inquiry and discussion and consideration? For if I then loved the pears which I stole and desired to enjoy them, I could have committed the theft by myself, supposing that I merely had to do this in order to get what I wanted to enjoy; there was no need to raise the pruriency of my desire by the excitement of having others to share the guilt. No, it was in the sin itself and not in those pears that my pleasure lay—a pleasure occasioned by the company of others who were sinning with me.

9   Now WHAT exactly was this feeling? Certainly it was a very bad one and a disgrace to me, who had it. But what exactly was it? *Who can understand his errors?* We laughed at it, as though our hearts were tickled at the thought that we were deceiving people who had no idea of what we were doing and who would

have strongly disapproved of it. Why, then, was my pleasure of such a kind that still I did not do the act by myself? Was it because people do not generally laugh by themselves? Generally they do not; but nevertheless there are times when, if something really ridiculous occurs to the mind or is presented to the senses, people, even quite alone by themselves, will be overcome by laughter. But I would not have done that alone; no, certainly, I would not.

See, my God, in front of you this vivid memory of my soul. By myself I would not have committed that theft, in which what pleased me was not what I stole, but that I stole; nor would I have got any pleasure out of it by myself, nor would I have done it at all by myself. What an unfriendly friendship is this! What a seduction of the soul and how difficult to track! That out of mere fun and play should proceed an eagerness to hurt and an appetite to do harm to others and with no sort of a desire either to avenge myself or to gain anything for myself! It has only to be said: "Come on, let's do it," and we become ashamed at not being shameless.

10 WHO CAN DISENTANGLE this most twisted and most inextricable knottiness? It is revolting; I hate to think of it; I hate to look at it. It is you that I desire, O justice and innocence, you who, to the eyes of the pure, are beauty and honesty, you, O plenteous unsating satisfaction. With you is true peace and life imperturbable. He who enters into you *enters into the joy of his Lord;* he shall have no fear; he shall be well indeed in him who is best of all. I slipped from you and went astray, my God, in my youth, wandering too far from my upholder and my stay, and I became to myself a wasteland.

Book III

1   I CAME TO Carthage, and all around me in my ears were the sizzling and frying of unholy loves. I was not yet in love, but I loved the idea of love, and from a hidden want I hated myself for not wanting more. Being in love with love I looked for something to love; I hated security and a path without snares. I was starved inside me for inner food (for you yourself, my God), yet this starvation did not make me hungry. I had no desire for the food that is incorruptible, and this was not because I was filled with it; no, the emptier I was, the more my stomach turned against it. And for this reason my soul was in poor health; it burst out into feverish spots which brought the wretched longing to be scratched by contact with the objects of sense. Yet if these had no soul, they could certainly not be loved. It was a sweet thing to me both to love and to be loved, and more sweet still when I was able to enjoy the body of my lover.

And so I muddied the clear spring of friendship with the dirt of physical desire and clouded over its brightness with the dark hell of lust. And still, foul and low as I was, I would, in the exorbitance of my vanity, give myself the airs of a fine man of fashion. Desiring to be captivated in this way, I fell headlong into love. My God and my mercy, how good you were to me in sprinkling so much bitterness over that sweetness! For I was loved myself, and I reached the point where we met together to enjoy our love, and there I was fettered happily in bonds of misery so that I might be beaten with rods of red-hot iron—the rods of jealousy and suspicions, and fears and angers and quarrels.

2   I WAS CARRIED away too by plays on the stage in which I found plenty of examples of my own miseries and plenty of fuel for my own fire. Why is it, I wonder, that people want to feel sad at miserable and tragic happenings which they certainly would not like to suffer themselves? Yet as spectators they do want to suffer the sadness and indeed their whole pleasure is just in this. What a wretched sort of madness! For if one is oneself subject to the kind of emotions one sees on the stage, one is all the more moved by them. Yet when one suffers in real life, this is described as "misery," and when one feels for others, we call it "compassion." But there can be no real compassion for fictions on the stage. A man listening to a play is not called upon to help the sufferer; he is merely invited to feel sad. And the sadder he feels, the higher is his opinion of the actor of this fantasy. If the disasters which happen to people on the stage (disasters which either took place in the remote past or else are pure inventions) are represented in such a way that the spectator does not feel sad, he will go out of the theater in disgust and speak disparagingly of the performance; but so long as he feels sad, he will stay fixed in his place, enjoying every moment.

Are we to say, then, that tears and sufferings are things which we love? Undoubtedly what every man wants is to be glad. Or is it that, while no one wants to be miserable, one still does want to have compassion, and, since one cannot feel compassion without feeling suffering, this and this alone is the reason why sufferings are loved?

This also springs from that vein and source of friendship. But in what direction does it flow? Why is it that it runs into that torrent of pitch which boils and swells with the high tides of foul lust, changing itself into them and of its own will altering its own nature from a heavenly clearness into a precipitation of depravity? Is compassion, then, to be cast out? Certainly not. We must therefore allow ourselves sometimes to love sufferings. But beware of uncleanness, my soul. Stay in the keeping of my God, the *God of our fathers, who is to be praised and exalted above all forever*. Beware of uncleanness.

I have not ceased to feel compassion now. But in those days in the theaters I used to sympathize with the joys of lovers, when they wickedly enjoyed each other, even though all this was purely imaginary and just a stage show, and when they were separated from one another, I used to sympathize with their misery, as though I felt real pity for them; yet I was thoroughly enjoying it in both cases. But now I feel more pity for someone who rejoices in his wickedness than for someone who is supposed to be suffering great hardships because of the lack of some harmful pleasure or the loss of some miserable felicity. This certainly is a truer form of compassion, but the pain in it does not give one pleasure. To feel grief for another's misery is a sign and work of charity and is therefore to be commended; but it is still true that a man who is genuinely compassionate would rather that there was nothing for him to feel grief about. Only if good will could will evil (which is impossible) could there be a man really and truly compassionate who would wish some people to be unhappy so that they could be objects for his compassion. Some sorrow, therefore, may be approved of, but none loved. For this, Lord God, is your way. You are wounded by no sorrow; yet you love souls far more deeply than we can, and your compassion is more lasting and indestructible than ours. *And who is sufficient for these things?*

But I, poor wretch, at that time loved to feel sad and went looking for something to feel sad about; in someone else's sorrow, which was purely fictitious and acted. I was best pleased and most strongly attracted by the performance of an actor who brought tears to my eyes. Unhappy sheep that I was, straying from your flock and impatient of your keeping! No wonder that I became infected with a foul disease, and this was the origin of my love for sorrows—not sorrows that really affected me deeply, for I did not like to suffer in my own person the things which I liked to see represented on the stage, but only those imaginary sorrows the hearing of which had,

as it were, the effect of scratching the surface of my skin.
And, as happens after the scratching of poisoned nails,
what came next were feverish swellings, abscesses, and
running sores. Such was the life I led. Was this, my God,
a life at all?

3   AND ABOVE ME hovered your mercy, faithful
however far I strayed. I wasted myself away in
great sins. I followed in the path of sacrilegious curiosity,
allowing it to lead me, in my desertion of you, down to the
depths of infidelity and the beguiling service of devils, to
whom I made my own evil deeds a sacrifice, and in all
these things you beat me with your rod. Once when your
solemnities were being celebrated within the walls of
your Church, I actually dared to desire and then to bring
to a conclusion a business which deserved death for its
reward. For this you lashed me with punishments that
were heavy, but nothing in comparison with my fault, O
you infinite mercy, my God, my refuge from those terrible destroyers, among whom I wandered with a stiff
neck on my path further and further away from you,
loving my own ways and not yours, loving the liberty
of a runaway.

Those studies of mine also, which were considered perfectly respectable, were designed to fit me for the law so
that I might gain a great name in a profession where those
who deceive most people have the biggest reputations.
Such is the blindness of men, that blindness should become an actual source of pride! And by now I was a
senior student in the School of Rhetoric and very pleased
with myself and proud and swelling with arrogance, although, as you know, Lord, I was a quieter character and
indeed entirely without any share in the subversive behavior of the "Subverters"—this being the savage and
diabolical name which was used as a kind of badge or mark
of a "man of the world." However, I kept company with
these Subverters and felt a kind of shameless shame for not
being like them. I went about with them and there were
times when I enjoyed their friendship, though I always
hated their actions—that is to say, their "subvertings,"

which were a kind of wanton persecution of the modesty of ordinary unknown people, a persecution carried out for no reason at all except that by jeering and mocking they were able to give themselves a malicious amusement. Nothing can be more like the behavior of devils than this. "Subverters," therefore, was a very good name for them. Most clearly they themselves were first subverted and entirely perverted, and on those occasions when they took pleasure in mocking and deceiving others, there were hidden within themselves deceiving spirits, laughing at them and leading them astray.

4   Among such companions in this unsettled age of mine I pursued my studies of the books of eloquence, a subject in which I longed to make a name for myself, though my reason for this was damnable and mere wind, being simply joy in human vanity. In the normal course of study I came across a book by Cicero, a man whose style, though not his heart, is almost universally admired. This book of his contains an exhortation to philosophy; it is called *Hortensius*. Now it was this book which altered my way of feeling, turned my prayers to you, Lord, yourself, and gave me different ambitions and desires. Every vain hope suddenly became worthless to me; my spirit was filled with an extraordinary and burning desire for the immortality of wisdom, and now I began to rise, so that I might return to you. I was in my nineteenth year (my father having died two years previously), and I might be assumed to be spending the money my mother sent me on sharpening my tongue; but it was not for the purpose of sharpening my tongue that I had used this book of Cicero's; what moved me was not the style, but the matter.

I was on fire then, my God, I was on fire to leave earthly things behind and fly back to you, nor did I know what you would do with me; for with you is wisdom. But that book inflamed me with the love of wisdom (which is called "philosophy" in Greek). There are some who lead us astray by means of philosophy and who use that great and pleasant and honorable name as a disguise or artificial coloring for their own errors, and nearly all such people, both of Cicero's time and before, are noted in that book and censured. There too is clearly stated that wholesome advice given to us by your good and faithful servant: *"Beware lest any man spoil you through philosophy and vain deceit, after the tradition of men, after the rudiments of the world, and not after Christ. For in Him dwelleth all the fullness of the Godhead bodily."* And as to me at that time (you know this, O light of my heart), I was still unacquainted with the Apostolic Scriptures. Yet the one thing in that exhortation which delighted me was this: I was not encouraged by this work of Cicero's to join this or that sect; instead I was urged on and inflamed with a passionate zeal to love and seek and obtain and embrace and hold fast wisdom itself, whatever it might be. And in my ardent desire only one thing held me back, which was that the name of Christ was not there; for this name, Lord, this name of my Saviour, your son, had been with my mother's milk drunk in devoutly by my tender heart, where it remained deeply treasured. So I could not be entirely swept away by anything, however learned or well written or true, which made no mention of this name.

5   I THEREFORE decided to give my attention to the study of the Holy Scriptures and to see what they were like. And what I saw was something that is not discovered by the proud and is not laid open to children; the way in is low and humble, but inside the vault is high and veiled in mysteries, and I lacked the qualities which would make me fit to enter in or stoop my neck to follow the pathway. For when I studied the Scriptures then I did not feel as I am writing about them now. They seemed to me unworthy of comparison with the grand style of Cicero. For my pride shrank from their modesty, and my sharp eye was not penetrating enough to see into their depths. Yet these Scriptures would grow up together with a little child; I, however, thought too highly of myself to become a little child; swollen with pride, I was, in my own eyes, grown-up.

6 AND so I fell in with a sort of people who were arrogant in their madness, too fond of the flesh and too fond of talking, in whose words were the snares of the devil and a kind of birdlime compounded out of a mixture of the syllables of your name and that of the Lord Jesus Christ and of the Holy Ghost, the Comforter. These names were never out of their mouths, but only so far as the sound went and the pronunciation of the words; in their hearts there was no truth whatever. And they kept on saying: "Truth, Truth"; they were forever dinning it in my ears, and *the truth was not in them.* What they said was false, and not only false about you but false about the elements of this world, your creation. And even those philosophers who speak the truth of such things ought to have been disregarded by me for the love of you, my Father and my highest good, O beauty of all things beautiful. O Truth, Truth, how I panted for you even then deep down in the marrow of my soul, when they were constantly and in all kinds of ways making use of the sound of your name—by voice and in their many books and huge tomes. On these dishes there was set before me, in my hunger for you, the sun and the moon, beautiful creations of yours, but nevertheless creations of yours and not you yourself, nor indeed the first of your creations. For your spiritual creations are before these physical creations, heavenly and shining as they are. But it was not even for these first creations of yours that I was hungry and thirsty; it was for you yourself, Truth, *in whom is no variableness neither shadow of turning.* But they in those dishes of theirs kept on putting before me glittering fantasies, and it would be better to love the actual sun, which is real to our sight at least, than those false fantasies which make use of the sight to deceive the mind. Nevertheless, since I thought that these were you, I fed on them, not with any great eagerness (for the taste in my mouth was not the real taste of you, just as you were not these empty fictions), and, so far from being nourished by them, I became the weaker. The food we dream about is very like the food we see in waking life; yet in our dreams we are not fed; we are, in fact, asleep. But (as you have since said to me) those things were not like you in any way; they were

fantasies made out of physical objects, false objects, since we can place more reliance in those real objects which we see, whether on earth or in the sky, with our fleshly sight; animals and birds perceive these objects just as we do, and they are more real when we see them than when we imagine them. And again we can have more confidence in our imagination of them than in conjectures made from them as to other greater and infinite objects which in fact do not exist at all.

It was on such things as these that at this time I was fed —fed without being nourished. But you, my love, for whom I faint that I may become strong, are not those objects which we see, though they are in heaven, nor are you those objects which we do not see there; for all these things are your creations, and you do not regard them as among the chief of your creations. How far then are you from those fantasies of mine, fantasies of objects which do not exist at all! More real than these are fantasies of objects that do exist, and the objects themselves are still more real; yet you are not they. Nor are you the soul, which is the life of bodies, and of course the life of bodies is better and more real than the bodies themselves. But you are the life of souls, the life of lives, the very living life; nor is there change in you, life of my soul. For me, then, at that time, where were you? How far away? Far indeed was I straying from you, debarred even from the husks of the swine whom I fed with husks. For even the stories of the poets and the masters of literature are better than these deceitful traps. Verses, poems, and "Medea flying through the air" are undoubtedly of more use to one than the Five Elements, variously tricked out to correspond with the Five Dens of Darkness—all of which have no existence at all and are death to the believer. For I can turn verses and poems into true nourishment, and if I declaimed "Medea flying," I was not asserting a fact, nor, if I heard someone else declaiming the lines, did I believe them to be true. But those other doctrines I did believe. And miserably indeed I feel now when I think of the steps by which I was brought down to the depths of hell. For want of truth I toiled and I tossed, for I was seeking for you, my God (this I confess to you who had pity on me even before I made my confession), not by means of the intellect and reason (which, according to your will, set us above the beasts), but by means of the bodily senses. But you were inside me, deeper than the deepest recesses of my heart, and you were above me, higher than the highest I could reach. I had fallen in with that bold woman in the allegory of Solomon who, *knowing nothing, sits at her door and says: Eat ye bread of secrecies willingly, and drink ye stolen waters which are sweet.* She it was who seduced me, for she found my soul dwelling out of doors, in the eye of my flesh, and chewing over in myself the cud of what I had eaten through that eye.

7   FOR I DID NOT know that other reality which truly is, and it was as though my own sharpness of intelligence was persuading me to agree with those stupid deceivers when they put forward their questions: "What is the origin of evil?" and "Can we imagine a God bounded by any physical shape and having hair and nails?" and "Should we consider good those who had many wives at the same time, who killed men and made animal sacrifices?" In my ignorance I was much disturbed by these questions, and, as I went further from the truth, I had the impression that I was drawing nearer to it. This was because I did not yet know that evil is nothing but a privation of good, which can continue to the point where a thing ceases to exist altogether. And how could I see this, when my eyesight could reach no further than bodies and the sight of my mind no further than a fantasy? I did not know that God is a spirit and not one with parts extended in length and breadth, nor one of whose being can be used such words as "size," "weight," "bulk." For everything of that kind must have parts which are less than the whole, and even if it is infinite there will be less of it in a part defined by a fixed space than in its total infinitude, and so it cannot be wholly everywhere, as Spirit is, as God is. Then too I was ignorant of what in us is the principle of our existence and what is meant by the words of Scripture "*after the image of God*"—as to that I was entirely ignorant.

I was ignorant also of that true and inward goodness which makes its judgments not from convention but from the most right and undeviating law of God Almighty. By this law the customs of different times and places are formed as is right for those times and those places, while the law is the same always and everywhere, not one thing in one place and one in another. According to this Abraham and Isaac and Moses and David and all those men praised by the mouth of God were good men, and to deny that they were good is a mark of ignorance, for it is to judge merely out of man's judgment and to measure the whole moral structure of the human race by one's own particular and partial standard of morality. It is as if someone who knew nothing about armor or what piece of armor was made for each limb were to try to put a shin guard on his head or a helmet on his foot and were then to complain that they fitted badly: or as if, when there was a public holiday in the afternoon, a shopkeeper were to object to not being allowed to keep his shop open then, because he had been allowed to keep it open in the morning; or when in a house one sees one servant handling something or other which the man who carries around the wine would not be allowed to handle; or something done behind the stables which would be forbidden in the dining room; or as if one should be indignant that in one house and one family there is not exactly the same system of distribution to everyone. All this is like the behavior of those who are offended when they hear that good men were allowed to do something in former ages which good men are not allowed to do today; or that, for reasons connected with time, God's commands to those in former times were not the same as his commands are to men of today; yet both in the past and in the present it is the same goodness to which obedience is due. And yet they can see in one man and one day and one household examples of different things being suited to different members, of one thing allowed at one time and not allowed an hour later, or of something permitted or commanded to be done in one corner which is forbidden under pain of punishment to be done in the next corner. Does this mean that justice is something which changes and varies? No, it does not; but

the times, over which Justice presides, do not pass by
evenly; for they are times. Men however, whose *days are
few upon the earth*, cannot by the use of their senses find
in previous ages and in other nations of which they have
no experience the same relations of cause and effect which
they observe in times and peoples of which they have
experience. In the case of one body or one day or one
house they can easily see what is fitting for each particular
member and time and part and person. This argument is
convincing, while the more remote argument is often a
stumbling block.

At that time I was ignorant of these things and unaware
of them. On all sides they were striking me in the eye, but
still I did not see them. For instance, when I wrote poetry,
I was not allowed to use every kind of foot wherever I
liked; different feet had to be used in different meters, and
even in the same meter one could not use the same foot
in every part of the line. Yet the art of poetry, in accordance with which I wrote, did not have different
principles for different occasions; it comprised all the rules
together in itself. And I still could not see that the rule of
righteousness, followed by these good and holy men,
comprised, in a much more lofty and sublime sense, all its
precepts together, and that in itself it never varied at all,
although at various times, instead of prescribing everything at once, it laid down rules and principles proper for
each occasion. So in my blindness I blamed these holy
Fathers who not only behaved in their own times as God
commanded and inspired them, but also foretold future
times as revealed by God.

8   CAN IT at any time or in any place be wrong *to
love God with all one's heart, with all one's soul,
and with all one's mind; and one's neighbor as oneself?*
Therefore, those crimes which are against nature must
everywhere and always be detested and punished. The
crimes of the men of Sodom are of this kind, and if all
nations in the world committed them they would all stand
guilty of the same crime against the law of God, which
did not design men so that they should use each other in

this way. Indeed even that bond which should exist between God and us is violated when the same nature, of which God is the author, is polluted by the perversity of lust. On the other hand in avoiding those actions which are offenses against the customs of men we must take due consideration of the diversity of customs. What has been laid down as a general rule, either by custom or by law, in any city or nation must not be violated simply for the lawless pleasure of anyone, whether citizen or foreigner. For there is faultiness and deficiency in every part that does not fit in with the whole, of which it is a part.

But when God commands that something should be done which is against the customs or institutions of any people, it must be done, even if it has never been done there before; if it is something that has fallen out of use, then it must be brought back into use, and if it was never a legal obligation, then it must now be made one. We know that it is lawful for a king in the state which he rules over to give an order which has never been given previously either by any of his predecessors or by himself, and that it is not against the general good of the state for him to be obeyed—or rather it would be against the general good if he was not obeyed, since there is a universal agreement in human society that obedience is due to kings. Then how much more unhesitatingly ought we to obey God, the Ruler of all creation, in everything which He commands! For, as in our human societies there are gradations of power, the greater being able to command more obedience than the lesser, so God is set over all.

One may also consider the various cases of sin, when there is a wish to hurt another person, either by insulting him or by injuring him. The motive may be either revenge, as in the case of one enemy against another; or to gain something which belongs to someone else, as with highwaymen against travelers; or to avoid trouble, as when one attacks someone whom one fears; or envy, as when the less fortunate turns against the more fortunate, or when the man who has been successful in something fears the prospect or is angry at the fact of having an equal; or simply the pleasure of seeing others suffer, as in the cases of those who watch gladiators or who mock and make fun of other people. Such sins fall under these headings and they spring from the lust of power, the lust of the eye, the lust of feeling—sometimes from one of these, sometimes from two, sometimes from all three. And so men live badly, against the Three and the Seven, that psaltery of ten strings, your Ten Commandments, O God most high and most sweet. But how can men's insults touch you, who are undefiled? Or what injury can be committed against you, who cannot be hurt? But your vengeance is in that which men do against themselves, because when they sin against you, they are acting wickedly against their own souls, and *iniquity gives itself the lie*. It may be by the corruption or perversion of their own nature, created and ordained by you, or in the immoderate use of things that are allowed, or in the burning lust for things not allowed and for that enjoyment which is against nature; or they may be found guilty of raging against you in their minds and in their words, *kicking against the pricks;* or when they take pleasure in the collapse of the standards of human society and brazenly set up, according to their own likes and dislikes, their private combinations or factions.

And these things are done when you are forsaken O fountain of life, who are the only and the true creator and ruler of the universe, and they proceed from the private and arrogant self-will which falsely attributes unity to a part and loves it. So then the way back to you is through humility and devoutness, and you cleanse us from our evil habits and look mercifully on the sins of those who confess them to you; you hear the groaning of the prisoners and you free us from those fetters which we have made for ourselves—so long as we do not raise against you the standards of an unreal liberty and, in desire for more, risk the loss of everything by setting our love more upon our own private good than upon you, the good of all things.

9   AMONG THE VICES and crimes and the many iniquities that there are must be counted the sins of those who are still making progress. These, if judged aright, will be condemned from the point of view of the

rule of perfection, but may be commended if they show hope of future fruit, as is the green blade of the growing corn. And there are some actions which look vicious and criminal and yet are not sins because they are not offenses either against you, our Lord God, or against human society. For example material goods necessary for maintaining life or for some special occasion may be accumulated, and we do not know whether or not the motive was the lust of possession; or, in a zeal for improvement, punishments may be inflicted by the proper authority, but we cannot be sure whether the real motive was or was not a desire to inflict pain. Many actions, therefore, which seem disreputable to men are, according to your testimony, to be approved, and many actions that are praised by men are, in your sight, to be condemned. The appearance of the act, the mind of the person who does the act, and the secret promptings of the occasion are all capable of great variations. But when you suddenly command that something unaccustomed and unforeseen should be done—even if this is something which at one time you forbade, and however much you may hide for the time being the reason for your command and however much it may run contrary to the convention of any particular human society—no one can doubt that this command of yours must be obeyed; since the only just society of men is the society which does your will. But happy are those who recognize your commands! For all the acts of your servants were done either to indicate something which needed showing in their own times, or else to foretell what was to come in the future.

10   I WAS IGNORANT of this, and so I used to mock at those holy servants and prophets of yours. And all my mocking of them meant nothing except that I myself was being mocked by you. Gradually and insensibly I was led on to believe a lot of nonsense, such as that a fig wept when it was picked and that the fig tree, its mother, shed milk-white tears. But if this fig were to be eaten by some Manichaean saint (always assuming that the picking of it was someone else's and not his guilt), it would be di-

gested and then at the end of the process this saint would breathe out from the fig angels, or rather actual particles of God, at every groan or sigh in his prayer, and these particles of the most high and true God would have remained bound up in the fruit if they had not been set free in this way by the mastication and digestion of some sainted "elect." Poor fool that I was, I believed that more mercy ought to be shown to the fruits of the earth than to men, for whom these fruits were created. For supposing some hungry person, not a Manichee, was to ask for a bit and were to be given it, the morsel given would be considered to be as it were condemned to capital punishment.

11   AND YOU stretched out your hand from on high and drew my soul out of that deep darkness. My mother, your faithful servant, was weeping for me to you, weeping more than mothers weep for the bodily deaths of their sons. For she, by that faith and spirit which she had from you, saw the death in which I lay, and you, Lord, heard her prayer. You heard her and you did not despise her tears which fell streaming and watered the ground beneath her eyes in every place where she prayed; indeed you heard her. How otherwise can one explain that dream of hers by which you comforted her and as a result of which she allowed me to live with her and eat at the same table in the house, a thing which she had begun to avoid, since she shrank from and detested the blasphemies of my error? For in her dream she was standing on a sort of wooden ruler, and there came to her a very beautiful young man with a happy face, smiling at her, though she herself was sad and overcome with her sorrow. He then asked her (his purpose being, as is usual in these visions, to instruct her rather than to be instructed) why it was that she was so sad, and she replied that she was weeping for my perdition. Then he told her to have no fear and instructed her to look carefully and see "that where she was, I was too," and when she did look she saw me standing close by her on the same ruler.

Now how could she have dreamed this unless your ears had been open to her heart, O omnipotent Good, you who care for each one of us as though he was your only care and who cares for all of us as though we were all just one person? And how too can this be explained? For when my mother told me her dream, I tried to twist it to a different meaning, namely, that it was she who need not despair of being one day what I was. But she at once and without the slightest hesitation said: "No; for what was told me was not, 'Where he is, you are too.' It was 'Where you are, he is too.'" I confess to you, Lord, that, to the best of my recollection (and I have often spoken of this), I was more moved by this reply given by you through my mother than I was by the dream itself. For my false interpretation was so plausible, yet she was not perplexed by it, and she saw so quickly what was to be seen and what I myself had certainly not perceived before she spoke. So for the consolation of her present distress, joy in the future was promised to this holy woman. And the prediction was made long before the event. For nearly nine years after this I wallowed in the mud of the pit and in the darkness of falsehood, often trying to rise and then being plunged back again all the more violently. Yet all this time that chaste widow, holy and sober (such as you love), though she had now more hope to cheer her, never slackened in her weeping and her lamentations, never ceased in all hours of her prayer to weep to you about me, and her prayers entered into your presence, and yet you still allowed me to roll over and over in that darkness.

12   AND IN THE meantime you gave her another answer, which I remember. For I am leaving out much, since I am hurrying on to those things which I want especially to confess to you, and also there is much that I have forgotten. You did then give her another answer through a priest of yours, a bishop who had been brought up in your Church and was well versed in your books. My mother asked this bishop to be so kind as to discuss things with me, to expose my mistakes, to unteach me what was bad, and to teach me what was good; for he used to do this, if he found suitable people for his instruction. However, he refused to do so in my case, and very

sensibly too, as I realized later. He told my mother that I was not yet fit to be taught, because I was full of self-conceit with the novelty of that heresy and had already, as she had told him, been disturbing the minds of people who were not skilled in argument by my captious questions. "But," he said, "let him alone for a while. Only pray to the Lord for him; he himself will find out by his reading what his mistake is and how great is its impiety." And at the same time he told her that he himself, when a small boy, had been handed over to the Manichees by his mother, who had been led astray by them; he had not only read nearly all their books but had actually copied them out, and (with no one to argue with him or attempt to convince him) it had become clear to him that that sect ought to be entirely avoided, and so he had left it. But when he had said this to her, my mother still refused to be satisfied. She kept on begging and praying him, weeping many tears, that he would see me and discuss matters with me. In the end he became somewhat annoyed and said: "Now go away and leave me. As you live, it is impossible that the son of these tears should perish."

And this answer (as she has often mentioned to me in our conversations) she took as though the words had sounded from heaven.

Book IV

1 So FOR THE SPACE of nine years (from my nine-teenth to my twenty-eighth year) I lived a life in which I was seduced and seducing, deceived and deceiving, the prey of various desires. My public life was that of a teacher of what are called "the liberal arts." In private I went under cover of a false kind of religion. I was arrogant in the one sphere, superstitious in the other, and vain and empty from all points of view. On the one hand I and my friends would be hunting after the empty show of popularity—theatrical applause from the audience, verse competitions, contests for crowns of straw, the vanity of the stage, immoderate lusts—and on the other hand we would be trying to get clean of all this filth by carrying food to those people who were called "the elect" and "the holy ones," so that in the factory of their own stomachs they could turn this food into angels and gods, by whose aid we should be liberated. This was my way of life and these were the things I did, I and my friends, who were deceived through me and with me. Let proud-hearted men laugh at me, and those who have not yet, for their own health, been struck down and crushed by you, my God. I shall still confess to you the story of my shame, since it is to your glory. Allow me this, I beg, and grant me the power to survey in my memory now all those wanderings of my error in the past and *to offer unto Thee the sacrifice of rejoicing*. For without you what am I to myself except a guide to my own downfall? Or what am I, even at the best, except an infant sucking the milk you give and feeding upon you, the food that is imperishable? And what sort of a man is any man one can name, seeing that he is only a man? So let the strong and the powerful laugh at us; but let us, weak and needy as we are, make our confession to you.

2   IN THOSE YEARS I taught the art of rhetoric. Overcome myself by a desire for gain, I took money for instructing my pupils how to overcome other people by speechmaking. Nevertheless, Lord, as you know, I preferred to have honest pupils (as honesty is reckoned nowadays); without deceit I taught them the arts of deception, to be used not against the life of any innocent man, though sometimes to save the life of the guilty. And, God, from afar you saw me stumbling in that slippery way and in all that smoke showing just a spark of honor; for in my teaching I did act honorably toward those who loved vanity and sought after a lie, being indeed their companion. In those years I lived with a woman who was not bound to me by lawful marriage; she was one who had come my way because of my wandering desires and my lack of considered judgment; nevertheless, I had only this one woman and I was faithful to her. And with her I learned by my own experience how great a difference there is between the self-restraint of the marriage covenant which is entered into for the sake of having children, and the mere pact made between two people whose love is lustful and who do not want to have children—even though, if children are born, they compel us to love them.

I remember too that once when I had decided to go in for a competition in poetry to be recited on the stage, some magician or other came to me and asked how much I would give him to be assured of winning the competition, but I loathed and detested the filthy ceremonies of these people, and I told him that, even if the crown to be won were golden and immortal, I would not allow a fly to be killed in order to give me the victory. For his inten-

tion was to kill some living creatures in the sacrifices he
was going to make and it seemed to me that he meant to
try to secure for me the favor of devils by honoring
them in this way. Yet in rejecting this evil thing, I was
not, O God of my heart, acting out of any pure feeling
toward you. I did not know how to love you. I did not
know how to think except in terms of a kind of corporeal
splendor. And a soul that pants for such figments of the
imagination is surely committing fornication against you,
is putting its trust in falsity and feeding upon the winds.
There was I not allowing this magician to sacrifice to
devils on my behalf; yet all the time I was, in that superstition of mind, sacrificing myself to them. For surely to
feed them is to feed the winds, and we do this when by
our own errors we become objects for their laughter and
contempt.

3   Thus I was ready enough to consult those im-
posters called astrologers, my reason being that
they made no sacrifices and addressed no prayers to any
spirit to assist them in their divinations. Yet true Christian
piety must necessarily reject and condemn their art. For
it is a good thing to confess unto Thee, and to say, *Have
mercy upon me, heal my soul, for I have sinned against
Thee*, and not to misuse your mercy so as to make it a
license for sinning, but to remember the Lord's words:
*Behold, thou art made whole, sin no more lest a worse
thing happen to thee*. But the astrologers try to do away
with all this wholesome truth when they say: "The cause
of your sin is inevitably determined by the stars" and
"Venus was responsible here, or Saturn or Mars." As
though man, who is flesh and blood and proud corruption, should be guiltless and the guilt should be laid upon
the creator and the ruler of heaven and of the stars—you,
our God, sweetness and fount of justice, *who shall render
to every man according to his works*, and *a broken and a
contrite heart wilt Thou not despise*.

The governor of the province at that time was a wise
man who had a great knowledge of medicine and was
very widely known for his skill. He it was who put on

my fevered head the crown which I won in the poetry
contest. But here he was not acting as a doctor for my
fever. That disease can only be cured by you, *who resist
the proud and give grace to the humble.* Nevertheless you
did not fail to help me by means of this old man, nor did
you let slip the opportunity of doing good to my soul.
I grew to know him better and I used to listen eagerly
and intently to what he said. His talk had no great literary
pretensions but was delightful to listen to and also very
much worth hearing because of the liveliness and force
of his opinions. When in the course of conversation he
discovered that I was an eager student of the books of
those who make horoscopes, he spoke to me in a most
kind and fatherly way, urging me to throw away these
books and not to waste on pure nonsense the care and
attention that should be devoted to something useful. He
told me that he himself had in his youth studied astrology
with the idea of adopting it as the profession by which he
would make his living. "And if," he said, "I could understand Hippocrates, there would certainly be no difficulty
in mastering that subject." Nevertheless he had abandoned
astrology and pursued his study of medicine, simply because he had discovered that astrology was a false science,
and, being an honest man, he had no wish to make his
living by deceiving other people. "But you," he said,
"have a profession, the profession of rhetoric, to support
yourself by. You are giving your time to this astrological
nonsense of your own free will and not for any reason of
financial necessity. So you ought to be all the more ready
to believe what I say; for I worked hard to gain a really
thorough knowledge of the subject, with a view to making it my one source of income." I asked him why it was
then that a number of true predictions were made by
astrology, and he, within the limits of his knowledge,
replied that this was due to the force of chance which
was, as it were, distributed through everything in nature.
Often, for instance, while turning over haphazardly the
pages of a book of poetry, one may come upon a line
which is extraordinarily appropriate to some matter which
is in one's own mind, though the poet himself had no
thought of such a thing when he was writing. So, he said,

there was no reason to be surprised if a man's soul, while quite unconscious of what was going on inside it, should be acted upon by some higher instinct and should, by chance and not by any kind of skill, produce an answer that would fit in well with the affairs or the doings of the inquirer.

This too, either by him or through him, you did for me, and it was you who traced in my memory the lines along which I was later to follow up the inquiry by myself. But at the time neither he nor my dear friend Nebridius (a really good and a really pure young man, who used to laugh at the whole business of divination) could persuade me to give up these studies. I was still too much impressed by the authority of the astrological writers, and I had not yet found the certain proof that I was looking for, which would make it clear to me beyond all doubt that when these men were consulted and gave a true answer this was by luck or by chance and not from a real science of stargazing.

4   In the time when I first began to teach rhetoric in the town where I was born, I had found a very dear friend who was following the same studies. We were both of the same age, now at the beginning of manhood; he had grown up with me as a child and we had gone to school together and played together. But he was not in those early days, nor even in this later time, a friend in the true meaning of friendship, because there can be no true friendship unless those who cling to each other are welded together by you in that love which is spread throughout our hearts by the holy spirit which is given to us. But still this friendship was something very sweet to us and had ripened in the enthusiasm of the studies which we had pursued together. For I had turned him away from the true faith (in which, being so young, he was not soundly or thoroughly grounded) and had led him into that deadly superstitious folly of my own, which had so saddened my mother. His mind was wandering astray with mine, and my soul could not be without him. But you were there, you who are always close upon the heels

of those who run away from you, you who are at the same time the God of vengeance and the fountain of mercy and who turn us to yourself in ways that are wonderful. You were there, and you took him away from this life, when he had scarcely had a year of this friendship with me, a friendship that was sweeter to me than all sweetnesses that in this life I had ever known.

Who can recount your praises? Who can recount the praises due for what he personally has experienced in himself? What was it, my God, that you did then? And how unsearchable is the abyss of your judgments! For a long time my friend suffered from a high fever and lay unconscious in a sweat that looked like death. When they despaired of his recovery, he was baptized. He knew nothing of this himself, and I paid little attention to the fact of his baptism. I assumed that his soul would retain what it had learned from me and would not be affected by something done to his body while he was unconscious. But it turned out very differently. For he got better and came back to life again, and, as soon as I could speak to him—which was as soon as he could speak to me, since I never left his side and indeed we depended too much on each other—I began to make jokes with him, assuming that he would join in, about the baptism which he had received when he could neither feel nor know what was being done, and yet had now been told that he had received it. But he shrunk back from me as though I were an enemy. With a sudden confident authority which took me aback he told me that, if I wanted to be a friend of his, I must give up talking to him in this way. I was astonished and amazed, and I put off telling him what was in my mind until he should get well again and should be strong enough in health for me to be able to discuss things with him as I wished. But he was taken away beyond the reach of my folly, so that with you he might be kept safe for my comfort. A few days later, when I was not there, his fever returned and he died.

My heart was darkened over with sorrow, and whatever I looked at was death. My own country was a torment to me, my own home was a strange unhappiness. All those things which we had done and said together became, now that he was gone, sheer torture to me. My eyes looked for him everywhere and could not find him. And as to the places where we used to meet I hated all of them for not containing him; nor were they able to say to me now, "Look, he will soon come," as they used to say when he was alive and away from me. I had become a great riddle to myself and I used to ask my soul why it was sad and why it disquieted me so sorely. And my soul did not know what to answer. If I said, "Trust in God," she very rightly did not obey me, because the man whom she had lost, my dearest friend, was more real and better than the fantastic god in whom she was asked to trust. Only tears were sweet to me, and tears had taken the place of my friend in my heart's love.

5   AND NOW, LORD, all that has passed and time has dulled my pain. May I learn from you, who are Truth, and may I put close to your mouth the ear of my heart so that you can tell me why it is that tears are sweet to us when we are unhappy? Or have you, in spite of the fact that you are present everywhere, put our unhappiness far from you? You abide in yourself, while we are tossed about from one trial to another. And yet if we could not speak our misery into your ears, there would be nothing at all left to us of hope. How is it, then, that from the bitterness of life we can pluck such sweet fruit in mourning and weeping and sighing and lamentation? Is the sweetness simply in the fact that we hope that you are listening to us? This is certainly so in the case of our prayers, since our prayers have a longing to reach you. But is it also so in the case of that sorrow and grief felt for something lost, in which I was overwhelmed at that time? For I had no hope that he would come back to life again, and this was not what I begged for with my tears; I merely felt sad and I wept; for I was in misery and I had lost my joy. Or is weeping really a bitter thing, and is it only pleasant to us at the moment when we are shrinking back from the things we once enjoyed and can scarcely bear to think of them?

6   BUT WHY am I saying all this? It is not the time now to be asking questions but for making my confession to you. I was unhappy and so is every soul unhappy which is tied to its love for mortal things; when it loses them, it is torn in pieces, and it is then that it comes to realize the unhappiness which was there even before it lost them. Such was I at that time, and I wept most bitterly, and I found repose in bitterness. Indeed I was unhappy, yet this unhappy life of mine was dearer to me than the friend whom I had lost. Certainly I would have liked to change my life, but not to part with it; I would prefer rather to part with my friend. And I doubt whether I would have parted with it even for his sake—as in the story, or fable, of Orestes and Pylades, who both wanted to die together, each for each, at the same time, since not to live together was worse to them than death. But I had a strange kind of feeling, which was just the opposite of theirs: I was at the same time thoroughly tired of living and extremely frightened of dying. The fact was, I think, that the more I loved my friend, the more I hated and feared death which, like a cruel enemy, had taken him away from me, and I imagined that, since it had been able to destroy him, it would quickly and suddenly destroy all men living. Yes; I remember it well; this was how I thought. Look, my God, into my heart; look inside it; see, because I remember, O my hope, you who cleanse me from the uncleanness of such affections, directing *mine eyes toward Thee and plucking my feet out of the snare*. I was surprised that other mortals could remain alive when the man, whom I had loved as though he would never die, was dead. And I was still more surprised that, when he was dead, I, who was his other self, should still live. I agree with the poet who called his friend "the half of his own soul." For I felt that my soul and my friend's had been one soul in two bodies, and that was why I had a horror of living, because I did not want to live as a half being, and perhaps too that was why I feared to die, because I did not want him, whom I had loved so much, to die wholly and completely.

7 WHAT MADNESS it is not to know how to love men as they should be loved! And how foolish man is to be violent and impatient with the lot of man. Mad and foolish I was at that time. I raged and sighed and wept and worried, I could not rest, I could not think intelligently. For I was carrying about with me my soul all broken and bleeding and not wanting to be carried by me; yet I did not know where to put it down. There was no rest for it anywhere—not in pleasant groves, not in games and singing, not in sweet-smelling gardens, not in fine banquets, not in the pleasures of the bed, not in the reading of books, nor in poetry. I loathed everything, even the light itself, and everything that was not he seemed to me painful and wearisome, except for my tears and my laments; for in these alone I did find a little peace. But as soon as my soul was distracted from weeping, I became overwhelmed by a great load of unhappiness. It was a load which I should have brought to you, Lord, for you to lighten. I knew this but I neither would nor could—all the more so because, when I thought of you, I was not thinking of something firm and solid. For it was not you yourself who were my God; my god was an empty fantasy, a creation of my own error. If I tried to lay down my burden there, that it might rest, it slipped through the void and came tumbling back upon me again. And myself to myself had become a place of misery, a place where I could not bear to be and from which I could not go. For my heart could not flee away from my heart, nor could I escape from myself, since wherever I ran, I should be following. Nevertheless I did flee from my native place; for my eyes did not search for him so much in places where they were not accustomed to see him. So I left the town of Tagaste and came to Carthage.

8 TIME IS NOT inactive. So far from passing through our senses without doing anything, it performs wonders in our minds. So now time came and went from one day to another, and in its coming and going it gave me other things to hope for and other things to remember, and gradually patched me up again with the sort of pleas-

ures which I had known before. To these pleasures my
great sorrow began to give way. But, though its place
was not taken by other sorrows, it was taken by things
which could cause other sorrows. For the reason why that
great sorrow of mine had pierced into me so easily and so
deeply was simply this: I had poured out my soul like
water onto sand by loving a man who was bound to die
just as if he were an immortal. Now certainly what did me
most good and helped most to cure me was the comfort
I found in other friends, in whose company I loved all the
things which, after this, I did love. And this was one huge
fable, one long lie; by its adulterous caressing, my mind,
which lay itching in my ears, was corrupted. Nor, if one
of my friends died, would that fable die out in me. There
were other things which more fully took up my mind in
their company—to talk and laugh and do kindnesses to
each other; to read pleasant books together; to make jokes
together and then talk seriously together; sometimes to
disagree, but without any ill feeling, just as one may disagree with oneself, and to find that these very rare dis-
agreements made our general agreement all the sweeter;
to be sometimes teaching and sometimes learning; to long
impatiently for the absent and to welcome them with joy
when they returned to us. These and other similar expressions of feeling, which proceed from the hearts of
those who love and are loved in return, and are revealed
in the face, the voice, the eyes, and in a thousand charming
ways, were like a kindling fire to melt our souls together
and out of many to make us one.

9   IT IS THIS which we love in our friends, and we
love it so much that a man's conscience will
condemn him if he fails to give or accept friendship
when it is sought for or offered; nor will he expect anything else of a physical nature from his friend except
these demonstrations of good feeling. It is for this that we
feel such sorrow if a friend dies, such darkness of pain,
the heart steeped in tears, all sweetness turned to bitterness, and for us a kind of living death because we have
lost in death one who was alive. Blessed is the man who

loves you, who loves his friend in you, and his enemy because of you. He alone loses no one dear to him, for they are all dear to him in one who is not lost. And who is this except our God, the God who made heaven and earth and who fills them, because it was by filling them that He created them? No one loses you, except one who voluntarily leaves you. And if he leaves you, where can he go, or where can he escape from you? He can only run from your kindness to your anger. Everywhere in his own punishment he will encounter your law. And your law is truth, and truth is you.

10 *Turn us, O God of hosts, show us thy countenance and we shall be whole.* For wherever man's soul turns, except toward you, it is fixed to sorrows, even if it fixes itself on things of beauty outside you and outside itself. These things of beauty would have no existence at all unless they were from you. They rise and set; in their rising they begin, as it were, to exist; they develop so as to reach their perfection, and after that they grow old and die; not all grow old, but all die. So, when they rise and reach their way into existence, the quicker they are to grow into being, the more they hurry toward ceasing to be. That is their law. So much you have given them, namely to be parts of a structure in which the parts are not all in existence at the same time; instead, by fading and by replacing each other, they all together constitute the universe of which they are parts. Our own speech too, which is constructed out of meaningful sounds, follows the same principles. There could never be a complete sentence unless one word, as soon as the syllables had been sounded, ceased to be in order to make room for the next. In these things let my soul praise you, God, creator of all things, yet let it not be stuck and glued too close to them in love through the senses of the body. For these things go along their path toward nonexistence, and they tear and wound the soul with terrible longings, since the soul itself desires to be and to find rest in what it loves. But in those things there is no place to rest, since they do not stay. They pass away and no one can follow them with his

bodily senses. Nor can anyone grasp them tight even
while they are present and in front of him.

Our bodily sense is slow because it is bodily sense and
is bounded by the physical. It is sufficient for the purpose
for which it was made, but it is quite incapable of grasping and holding things as they run on their appointed way
from their beginnings to their endings. For in your word,
by which they are created, they hear their decree: "From
this point; and not beyond that."

11   DO NOT BE FOOLISH, my soul, and do not let the
ear of your heart be deafened by the din of your
folly. Listen now. The Word itself calls you to come
back; and there is the place of peace that is imperturbable,
where love cannot be forsaken unless it first forsakes.
See how things pass away so that other things may take
their places and that so this lower universe may be established in all its parts. "But do I ever depart," says the
Word of God, "and is there any place to which I could
depart?" There fix your dwelling place, my soul, and
there store up everything which you have received from
there. Do it now at least, tired out as you are with falsities.
Entrust to truth whatever truth has given you, and you
will lose nothing. What is withered in you will flower
again, and all your illnesses will be made well, and all
that was flowing and wasting from you will regain shape
and substance and will form part of you again, and they
will not lay you down in the place where they themselves
descend, but will stand fast with you and abide with you
forever before God who stands and abides forever.

Why then be perverse, my soul, and why follow your
own flesh? Will you not rather turn and let your flesh
follow you? Whatever you perceive through the flesh
you perceive only in part, and you are ignorant of the
whole, of which these are parts; yet still these parts delight
you. But if your bodily sense were capable of comprehen-
ding the whole—instead of being, for your punishment,
justly restricted itself to a part of the universe—
you would wish that everything in existence at the present moment would pass and go, so that you might have

the greater pleasure of perceiving the entirety of things. For these words we speak are perceived by you through your bodily sense, and you certainly do not want to hear the same syllables forever; you want them to pass away so that others may come and so that you may hear the whole sentence. And this is always the case when one thing is made up of many parts and all the parts do not exist together at the same time. To perceive all the parts together at once would give more pleasure than to perceive each individual part separately. But far better than these is He who made all things, and He is our God. And He does not pass away, because there is nothing to take His place.

12 IF BODIES PLEASE YOU, praise God for them and turn your love back from them to their maker, lest you should displease Him in being pleased by them. If souls please you, love them in God, because by themselves they are subject to change, but in Him they are established firm; without Him they would pass away and be no more. So you must love them in Him and take with you to Him as many souls as you can and say to them: "It is He whom we must love; He made all this and He is not far off." For He did not make things and then go away; things are from Him and also in Him. See where He is: He is everywhere where there is the least trace of truth. He is right inside the heart, but the heart has wandered away from Him. Return, sinners, to your own heart and cling to Him who made you. Stand in Him, and you shall stand fast; rest in Him, and you shall find peace. Where are you going to over those rough paths? Where are you going? The good that you love is from Him; but its goodness and sweetness is only because you are looking toward Him; it will rightly turn to bitterness if what is from Him is wrongly loved, He Himself being left out of the account. What are you aiming at, then, by going on and on walking along these difficult and tiring ways? There is no rest to be found where you are looking for it. Seek what you seek, but it is not there where you are seeking. You seek a happy life in the country of death. It is not there. For how can life be happy, where there is no life?

But our Life came down to us and suffered our death and destroyed death by the abundance of His own life: and He thundered, calling us to return to Him into that secret place from which He came out to us—coming first into the Virgin's womb, where humanity was married to Him, our mortal flesh, that it might not be forever mortal, and from there *like a bridegroom coming out of His chamber, rejoicing as a giant to run His course.* For He was not slow; He ran, crying aloud in His words, in His deeds, in His death, in His life, in His descent, in His ascension, crying and calling us to return to Him. And He withdrew Himself from our eyes so that we might return to our heart and find Him. He went away, and, look, He is here. He did not want to be with us long, and He has not left us. He went back to a place which He had never left, since the world was made by Him and He was in this world, and He came into this world to save sinners. It is to Him that my soul makes confession, and He heals my soul, for it has sinned against Him. Sons of men, how long will you be so slow and heavy of heart? Now that Life has come down to you, will you not raise yourselves and live? But how can you raise yourselves, when you are already high in the air and have *set your mouth against the heavens?* Come down, so that you may go up and go up toward God. For in climbing up against God, you fell. Say this to the souls you love. Tell them to weep in this valley of tears, and so carry them up with you to God, because it is by His spirit that you are saying this to them, if, while you say it, you are burning with the fire of charity.

13   AT THAT TIME I did not know this and I loved these lower beauties and I was sinking down to the depths. I used to say to my friends, "Do we love anything except what is beautiful? What, then, is the beautiful? And what is beauty? What is it that attracts us and wins our affection for the things we love? For unless there were grace and beauty in them, they could not

possibly draw us to them." And, observing things closely, I saw that in bodies themselves there was one sort of beauty which comes from a thing constituting a whole, and another sort of grace which comes from the right and apt relationship of one thing to another, such as one part of a body to the whole body, or a shoe to the foot, and so on. This idea sprang up into my mind from the depths of my heart, and I wrote some books on "The Beautiful and the Fitting"—two or three books, I think. You know, God, for I cannot remember. I no longer have the books. Somehow or other they have disappeared.

14 WHY WAS IT, Lord my God, that I decided to dedicate these books to Hiereus, who was an orator at Rome? I had never seen the man, but I had come to love him because of his very great reputation for learning, and I had heard and very much admired some of the things he had said. But the greater part of my admiration came from the fact that others admired him. He was praised to the skies and people were astonished that he, a Syrian who was brought up as a master of Greek oratory, should later become such a wonderful speaker in Latin and should also possess such a wide knowledge of philosophy. So he was praised and, without ever having been seen, was loved. Does this kind of love come into the heart of the hearer straight from the words of praise which he hears? Not at all. What happens is that love is kindled by love. We only love someone whom we hear praised when we believe that the praise comes from a sincere heart, that is to say, when the man who gives the praise loves the man whom he is praising.

So at that time I loved men on the strength of the judgment of other men—not on your judgment, my God, in whom no one is deceived. Yet my feeling was not like that which one may have for a famous charioteer or a fighter with wild beasts in the theater who is the idol of the crowd. My feelings were different and more serious, and I admired others as I would have liked to be admired myself. For I would not have wanted to be praised and loved as actors are, though I myself would certainly praise and love actors. But I would rather have been quite unknown than known in that way, rather have been hated than loved like that. How does it come about that the weights and impulses toward all these different kinds of love are distributed in one soul? Why is it that I love some quality in another man and yet would appear to hate it too, since I should reject it and detest it in myself? We are both of us human; the actor and I share the same nature, so one cannot compare my feeling about him with the feeling of a man who loves a good horse but would not like to be a horse, even if he could. How is it then that I love in a human being something which I should hate in myself, though I also am a human being? Man himself is a great deep, and you, Lord, number the very hairs of his head and in your sight they are not lost. Yet the hairs of man's head are easier to number than are his affections and the impulses of his heart.

That orator, however, whom I loved so much, was the kind of man that I would have wished to be myself. And I erred through swelling pride; I was tossed about by every wind, and it was too difficult for me to feel your steering hand. Why is it that I know now, and can confess it to you confidently, that I loved that man more because of the love of those who praised him than because of the actual qualities for which he was praised? The fact is that if the same people, instead of praising him, had abused him and had said just the same things about him in an abusive and contemptuous spirit, I should not have been so set on fire with admiration for him; yet his qualities would have been just the same; the man himself would have been no different; the only differences would have been in the feelings of the speakers. See how abject and helpless the soul is before it learns to cling to the solidity of truth! As the winds of speech blow from the hearts of those who hold their varying opinions, so the soul is carried this way and that, changing its course now here, now there; its light is clouded over, and it cannot see the truth. And there is the truth, right in front of us. And to me it was a matter of great importance for my style and my work to become known to that famous orator, and if he liked them, I should be all the more ardent about him; though if he thought little of them, then my vain heart, quite empty of your solidity, would be wounded. Yet still I enjoyed my meditations on "The Beautiful and the Fitting," which I dedicated to him, and, if there was no one else to admire the work, I thought it very good myself.

15   BUT, ALMIGHTY, I did not yet see that all this great matter has its hinge in your workmanship; for you alone make wonders, and my mind was ranging over corporeal forms. I defined and distinguished the beautiful as being that which is beautiful in itself and the fitting as being that which derives its grace from its appropriateness to something else, and I used corporeal examples in support of my argument. I also considered the nature of the mind, but the false view I had of spiritual things prevented me from seeing the truth. And the very force of truth itself was staring me in the face, but I turned my panting mind away from what was incorporeal and concentrated on line and color and swelling magnitudes, and because I could not see these in my mind, I concluded that I could not see my mind. And as in virtue I loved peace and in vice I hated discord, so I noted the unity in the one and the division, as it were, in the other, and it seemed to me that in the unity lay the rational mind and the nature of truth and the supreme good; but in the division I was wretched enough to imagine that I saw some sort of substance of the irrational life and a nature of the supreme evil, which was not only substance but actually life—yet not proceeding from you, my God, from whom proceed all things. I called the first a Monad, conceiving of it as a mind without any sex, and I called the other a Dyad—anger as in deeds of violence, and lust as in sins of impurity. I was talking ignorantly. I did not know and I had not yet been taught that evil is not a substance at all nor is our soul that supreme and unchangeable good.

For just as acts of violence are done if the emotion, in which lies the impulse to act, is vicious and aggressive and muddled, and just as sins of impurity are done if the affection of the soul from which carnal pleasures are derived is uncontrolled, so errors and false opinions contaminate life if the rational soul itself is corrupted. And so it was with me at that time, when I did not know that my soul needed to be illumined by another light, if it was to be a partaker of truth, since it is not itself the essence of truth. *For Thou shalt light my candle, O Lord my God, Thou shalt enlighten my darkness:* and *of Thy fullness have we all received, for Thou art the true light that lighteth every man that cometh into the world; for in Thee there is no variableness, neither shadow of change.*

But I was aiming to reach you and at the same time was being forced back from you, so that I might taste death; for *Thou resistest the proud.* And how could anything be more proud than to assert, as I did in my incredible folly, that I was by nature what you are? For, being subject to change myself (as was obvious from the mere fact that I wanted to become wise and so proceed from worse to better), I preferred to think that you also were subject to change rather than I was not what you are. And so I was forced back from you and you resisted my vain stiff-neckedness, and I imagined corporeal forms, and, being myself flesh, I accused the flesh, and, being a wayfaring spirit, I did not return to you, but went on and on wandering into fancies which have no existence either in you or in me or in the body and, so far from being created for me by your truth, were figments constructed by my imagination out of corporeal things. And I used to speak to the little ones of your faith—my own fellow citizens, though I, without knowing it, was in exile from them—and, like a talkative ass, I used to say, "How is it, then, that the soul makes a mistake if it was created by God?" But I would not allow myself to be asked, "How is it, then, that God makes a mistake?" And I preferred to maintain that your unchangeable substance went astray under compulsion, rather than admit that my own changeable substance had deviated of its own accord and for its punishment had fallen into error.

I was about twenty-six or twenty-seven when I wrote those books. As I wrote them I turned over in my mind all those corporeal fictions which made such a noise that the ears of my heart were deafened. Yet, sweet truth, I was straining these ears to try to hear your inner melody, as I meditated upon "The Beautiful and the Fitting"; and I longed to stand and hear you and rejoice with joy at the voice of the bridegroom; but I could not. I was being dragged out and away by the voices of my own error, and I was sinking down to the depths under the weight of my own pride. You did not *make me to hear joy and gladness* nor did *the bones exult which were not yet humbled.*

16 AND WHAT GOOD did it do me that at about the age of twenty I was able to read and understand without any help that book of Aristotle's called *The Ten Categories* when it came into my hands? My rhetoric master at Carthage and others too with a reputation for learning would puff out their cheeks with pride whenever they mentioned this book, and so I was looking forward to it eagerly as though it was something wonderful and inspired. Later I compared notes with people who told me that they had had the greatest difficulty in understanding this book, even with the help of most learned commentators who had explained matters not only in words but by diagrams drawn in the sand. However they could tell me no more about the book than what I had discovered by reading it myself. Indeed the book seemed to me to deal very clearly with substances, such as "man," and with their qualities, such as the figure of a man; what sort of man he is; his height, how many feet; his family relationships, whose brother he is; where he is placed; when he was born; whether he is standing or sitting; whether he is wearing shoes or armor; whether he is doing something or having something done to him—and all the other innumerable things that can be put either in these nine categories of which I have given examples, or else in the main category of substance.

All this, so far from doing me any good, actually did me harm. For, imagining that everything in existence could be placed under these ten categories, I attempted by this method to understand you, my God, in your wonderful simplicity and changelessness, as though you were a substance with the qualities of your own greatness or your own beauty, as we find qualities in a body. But you yourself are your greatness and your beauty, but a body is not great or beautiful simply by the fact of being a body, since it would still be a body if it were less great or less beautiful. My thoughts of you were falsehood and not truth, fictions of my misery and not the realities of your blessedness. You gave the order, and so it was done in me, that the *earth should bring forth briars and thorns to me* and that *in the sweat of my brows I should eat my bread*.

And what good did it do me that I, at a time when I was the vile slave of evil desires, read and understood for myself every book that I could lay my hands on which dealt with what are called the liberal arts? I enjoyed these books and did not know the source of whatever in them was true and certain. For I had my back to the light and my face to the things on which the light shone; so the eyes in my face saw things in the light, but on my face itself no light fell. I could understand quite easily and without the aid of an instructor every work on rhetoric or logic, geometry, music, and arithmetic. This you know, my Lord God, since quickness of intelligence and precision in understanding are your gifts. But I did not use these gifts by making an offering of them to you. And so it all turned more to my destruction than to my profit, because I labored to secure so good a portion of my substance in my own power, and, instead of preserving my strength for you, I went away from you into a far country to waste my substance upon false and prostitute desires. For what good could my good abilities do me if I did not use them well? I never realized that even hard-working and talented people find these arts very difficult to understand until I began to try to explain them to others; then I found that the real experts in them were the ones who could follow my explanations reasonably quickly.

But what good was all this to me, holding, as I did, that you, Lord God and Truth, were a vast luminous body and that I was a sort of piece broken off from this body? What an extraordinary perversity I showed! Yet this was what I was then. And now, my God, I do not blush to confess to you the mercies which you have shown me and to call upon you—I who did not blush then, when I was professing my blasphemies before men and raising my barking voice against you. What good to me then was that intelligence of mine, so quick and nimble in those arts and sciences? What good to me were all those knotty volumes which I unraveled without the aid of any human teacher, when all the time I was so disgracefully, so sacrilegiously, and so foully wrong in the doctrine of piety? Or what great harm was it to your little ones, if they had a far slower intelligence than mine, since they did not go far from you, and so were able safely to become fledged in the nest of your Church and nourish the wings of charity on the food of a sound faith?

O Lord our God, *under the shadow of Thy wings let us hope.* Protect us and bear us up. You will bear us up, yes, from our infancy until our gray hairs you will bear us up. For our strength, when it is from you, is strength indeed; but when it is our own, it is weakness. With you our good is ever living, and when we turn our backs on it, then we are perverse. Let us return now to you, Lord, so that we may not be overturned, because our good is with you, living and without any defect, since you yourself are our good. And we need not be afraid of having no place to which we may return. We of our own accord fell from that place. And our home, which is your eternity, does not fall down when we are away from it.

Book V

1 ACCEPT THE SACRIFICE of my confessions which my tongue sets before you. You formed the tongue and moved it to make confession to your name. *Heal Thou all my bones, and let them say, O Lord, who is like unto Thee.* When we confess to you, we do not inform you of what is happening inside us; for the closed heart does not shut out your eye, and man's hardness cannot resist your hand. You dissolve it at your pleasure, either in pity or in punishment, and *nothing can hide itself from Thy heat.* But let my soul praise you so that it may love you, and let it confess to you your acts of mercy, so that it may praise you. Your whole creation is never silent and never ceases to praise you. The spirit of every man utters its praises in words directed to you; animals and material bodies praise you through the mouth of those who meditate upon them, so that our soul may rise out of its weariness toward you, first supporting itself upon the things which you created, and then passing on to you yourself who made them marvelously. And there is refreshment and true strength.

2 LET THE WICKED and the restless go from you and run away. Yet still you see them, piercing through their shadows and all about them all things are beautiful and they themselves are deformed. And what harm have they done you or in what respect have they

brought dishonor on your government which from the
heavens down to the lowest things of earth is just and
perfect? For where did they run, when they ran from
your face? Is there anywhere where you do not find
them? In fact they ran away so as not to see you, though
all the time you saw them, and that, in their blindness,
they might stumble on you (since *Thou forsakest
nothing Thou hast made*), that in their injustice they
might stumble on you and by your justice they might
suffer for it, withdrawing themselves from your gentleness and stumbling on your uprightness and falling into
your anger. Little do they know that you are everywhere, that it is impossible to draw a line of circum-
scription about you, and that you alone are always
present even to those who have put themselves furthest
from you. Let them turn, then, and seek for you, since
you have not deserted your creation in the same way as
they have deserted their creator. Let them turn and see,
you are there, you are in their hearts, in the hearts of
those who confess to you and who throw themselves upon
your mercy and weep upon your breast after the difficult
ways which they have trod. And you in your gentleness
wipe the tears from their eyes, and they weep the more
and rejoice in their weeping, since it is you, Lord, and
not any man of flesh and blood, but you, Lord, their
creator, who are giving them refreshment and consolation. And where was I when I was seeking for you? You
were there, in front of me; but I had gone away even
from myself. I could not even find myself, much less find
you.

3   I now set down in the sight of my God the story
    of my twenty-ninth year. At this time there had
come to Carthage a Manichaean bishop called Faustus. He
was a great snare of the devil and many were caught in
the snare. What charmed people was the smoothness of
his language, and I certainly admired this myself; but I
was able to distinguish between it and the truth about
those matters which I was so eager to learn; I was interested not so much in the dish and adornment of a fine

style as in the substance of the knowledge which this
celebrated Faustus of theirs was setting before me. For
his reputation had preceded him, and I had been told that
he was a really remarkable scholar in all branches of learning and particularly learned in the liberal sciences.

Now I had read a lot of philosophy, and I retained in
my memory a great deal of what I had read. I began to
compare some of the things said by the philosophers with
those interminable fables of the Manichees, and it seemed
to me that what the philosophers said was the more probable, even though their powers were limited to the in-
vestigation of this world and they could not possibly
discover its Lord and Master. *For Thou art great, O Lord,
and hast respect unto the humble, but the proud Thou
beholdest afar off.* Nor do you draw near except to the
contrite in heart. The proud cannot find you, however
deep and curious their knowledge, not even if they could
count the stars and the grains of sand, or measure the con-
stellations in the sky and track down the paths of the
stars. Into all these things they look with the mind and
understanding which you gave them; they have discovered much and many years in advance of the event have
predicted eclipses of the sun and moon, setting down the
day, the hour, and the extent of these eclipses. Their calculations have been proved correct; everything took
place as they had foretold; they put into writing the
rules which they had discovered, and these rules are read
today; on the basis of these rules one can foretell the year,
the month, the day, and the hour when there will be an
eclipse of the sun or moon and whether the eclipse will be
total or partial. And everything will take place as predicted. And men who are ignorant of the subject are full
of astonishment and admiration, while those who know
will boast of their knowledge and will be praised for it,
thus turning away from you in their evil pride and losing
the light that comes to them from you. They can see an
eclipse of the sun long before it happens, but cannot
see their own eclipse when it is actually taking place.
For they do not approach the matter in a religious spirit
and ask what is the source of the intelligence which they
use to inquire into all this, and then, finding that it is

you who made them, they do not give themselves up to
you for you to preserve what you have made; nor do they
sacrifice to you what they have made of themselves; nor
do they slaughter their flighty imaginations like birds,
and their inquisitivenesses, by which they wander through
the secret paths of the abyss, like the fish of the sea, and
their lusts like the beasts of the field, so that you, God,
the consuming fire, may burn up those dead cares of
theirs and recreate the men themselves immortally.

But they do not know the way, which is your word,
and by your word you made the things which they number and themselves who do the numbering and the sense
by which they see what they number and the understanding from which comes the ability to number, *and of Thy
wisdom there is no number*. But the Only Begotten is
Himself *made unto us wisdom, and righteousness and
sanctification*, and was numbered among us, and *paid
tribute to Caesar*. They do not know this way, the way to
descend from themselves to Him, and by Him ascend to
Him. They do not know this way; they fancy that they
are high up and shining with the stars, and in fact they
have fallen to the ground and *their foolish heart is
darkened*.

Much that they say about what is created is true; but
they do not seek religiously for the truth which is the
maker of creation, and therefore they do not find Him,
or, if they do find Him and know Him to be God, they
do not honor Him as God and give Him thanks; instead
they become vain in their imaginations and consider
themselves to be wise; they attribute to themselves what
is yours, and in this way, such is the perversity of their
blindness, they actually attribute their own qualities to
you, making you, who are Truth, responsible for their
own falsehoods, and *changing the glory of the uncor-
ruptible God into an image made like corruptible man,
and to birds, and four-footed beasts, and creeping things,
changing Thy truth into a lie, and worshiping and serving the creature more than the Creator*.

Nevertheless, I could remember many true things
which the philosophers have said about this created world,
and I could see the reason for what they said in calcula-

tion, in the order of time, and in the visible evidence of
the stars. I compared their views with those of Manes,
who, drawing on a rich vein of pure fantasy, has had a
lot to say on these subjects. I found in him no reason
given for the solstices and the equinoxes or the eclipses of
the sun and moon or anything else of this kind which I
had learned in the books of secular philosophy. I was told
to believe in these views of Manes; but they did not correspond with what had been established by mathematics
and my own eyesight; in fact they were widely divergent.

4   BUT, LORD GOD of truth, does a man please you
by knowing all these things? For the man who
knows them all, but does not know you, is unhappy, and
happy is the man who knows you, even if he does not
know these other things. And he who knows both you
and them is not the happier because of them but is only
happy because of you, if *knowing Thee, he glorifies
Thee as God, and is thankful* and becomes not vain in his
imaginations. The man who consciously owns a tree and
knows how to use it and gives you thanks for it may not
know its exact height or how widely the branches spread;
but he is better off than the man who, while he has
measured the tree and counted all its branches, neither
owns it nor knows and loves its creator. In just the same
way a faithful servant of yours, who has the whole
world of wealth and who though apparently possessing
nothing yet possesses everything because he clings to you,
whom all things serve, may not even know about the
circles of the Great Bear; but it would be absurd to doubt
that he is better off than the man who, though he can
measure the heaven and count the stars and weigh the
elements, is forgetful of you, who have *made all things in
number, weight, and measure.*

5   WHAT THEN WAS the point of this Manes writing
on these subjects, which are not necessary for the
learning of goodness and piety? For you have said to
man: *Behold, piety is wisdom.* And Manes, even if he had

known all these subjects perfectly, might still have been
without wisdom; but in impudently presuming to teach
them, when he did not know them, he certainly revealed
an incapacity for piety. For the profession of these subjects, even when one knows them, is worldly vanity; confession to you is piety. So he had gone astray, and all he
achieved by his numerous statements on these matters
was this: he was shown up by people who had an accurate
knowledge of them, and it was thus made perfectly plain
how much reliance could be placed on his understanding
of other more abstruse matters. He certainly did not
wish to be thought little of; for he made it his business
to persuade people that the Holy Ghost, the comforter
and enricher of your faithful ones, was personally and
with plenary authority resident in himself. And so when
he was caught out making false statements about the
heaven and the stars and the movements of the sun and
moon, even though these things are not an integral part
of religious doctrine, yet it was clear enough that his presumption was sacrilegious: he was talking about things
he did not know; he was making false statements about
them, and so mad was the vanity of his pride that he attempted to have these statements attributed to him as
though he were a divine person.

Now whenever I come across any Christian brother,
whoever it may be, who is ignorant of these sciences and
has mistaken views on them, I can listen to him patiently
enough as he delivers his opinions. So long as he does not
hold any unworthy beliefs about you, Lord and Creator
of all things, I cannot see that it does him any harm if
he is rather ignorant about the situation or conditions of
material objects. But it does do him harm if he imagines
that this scientific knowledge is an integral part of the
structure of the doctrine of piety, and then has the
audacity to make overconfident assertions on subjects of
which he knows nothing. Yet even such weakness as this
is borne patiently by our mother Charity while a man's
faith is in its infancy until the new man rises up into
the perfect man, so as not to be carried about with every
wind of doctrine. Manes, however, set himself up as the
teacher, the first authority, the leader, and the guide of

his disciples, and he did it in such a way that his followers imagined that they were following not a mere man, but your Holy Spirit. Obviously, once he was convicted of having made false statements, one must consider this extraordinary madness of his as something detestable and something which ought to be utterly rejected. Nevertheless I had not as yet reached a firm conclusion as to whether or not it might be possible to explain the changes in the lengths of days and nights, the alternation of night and day, eclipses of sun and moon and other such things of which I had read in a manner that would be consistent with the doctrines of Manes. If it were possible, then it would still be an open question to me whether his solution was correct; yet, because of his reputation for sanctity, I would still prefer to trust in him as an authority.

6   FOR ABOUT NINE YEARS, in my mental aberration, I was a disciple of the Manichees, and for nearly all of this time I had been waiting with a kind of boundless longing for the coming of this man Faustus. For the other Manichees whom I met and who failed to produce any answers to the questions I was raising on these subjects were always putting forward his name and promising me that as soon as Faustus arrived and I was able to discuss matters with him, all these difficulties of mine, together with any more weighty questions that I might care to ask, would be very easily dealt with and very lucidly explained. Well, he did arrive, and I found him a charming man with a very pleasant choice of words; he came out with exactly the same things as the others are always saying, but he did it much more elegantly.

However, my thirst could not be relieved by expensive drinking vessels and a well-dressed waiter. My ears were full already of this stuff, and the arguments themselves did not appear to me to be any better simply because they were better expressed; eloquence did not make them true; nor could I consider the soul wise because the face was attractive and the words well chosen. And as to those who promised me so much of him, they were not good judges of things. Their reason for thinking him wise and intelligent was simply that his way of speaking gave them pleasure.

I have had experience too of a quite different kind of person, the sort who will bring truth itself into suspicion and refuse to assent to it, if it is expressed in a good and ordered style. But you, my God, had already taught me in wonderful and hidden ways, and I believe that it was you who taught me because it is the truth and apart from you there is no other teacher of the truth, wherever or however it may be revealed. I had now learned this from you: that a thing is not necessarily true for being expressed eloquently, nor necessarily false if the sounds made by the lips are imperfectly pronounced; nor, on the other hand, is a thing true simply because it is expressed in a rough and ready way, nor false because it is uttered in a fine style. For with wisdom and folly the same thing holds good as with wholesome and unwholesome food. You can have silver or earthenware dishes on the table, just as you can have a decorated or undecorated use of language; either kind of food can be served in either kind of dish.

So those eager feelings of mine, with which I had so long been waiting for this man, were certainly gratified when I saw the way he carried himself and the way he behaved in a discussion, and when I saw how readily he found just the right words for expressing his thought I was delighted, and with many others, indeed more than most, I praised him and spoke highly of him. But I was upset when I found that, with all his disciples around him, I was not allowed to put a question to him and communicate to him the perplexities which troubled me by talking to him as man to man with each of us speaking in turn. In the end I did get a chance to do this and, with some friends of mine, was able to engage his attention at a time when it was not incorrect for him to discuss matters by means of question and answer. I put forward some of the things which were disturbing me and at once discovered that this man was not educated in any of the liberal sciences except literature, and even here his learning was of a very conventional kind. He had read some of Cicero's speeches, a very few books by Seneca, some poetry, and those volumes written by people of his own persuasion which were in Latin and were neatly constructed; he also had daily practice in making speeches, and all this was the source of his eloquence, which was made the more agreeable and charming by being directed by a good intelligence and expressed with a kind of grace which was natural to the man.

Is it not so, as I remember it, Lord my God, judge of my conscience? My heart and my memory are open before you, and you in the hidden secrecy of your providence were working upon me then and setting in front of my face those shameful errors of mine, so that I might see them and hate them.

7   FOR AFTER IT became quite clear to me that he was ignorant of those subjects in which I had thought him to be so particularly learned, I began to lose hope in his being able to solve my perplexities and explain to me the questions that troubled me—though, as I see now, he could have been ignorant of all this and still held the truth of piety, if only he had not been a Manichee. The books of the Manichees are indeed full of lengthy fables about the heaven and the stars and the sun and the moon, and I now thought that he could not possibly give me a reasoned answer to what I wanted to know, which was whether, after comparing all this with the calculations I had read of elsewhere, the facts were as stated in the books of Manes, or if, at any rate, some explanation equally good could be discovered in these books. When I put forward this question as something to be considered and discussed he behaved with great modesty and would not venture to take up the burden. He knew that he was ignorant of these things and was not ashamed to admit it. He was not one of those talkative people (I had had to put up with a great many of them) who attempted to instruct me in these subjects but had no instruction to give. Indeed he had a heart which, while not right toward you, was quite well prepared to look after himself. He was not altogether ignorant of his own ignorance, and he had no wish to get rashly involved in a controversy

which he could not possibly win and from which he would find it difficult to retire. For this too I liked him all the better; for there is more beauty in the modesty of a mind that admits its faults than in the knowledge that I was seeking for. So I found him too when it came to all the more difficult and subtle questions.

As a result of this I lost the enthusiasm which I had had for the writings of Manes, and I had all the less confidence in the other Manichaean teachers after I found that the famous Faustus had shown up so badly in many of the questions which perplexed me. However I began to spend much time with him because of his own kind of enthusiasm, which was for literature, and it was literature which I, as professor, was at that time teaching to the young at Carthage. I used to read with him what he wanted to have read or what I considered right for his kind of intelligence. But all the ambition I had had to go far in that sect simply collapsed once I had got to know the man. Not that I broke completely with the Manichees. It was simply that, not being able to find anything better than the course on which I had somehow or other become set, I had decided to stay as I was for the time being, unless something else should happen to appear which seemed preferable. So this Faustus, who to many people had been a real snare of death, now began, without willing it or knowing it, to unloosen the snare in which I had been caught. Your hands, my God, in the secrecy of your providence never abandoned my soul; from the blood of my mother's heart, by the tears which she shed day and night, sacrifice for me was offered to you, and in wonderful ways you dealt with me. It was your doing, my God: for *the steps of a man are ordered by the Lord, and He shall dispose his way*. Or how shall we find salvation except by your hand's remaking what you made?

8   YOU ACTED UPON ME in such a way that I was persuaded to set out for Rome to teach there the same subjects as I had been teaching in Carthage. How it was that I came to be persuaded to do this must not be passed over in my confession to you; here too I must

ponder over and openly declare the deep secrecy of your ways and your mercy which is always so close to us. I wanted to go to Rome not only because of the higher earnings and the greater reputation which my friends, who persuaded me to go, thought I would get there, though these reasons did have some weight with me at that time; in fact, however, my main and almost my only reason for going was that I heard that in Rome the young men followed their studies in a more orderly manner and were controlled by a stricter discipline. They were not allowed, for instance, insolently and at their own pleasure to come rushing into the school of a man who was not their own teacher; in fact they were not allowed to enter the school at all without the master's permission.

At Carthage, on the other hand, the students are disgracefully out of control. They come breaking into a class in the most unmannerly way and, behaving almost like madmen, disturb the order which the master has established for the good of his pupils. They commit a number of disorderly acts which show an incredible stupidity and which ought to be punished by law. However, custom protects them, and this is a fact which makes their state even more wretched, because the things they do appear to them permissible, though by your eternal law such things can never be permitted, and they imagine that they are getting away scot-free with what they do, whereas the very blindness with which they act is their punishment, and the harm which they do to themselves is incomparably worse than what they do to others. When I was a student myself I refused to become one of those who behaved in this way, though when I became a teacher I had to put up with this behavior from other people, and so the reason why I wanted to go to Rome was that all who knew about it told me that there these things were not done. But you, my hope and my portion in the land of the living, were urging me to change countries for the salvation of my soul. In Carthage you prepared goads for me, so that I should be driven from the place, and at Rome you provided attractions which would draw me there, and in both cases you made use of men who were in love with this deathly life; on the one side were people acting like lunatics and on the other people who promised me mere vanities. So, to reform my ways, you secretly made use both of their perversity and of my own. For those who were disturbing my peace were blinded by a disgraceful frenzy, and those who urged me to go elsewhere savored of earth. And I, hating my real misery in Carthage, looked for a false happiness in Rome.

But you, God, knew why it was that I was going from the one place to the other, and you did not reveal the reason either to me or to my mother, who was most bitterly distressed at my going away and who followed me right down to the seacoast. She clung to me with all her force, begging me either to return or to take her with me, but I deceived her and pretended that I had a friend whom I did not want to leave until the wind was right for him to set sail. So I told a lie to her, my mother, and such a mother, and I got away from her. And this too you have mercifully forgiven me. You saved me, full as I was with the most execrable uncleanness, from the waters of the sea and brought me to the water of your grace, so that, when I was washed in this water, the rivers that flowed from my mother's eyes, tears daily shed for me that watered the ground below her downcast looks, should be dried up. Still she refused to go home without me, and I had much difficulty in persuading her to stay that night in a place near the ship where there was an oratory in memory of St. Cyprian. That night I stole away, leaving her behind; she stayed there weeping and praying. And the whole purport, my God, of the prayers which she addressed to you with so many tears was that you would not allow me to sail. But your counsels are deep; you granted what was the key point of her prayer and did not do what she was asking for at that moment so that you might make me what she always wanted me to be. The wind blew and filled our sails; we lost sight of the land where, that morning, my mother was frantic with grief and filled your ears with her lamentations and complaints, and you seemed not to hear her, yet all the time you were dragging me away by the force of my own desires in order that these desires might be brought to an end, and you were justly punishing her with the whip of sorrow for an affection that was too much of the flesh. For she loved having me with her, as all mothers do, only she much more than most, and she did not know what great joys you were preparing for her by my going away. This she did not know, and so she wept and cried aloud and by all this agony she showed in herself the heritage of Eve, seeking in sorrow what in sorrow she had brought forth. Nevertheless, after accusing me of treachery and cruelty, she turned once more to her prayers to you for me. She went home and I went on my way to Rome.

9   THERE THE FIRST THING that happened to me was that I was struck down by a sickness of the body, and I very nearly went to hell, carrying with me all the sins I had committed against you and against myself and against others. Many and grievous they were, over and above the bond of original sin whereby we all die in Adam. For you had not yet forgiven me any of them in Christ, nor had He abolished by His cross the enmity which by my sins I had incurred with you. Indeed how could He do so by the cross of a phantom, which was how I thought of Him? Just as the death of His flesh seemed to me not true, so true was the death of my soul, and just as the death of His flesh was true, so false was the life of my soul, which did not believe in it. My fever grew worse and worse. I was very nearly gone and very nearly lost. For, if I had gone then, where should I have gone except to the fire and the torments which in the truth of your ordinance my deeds deserved? My mother knew nothing of my illness, yet, though she was far away, she continued to pray for me. But you, who are present everywhere, heard her where she was and pitied me where I was, so that I regained my bodily health, though I was still sick enough in my sacrilegious heart. For even in this great danger I did not long for your baptism. Indeed I was better when I was a boy and begged for this from my mother's piety, as I have already recalled in my confession. But I had grown up into my own shame; I madly mocked at the medicine prescribed by you, who

would not allow me in my present state to die a double
death. If I had so died and my mother's heart had been
struck with that wound, it would never have been cured
again. For I cannot express how she loved me and how she
labored with much greater pain to give me birth in the
spirit than she had suffered when giving birth to me in the
flesh. So I cannot see how she could have been cured, if
I had died a death like this and the very core of her love
for me had been pierced through by it. And where then
would have been all those prayers of hers which she
uttered day and night without ceasing? Nowhere but
with you. But would you, God of mercies, despise the
contrite and humbled heart of that chaste and good
widow, who was so constant in almsgiving, so willing
and ready in the service of your saints, who never let a
day pass without making her oblation at your altar, who
used to go twice a day, without any exception, in the
morning and in the evening, to your Church, not to listen
to idle gossip and old wives' tales, but that she might listen
to you in the sermons preached and that you might
listen to her as she prayed? Could you refuse your help
to her or despise her tears with which she asked from
you, not gold or silver or any mutable and transitory
good, but the salvation of her son's soul—for it was by
your grace that she was like this? No, Lord, you could
not. It is certain that you were with her and heard her
and that you were doing everything in the order which
you had predestined. It would be impossible that you
should deceive her in the visions and answers which you
gave her—both those which I have mentioned and others,
all of which she laid up in her faithful heart and would
constantly bring them forward to you in her prayers, as
though they were promises written in your own handwriting. For you (since your mercy endures forever)
will deign to become by your promises actually the
debtor of those whose debt of sin you have entirely
forgiven.

10   So YOU BROUGHT me back from that illness, and
you gave the son of your handmaid his bodily
health at that time, so that he might live for you to give
him a better and a more certain health. Even then, in
Rome, I associated myself with those false and deceiving
"saints," not only with the "hearers" (one of whom was
the man in whose house I had been ill and had recovered),
but also with the ones whom they call "the elect." For
I was still of the opinion that it is not we ourselves who
sin, but some other nature which is in us; it gratified my
pride to think that I was blameless and, if I did something
wrong, not to confess that I had done it, so that you might
heal my soul, because my soul had sinned against you.
Instead I liked to excuse myself and accuse something else
—something that was in me, but was not really I. But in
fact I was wholly I and it was my impiety which had
divided one me from another me. My sin was all the more
incurable because I imagined that I was not a sinner, and
it was most execrable wickedness in me that I preferred
that you, you, Almighty God, should be overcome in me
to my destruction rather than that I should be overcome
by you for my salvation.

You had not yet *set a watch before my mouth and a
door of safekeeping around my lips, that my heart might
not turn aside to wicked speeches, to make excuses of sins,
with men that work iniquity*. And for this reason I was
still in the fellowship of their Elect. However, I saw no
prospect of being able to go far in that false doctrine, and
I began to have less and less interest in and enthusiasm
for even those principles of theirs with which I had
decided to be content, if I could find nothing better.

The thought occurred to me that those philosophers
who are called the Academics were wiser than the rest,
because they held that everything should be considered
doubtful and had come to the conclusion that no truth
could be comprehended by man. For it seemed to me
quite clear that this (as is the general belief) was the view
they held, though in fact I had not yet even grasped what
they were driving at. Certainly I quite openly persuaded
this man in whose house I was staying not to have such
excessive faith, which I could see that he had, in all those

fables of which the books of Manes are full. Yet I still lived on more friendly terms with the Manichees than with others not of that heresy. I was no longer defending it with my old fervor, but my friendship with those people (and Rome shelters a great many of them) made me slower to look for some other belief, especially since, Lord of heaven and earth, Creator of all things visible and invisible, I had no hope of finding the truth in your Church. For they had turned me against it, and I thought it most unseemly to believe that you had the shape of our human flesh and were bounded by the bodily outlines of our limbs. When I wanted to think of my God, I did not know how to think of him except as a mass of bodies, for it seemed to me that what was not this was nothing. And this was the chief, indeed almost the only, cause of my inevitable error.

Because of this I believed that evil also was some such a kind of substance, with its own foul and hideous bulk, which might be either gross (which they called earth) or thin and subtle like the body of air; for they imagine it to be a kind of malignant mind creeping through the earth. And because this strange form of piety of mine led me to believe that a good God had never created any evil nature, I came to the conclusion that there were two masses in opposition to each other, both infinite, but the evil one more contracted and the good one more expansive. And from this pestilent beginning other sacrilegious notions followed naturally.

When my mind tried to revert to the Catholic faith, it was driven back again, because I had a false idea of what the Catholic faith really was. It seemed to me more reverent to believe that you, God (to whom I now confess your mercies done in me), were infinite in all parts except one—for I should be forced to confess that you were finite in respect to that part where the mass of evil was set in opposition to you—rather than to hold the view that you were in all your parts finitely contained in the shape of a human body. And it seemed better to believe that you had created no evil than to believe that what I conceived to be the nature of evil was from you, and evil seemed to me in my ignorance to be not only a substance, but actually a physical substance; for I could not even think of mind except as a rarified form of body with extension in space. And I thought of our Saviour Himself, your Only-begotten Son, as if He were for our salvation stretched out to us, as it were, from the mass of your bright and shining substance, and as a result I could believe nothing of Him except what would fit in with my empty imagination. I considered that such a nature could not possibly be born of the Virgin Mary, unless it were mingled with her flesh, and I could not see how the nature which I had imagined to myself could be mingled without being defiled. Thus I was afraid to believe that He was born in the flesh lest I should be forced to believe that He was defiled by the flesh. I know that your spiritual ones will be smiling at me, though kindly and lovingly, if they read the story of these confusions of mind. But this was what I was like at that time.

11 THEN TOO I thought that some of the Manichaean criticisms of your Scriptures were unanswerable. Yet there were times when I certainly would have liked to discuss each point separately with someone really learned in those books and to find out what he thought about it. Even at Carthage I had begun to be disturbed by listening to a man called Elpidius who spoke and argued openly against the Manichees and produced evidence from the Scriptures which was not easy to resist. And the answer which they did give seemed to me a very feeble one; indeed they preferred not to give it at all in public, but only in private gatherings of ourselves. What they said was that the Scriptures of the New Testament had been corrupted by people who wanted to insert the Jewish law into the Christian faith; yet they themselves could not produce any copies that had not been corrupted. But, as I still thought only in terms of bodies, it was chiefly these "masses" which held me down a prisoner and were practically stifling me; under their weight I panted for the fresh air of your truth, but was unable to breathe it pure and untainted.

12 I STARTED AT ONCE to do what I had come to do,
    namely to teach rhetoric at Rome. First of all I
collected a few pupils at my house and by means of them
I began to become known. I soon found out that things
went on in Rome which I had not had to put up with in
Africa. True enough I discovered that in Rome there was
none of that subversive behavior which I knew on the
part of the worst types of young men; but, so I was told,
"in order to avoid paying their fees to the professor, a
number of young men form a conspiracy and suddenly
go off to study under another professor, thus breaking
their pledged words and showing that to them justice is
cheap compared with the love of money." I hated them
too in my heart, though the hatred I felt was not a perfect
hatred. I think that I hated them more because of what I
was likely to suffer from them personally than because
of the wrong they did to everyone concerned. Such people, however, are certainly vile characters; they fornicate
against you in loving the fleeting mockeries of time and
the filthy lucre which soils the hand that holds it and in
embracing this fleeting world and in despising you who
abide and who call them back to you and who give
pardon to the adulterous soul of man when it returns to
you. I still hate wicked and depraved people of this sort,
though I love the thought of their being corrected and
taught to love learning more than money and to love
you, God, the truth and fullness of certain good, and the
purest peace, more than learning. But at that time I was
more anxious not to have to put up with their evil ways
for my own sake than that they should learn good for
your sake.

13 SO WHEN THE prefect of the city in Rome re-
    ceived a message from Milan, asking him to
provide them with a professor of rhetoric and promising
to pay the expenses of his journey out of public funds, I
applied for the post myself. My application was supported
by those very people who were intoxicated with the
vanities of Manichaeism, and it was just to be rid of
these people that I was going—though neither they nor I

realized the fact. So I had the opportunity to make a speech on a set subject; Symmachus, who was then prefect, approved of it, and I was sent to Milan. And at Milan I came to Bishop Ambrose, who had a worldwide reputation, was a devout servant of yours and a man whose eloquence in those days gave abundantly to *Thy people the fatness of Thy wheat, the gladness of Thy oil and the sober intoxication of Thy wine.* Though I did not realize it, I was led to him by you so that, with full realization, I might be led to you by him. That man of God welcomed me as a father and, in his capacity of bishop, was kind enough to approve of my coming there. I began to love him at first not as a teacher of the truth (for I had quite despaired of finding it in your Church) but simply as a man who was kind and generous to me. I used to listen eagerly when he preached to the people, but my intention was not what it should have been; I was, as it were, putting his eloquence on trial to see whether it came up to his reputation, or whether its flow was greater or less than I had been told. So I hung intently on his words, but I was not interested in what he was really saying and stood aside from this in contempt. I was much pleased by the charm of his style, which, although it was more learned, was still, so far as the manner of delivery was concerned, not so warm and winning as the style of Faustus. With regard to the actual matter there was, of course, no comparison. Faustus was merely roving around among Manichaean fallacies, while Ambrose was healthily teaching salvation. But salvation is far from sinners of the kind that I was then. Yet, though I did not realize it, I was drawing gradually nearer.

14   FOR ALTHOUGH my concern was not to learn what he said but only to hear how he said it (this empty interest being all that remained to me, now that I had despaired of man's being able to find his way to you), nevertheless, together with the language, which I admired, the subject matter also, to which I was indifferent, began to enter into my mind. Indeed I could not separate the one from the other. And as I opened my heart in order

to recognize how eloquently he was speaking it occurred
to me at the same time (though this idea came gradually)
how truly he was speaking. First I began to see that the
points which he made were capable of being defended.
I had thought that nothing could be said for the Catholic
faith in the face of the objections raised by the Manichees,
but it now appeared to me that this faith could be main-
tained on reasonable grounds—especially when I had heard
one or two passages in the Old Testament explained,
usually in a figurative way, which, when I had taken
them literally, had been a cause of death to me. So, after
a number of these passages had been explained to me in
their spiritual sense, I began to blame that despairing
attitude of mine which had led me to believe that the
Law and the Prophets could not possibly stand up to
hostile and mocking criticism. However, I did not feel
that I ought to take the way of the Catholics simply
because they too could produce learned men to maintain
their belief and to answer objections skillfully and without absurdity; nor did I think that the faith which I held
should be condemned simply because the Catholics were
just as well able to defend theirs. So, though the Catholic
cause did not seem to me defeated, it did not yet seem
to me to have won.

Then indeed I began to bend my mind earnestly to the
question: Could I find any sure proofs by which to con-
vict the Manichees of falsehood? If only I had been able
to form the idea of a substance that was spiritual, all their
strongholds would have collapsed at once and been
thrown out of my mind. But I could not.

However, with regard to the body of this world and
the whole of nature that is within the reach of our bodily
senses, I considered, after much consideration and fre-
quent comparisons, that very many of the philosophers
held views which were much more probable than those
of the Manichees. So, in what is assumed to be the manner
of the Academics, while doubting everything and wavering between one thing and another, I did at least decide
that I must leave the Manichees. For even in this period
of doubt, I did not consider that I ought to remain in
that sect when I already thought more highly of some of

the philosophers than of the Manichees. Though still I absolutely refused to allow these philosophers to take care of my sick soul, because they were without the saving name of Christ. I decided, therefore, to be for the time being a catechumen in the Catholic Church (the Church which my parents had encouraged me to join) until I should see some certain light by which to steer my course.

Book VI

1 HOPE OF MINE from my youth, where were you and where had you gone from me? Was it not you who had created me and distinguished me from the beasts of the field and made me wiser than the birds of the air? Yet I walked through shadows and on slippery ways, and I searched for you outside me and did not find the God of my heart. I had come to the depths of the sea, and I had no confidence or hope of discovering the truth.

By this time my mother had joined me. Her piety had given her strength and she had followed me over land and sea, confident in you throughout all dangers. In the perils of the sea it was she who put fresh heart into the sailors although as a rule it is for the sailors to reassure the passengers who are inexperienced on the high seas. But she promised them that they would get safely to land because you had promised this to her in a vision. She found me in grave danger indeed, my danger being that of despairing of ever discovering the truth. I told her that, though I was not yet a Catholic Christian, I was certainly no longer a Manichaean; but she showed no great signs of delight, as though at some unexpected piece of news, because she already felt at ease regarding that particular aspect of my misery; she bewailed me as one dead, certainly, but as one who would be raised up again by you; she was in her mind laying me before you on the bier so that you might say to the widow's son: "*Young man, I say unto thee, Arise,*" and he should revive and begin to

111

speak and you should give him to his mother. So her heart was shaken by no storm of exultation when she heard that what she had daily begged you with her tears should happen had in so large a part taken place—that I was now rescued from falsehood, even though I had not yet attained the truth. She was indeed quite certain that you, who had promised her the whole, would give her the part that remained, and she replied to me very calmly and with a heart full of confidence that she believed in Christ that, before she departed from this life, she would see me a true Catholic. So much she said to me. But to you, fountain of mercies, she poured out her prayers and her tears more copiously than before, begging you to hasten your help and to lighten my darkness, and she would hurry more eagerly than ever to church and hang upon the words of Ambrose, praying for *the fountain of that water, which springeth up into life everlasting.* For she loved that man as though he were an angel of God, because she knew that it was through him that I had been brought for the time being to this doubtful wavering state of mind, and she was perfectly certain that I would pass through this from sickness to health, though before then I should be exposed to a more serious attack, like that which doctors call "the crisis."

2   THERE WAS an occasion when my mother had brought, as was her custom in Africa, cakes and bread and wine to some of the chapels built in memory of the saints and was forbidden to do this by the door-keeper. When she found that it was the bishop who had forbidden this practice, she accepted his ban so devoutly and so willingly that I myself was amazed to see how much more readily now she would condemn her own practice of the past than dispute the bishop's prohibition. For her soul was not a victim to the craving for wine, and no liking for wine stimulated her into a hatred for the truth—a thing which happens to many people of both sexes who are just as disgusted by a hymn of sobriety as real drunkards are if their wine is mixed with water. But when my mother brought her basket with the usual sorts

of food, which were first to be tasted by her and then given away, she never took more than one small cup well watered down to suit her sober taste, and this was just for the sake of courtesy. And if there were many memorial chapels which she thought ought to be honored in this way, she still carried this same cup around with her to be used at each place; in the end it would be not only nearly all water, but also lukewarm, and she would share this out in small sips with those around her; for she came then to look for piety, not for pleasure. But when she found that that famous preacher and that great example of piety had forbidden the practice even to those who used it soberly—so that drunkards should not be given an occasion for excess and also because this kind of anniversary funeral feast is very much like the superstitious ceremony of the pagans—she most willingly gave up her old habit. Instead of a basket filled with the fruits of the earth, she had learned to bring to the chapels of the Martyrs a breast full of something much purer, her prayers. So she was able to give what she could spare to the poor, and so the communion of the Lord's body might be celebrated in those places where, in imitation of His passion, the martyrs had lost their lives and won their crowns.

And yet it seems to me, my Lord God—and on this matter my heart lies open in your sight—that in abandoning this old custom of hers my mother might possibly not have given way so easily if the prohibition had come from someone else whom she did not love as she loved Ambrose. For she loved him very greatly on account of my salvation, and he loved her for her religious way of life; for she was always doing good works, was fervent in spirit, and constantly at church. So that when he saw me he often used to burst forth in her praises, congratulating me on having such a mother, though he was unaware of what sort of a son she had in me—one who was in doubt on all these matters and who thought that there was no possibility of finding the way of life.

3 I WAS NOT YET groaning in prayer for you to help me. My mind was intent on inquiry and restless in dispute. I considered Ambrose himself, who was honored by people of such importance, a lucky man by worldly standards; only his celibacy seemed to me rather a burden to bear. But I could neither guess nor tell from my own experience what hope he had within him, what were his struggles against the temptations of his exalted position, what solace he found in adversity; nor could I tell of that hidden mouth of his (the mouth of his heart), what joys it tasted in the rumination of your bread. And he on his side did not know of the turmoil in which I was or the deep pit of danger before my feet. I was not able to ask him the questions I wanted to ask in the way I wanted to ask them, because I was prevented from having an intimate conversation with him by the crowds of people, all of whom had some business with him and to whose infirmities he was a servant. And for the very short periods of time when he was not with them, he was either refreshing his body with necessary food or his mind with reading. When he was reading, his eyes went over the pages and his heart looked into the sense, but voice and tongue were resting. Often when we came to him (for no one was forbidden to come in, and it was not customary for visitors even to be announced) we found him reading, always to himself and never otherwise; we would sit in silence for a long time, not venturing to interrupt him in his intense concentration on his task, and then we would go away again. We guessed that in the very small time which he was able to set aside for mental refreshment he wanted to be free from the disturbance of other people's business and would not like to have his attention distracted; also we thought that he might be taking precautions in case, if he read aloud in the presence of some eager and interested person, he might have to give a lecture on the obscure points in the author whom he was reading, or enter into a discussion on the questions of difficulty, with the result that, after he had spent time on this, he would not be able to read as many books as he wanted to read. Though perhaps a more likely reason for his reading to himself was that he wanted to preserve

his voice, which grew tired very easily. But whatever his
reason was for acting in this way it would certainly be
a good one.

Anyhow, I was given no chance of making the inquiries
I wished to make from that holy oracle of yours, his
breast. I could only ask things that would not take long
in the hearing. But I needed to find him with plenty of
time to spare if I was to pour out to him the full flood
of agitation boiling up inside me, and I could never find
him like this. Yet every Sunday I listened to him rightly
preaching to the people the word of truth, and I became
more and more sure that all those knots of cunning cal-
umny which, in their attacks on the holy books, my
deceivers had tied could be unraveled. In particular I discovered that the phrase "man, created by Thee, after
Thine own image" was not understood by your spiritual
children, whom you have made to be born again by grace
through the Catholic mother, in such a way as to mean
that you are bounded by the shape of a human body. And
although I had not the faintest or most shadowy notion
about what a spiritual substance could be, nevertheless
with a kind of pleasant shame I blushed to think of how
for all these years I had been barking not against the
Catholic faith but against figments of carnal imaginations.
And indeed I had been rash and impious; for I had spoken
in condemnation of things which I ought to have taken
the trouble to find out about. But you, the highest, and
the nearest, most hidden and most present, have no limbs
or parts greater and smaller; you are everywhere in your
entirety, yet limited by no particular space; you are not
of any bodily form, yet you made man "after your own
image" and, see, man is in space from head to foot.

4   BEING IGNORANT, then, of how this image of yours
       could subsist, I ought to have knocked at the
door and asked in what sense the doctrine was to be believed, instead of insulting and attacking what I assumed
to be the accepted doctrine. And so my anxiety as to
what I could hold for certain gnawed at my inmost heart
all the more keenly as I felt the more ashamed of myself

for having been so long deluded and deceived by the
promise of certainties and then having, with a quite
childish inaccuracy and enthusiasm, gone on and on pro-
claiming uncertainties as though they were truths. That
they were actual falsehoods only became clear to me
later. What was certain was that they were uncertain
and that I for some time had accepted them as certainties
when, in my blind zeal for contention, I was attacking
your Catholic Church. I had not yet discovered that this
Church was teaching the truth, but at least I now knew
that it was not teaching the things which I had so vigor-
ously attacked. So I was both confounded and converted,
and I was glad, my God, that your only Church, the body
of your only son—that Church in which the name of
Christ had been put upon me as an infant—was not
flavored with this childish nonsense and did not, in her
healthy doctrine, maintain the view that you, the Creator
of all things, could be, in the form of a human body,
packed into a definite space which, however mighty and
large, must still be bounded on all sides.

I was glad too that the old Scriptures of the Law and
the Prophets were set before me in such a way that I
could now read in a different spirit from that which I had
had before, when I used to criticize your holy ones for
holding various views which, plainly, they never held at
all. And I was happy when I heard Ambrose in his sermons, as I often did, recommend most emphatically to
his congregation this text as a rule to go by: *The letter
killeth, but the spirit giveth life.* So he would draw aside
the veil of mystery and explain in a spiritual sense the
meanings of things which, if understood literally, appeared to be teaching what was wrong. And I could
raise no objections to what he said, even though I was
still not sure whether what he said was true or not. I held
my heart back from positively accepting anything, since
I was afraid of another fall, and in this condition of
suspense I was being all the more killed. I wanted to be
just as certain about things which I could not see as I was
certain that seven and three make ten. For I was not quite
mad enough as to think that even this proposition is
beyond our comprehension; but I did demand the same

degree of certainty with regard to other things, whether they were material things not present to my senses or spiritual things, of which I could form no conception except in material terms. By believing I might have been cured, so that the sight of my mind would be clearer and might be somehow or other directed toward your truth which is the same forever and in no point fails. But it was the same with me as with a man who, having once had a bad doctor, is afraid of trusting himself even to a good one. So it was with the health of my soul which could not possibly be cured except by believing, but refused to be cured for fear of believing something falser. So I resisted your hands, for it was you who prepared the medicines of faith and applied them to the diseases of the world and gave them such potency.

5   FROM NOW ON, however, I began to prefer the Catholic faith. In requiring belief in what was not demonstrated (and this includes both things that cannot be proved at all and things which, though capable of being proved, cannot be proved to everyone) I felt that the Catholic faith showed more modesty and more honesty than did the Manichees, who made rash promises of certain knowledge, derided credulity, and then produced a lot of fabulous absurdities in which we were required to believe because they were not susceptible of proof. Finally it was you, Lord, who with your most tender and merciful hand gradually laid hold upon my heart and settled it in calm. I considered what a countless number of things there were which I believed though I had not seen them and had not been present when they had taken place—so many historical events, so many facts about countries and cities which I had never seen, so many things told me by friends, by doctors, by one man or another man—and unless we believed these things, we should get nothing done at all in this life. Then in particular I considered how fixed and unalterable was the belief I held that I was the son of a particular father and mother, a thing which I could not possibly know unless I had believed it on the word of others. And so by these

considerations you led me to see that the people to be
blamed were not those who believed in those books of
yours, which you have established with such authority in
nearly every nation of the world, but those who did not
believe in them, and that I ought not to pay any attention
to anyone who might say to me: "How do you know that
those books were bestowed on mankind by the spirit of
the one true and most true God?" It was indeed just this
point which in particular must be believed. Since however
much I might be assaulted by calumnious questionings
(and I had read much in the works of philosophers as
they contradicted each other), nothing could shake these
two beliefs—first, that you exist (though I did not know
what your nature was), and secondly, that the government of human affairs is in your hands.

I believed this sometimes more and sometimes less
strongly. Nevertheless, I always did believe that you
exist and that you have a care for us, even though I did
not know what to think about your substance or what
way leads, or leads back, to you. So, since we were too
weak to discover truth by pure reason and therefore
needed the authority of Holy Writ, I now began to
believe that you could not possibly have given such supreme authority to these Scriptures all over the world,
unless it had been your wish that by means of them men
should both believe in you and seek after you. As for
the absurdities which used to offend me in Scripture, I
had heard many of them explained in a convincing way
and I now looked for their meanings in the depth of
mystery. In fact the authority of Scripture seemed to me
the more venerable and the more worthy of religious
faith because, while it was easy to read for everybody,
it also preserved in the more profound sense of its meaning the majesty of something secret; it offers itself to all
in plain words and a very simple style of speech, yet
serious thinkers have to give it their closest attention.
Thus its arms are wide open to receive everyone, yet
there are a few whom it draws to you along narrow ways,
and these few would be fewer still if it were not for
the fact that at the same time it stands on such a peak of
authority and also draws crowds into its bosom because

of its holy humility. These were my thoughts, and you were by me; I sighed and you heard me; I was storm tossed and you held the tiller; I was going on the broad path of this world and you did not forsake me.

6 I PANTED FOR HONORS, for money, for marriage, and you were laughing at me. I found bitterness and difficulty in following these desires, and your graciousness to me was shown in the way you would not allow me to find anything sweet which was not you. Look into my heart, Lord; for it was you who willed me to remember all this and to confess it to you. And let my soul cling to you now that you have freed it from that gripping birdlime of death! How unhappy it was then! And you pricked its wound on the quick, so that it might leave everything else and turn to you, who are above all things and without whom all things would be nothing—so that it might turn to you and be cured. I was unhappy indeed, and you made me really see my unhappiness. It was on a day when I was preparing a speech to be delivered in praise of the emperor; there would be a lot of lies in the speech, and they would be applauded by those who knew that they were lies. My heart was all wrought up with the worry of it all and was boiling in a kind of fever of melting thoughts. I was going along one of the streets of Milan when I noticed a poor beggar; he was fairly drunk, I suppose, and was laughing and enjoying himself. It was a sight which depressed me, and I spoke to the friends who were with me about all the sorrows which come to us because of our own madness. I thought of how I was toiling away, spurred on by my desires and dragging after me the load of my unhappiness and making it all the heavier by dragging it, and it seemed to me that the goal of this and all such endeavors was simply to reach a state of happiness that was free from care; the beggar had reached this state before us, and we, perhaps, might never reach it at all. With the few pennies that he had managed to beg he had actually obtained what I, by so many painful turns and such devious ways,

was struggling to reach—namely, the joy of a temporary happiness.

No doubt the beggar's joy was not true joy; but it was a great deal truer than the joy which I, with my ambition, was seeking. And undoubtedly he was happy while I was worried; he was carefree while I was full of fears. And if I were asked which I would prefer, to be merry or to be frightened, I should reply "to be merry." But if I were asked next whether I would prefer to be a man like the beggar or a man like I then was myself, I should choose to be myself, worn out as I was with my cares and my fears. Was not this absurd? Was there any good reason for making such a choice? For I had no right to put myself in front of the beggar on the grounds that I was more learned than he, since I got no joy out of my learning. Instead I used it to give pleasure to men—not to teach them, only to please them. And therefore you were breaking my bones with the rod of your discipline.

So I will not allow my soul to listen to those who say to her: "The difference is in the source of a man's happiness. That beggar found his joy in being drunk, you were looking for your joy in winning glory." What glory, Lord? A glory that was not in you. For just as the beggar's joy was not true joy, so my glory was not true glory. Moreover it had a worse effect on my mind. The beggar would sleep off his drunkenness that very night; but I had gone to bed with mine and woken up with it day after day after day and I should go on doing so. Certainly it makes a difference what is the source of a man's happiness. I know it does. And the joy of a faithful hope is incomparably beyond all such vanity. Yes, and so was the beggar then beyond me; without any doubt he was the happier, not only because he was drenched in merriment while I eaten up with anxieties, but also because he by wishing people good luck had got some wine for himself while I by lying was seeking for an empty bubble of praise.

I said much along these lines to my intimate friends at the time, and I often noticed that it was the same with them as it was with me, and I found that things were not at all well with me, and I worried about it and by worrying made matters twice as bad, and if fortune seemed to smile on me at all, I felt too tired to grasp my opportunity, for it fled away almost before I could take hold of it.

7   ALL OF US who were friends together were depressed by these thoughts. The ones I talked to most about it were Alypius and Nebridius. Alypius was born in the same town as I, and his parents were important people there. He was younger than I. Indeed he had studied under me when I began teaching in our town and later in Carthage. He was very fond of me, because he thought me good and learned, and I was very fond of him because of his natural tendency toward virtue which was really remarkable in one so young. Nevertheless, he had been sucked into the whirlpool of Carthaginian bad habits, and in particular the empty enthusiasm for shows in the Circus. At the time when he was becoming involved in this wretched passion I had set up as a teacher of rhetoric there with a school open to the public, but he did not come to me as a pupil because of some difference which had arisen between his father and me. I had found out that he had got this fatal passion for the Circus and I was greatly disturbed about it, because it seemed to me that he was likely to throw away, if he had not thrown away already, all those high hopes we held of him. But I had no means of giving him advice or of using any kind of authority to restrain him; I could not appeal to his good will as a friend or to his duty as a pupil. For I thought that he shared his father's views about me. In fact he did not, and so, not allowing himself to be influenced by his father's quarrel, he began to greet me when we met and used to come into my school and sit listening for a time before going away.

Nevertheless, I had forgotten about any idea I might have had for trying to influence him so as to prevent the waste of such a good intelligence on a blind and headstrong enthusiasm for empty shows. But you, Lord, you, whose hand is on the helm of all that you have created, had not forgotten him, who was to become one day a member of your family and a high priest of your sacrament. And his reform must quite clearly be attributed to you, as is shown by the fact that, though you brought it about by means of me, I did not know what I was doing. This was what happened. One day when I was sitting in my usual place with my pupils around me, Alypius came in and, after saluting me, sat down and listened to what was going on. In the course of my exposition of the passage of literature with which I happened to be dealing it occurred to me that I could make an apt use of a comparison taken from the games in the Circus; this would make my point clearer and more amusing, and I could combine it with some bitter sarcasm at the expense of those who were the prey of this kind of madness. You, God, know that at that time I had no thought of curing Alypius of that disease. But he took my remarks personally and believed that it was only because of him that I had made them. Another person would have taken this as a reason for being angry with me, but this fair-minded young man took it as a reason for being angry with himself and for loving me all the more. For you said long ago, and you had it put in your book: *Rebuke a wise man, and he will love thee.*

In fact I had not been rebuking him, but you make use of all men, whether or not they are aware of it, according to a method that is known to you, and that order and method is just. So out of my heart and tongue you made burning coals to cauterize and to cure that promising mind of his as it lay sick. Who can fail to praise you if he considers your mercies, mercies which I myself confess to you from the very marrow of my bones? For after those words of mine Alypius clambered out of that deep pit into which he had been glad enough to sink and in which he was being blinded by his pleasures; he took a firm hold on his mind and shook it; all the filth of the Circus fell off and he never went there again. Then he won over his father so that he might be allowed to attend my classes as a pupil. His father was unwilling enough, but gave way and gave in. Alypius was once more my pupil and became involved with me in the same superstition. He loved the Manichaean pretense of continence, considering it to be real and genuine, though

in fact this kind of continence was senseless and mis-
leading and ensnared precious souls which were not yet
able to reach the depth of virtue but could easily be
deceived by the superficial appearance of a virtue which
was shadowy and pretended.

8   BUT THERE WAS no abandoning of the worldly
      career which his parents were always talking to
him about. He had gone to Rome before me in order to
study law and in Rome he had been quite swept away, in-
credibly and with a most incredible passion, by the gladi-
atorial shows. He was opposed to such things and detested
them; but he happened to meet some of his friends and
fellow pupils on their way back from dinner, and they,
in spite of his protests and his vigorous resistance, used a
friendly kind of violence and forced him to go along with
them to the amphitheater on a day when one of these
cruel and bloody shows was being presented. As he went,
he said to them: "You can drag my body there, but don't
imagine that you can make me turn my eyes or give my
mind to the show. Though there, I shall not be there,
and so I shall have the better both of you and of the
show."

After hearing this his friends were all the keener to
bring him along with them. No doubt they wanted to
see whether he could actually do this or not. So they
came to the arena and took the seats which they could
find. The whole place was seething with savage enthusiasm, but he shut the doors of his eyes and forbade
his soul to go out into a scene of such evil. If only he
could have blocked up his ears too! For in the course
of the fight some man fell; there was a great roar from
the whole mass of spectators which fell upon his ears;
he was overcome by curiosity and opened his eyes, feeling perfectly prepared to treat whatever he might see
with scorn and to rise above it. But he then received in
his soul a worse wound than that man, whom he had
wanted to see, had received in his body. His own fall was
more wretched than that of the gladiator which had
caused all that shouting which had entered his ears and

unlocked his eyes and made an opening for the thrust which was to overthrow his soul—a soul that had been reckless rather than strong and was all the weaker because it had trusted in itself when it ought to have trusted in you. He saw the blood and he gulped down savagery. Far from turning away, he fixed his eyes on it. Without knowing what was happening, he drank in madness, he was delighted with the guilty contest, drunk with the lust of blood. He was no longer the man who had come there but was one of the crowd to which he had come, a true companion of those who had brought him.

There is no more to be said. He looked, he shouted, he raved with excitement; he took away with him a madness which would goad him to come back again, and he would not only come with those who first got him there; he would go ahead of them and he would drag others with him. Yet you, with your most strong and merciful hand, rescued him from this, and you taught him to put his trust not in himself but in you. This, however, was much later.

9   NEVERTHELESS, this was already being stored up in his memory for his future healing. So also was something which happened to him when he was still a pupil of mine at Carthage. He was in the market place in the middle of the day, thinking over the words of a passage which in the ordinary course of his education he would have to say by heart. You then allowed him to be arrested by the market police as a thief, and, our God, I think that the only reason why you allowed this to happen was that one who was going to become such a great man should even then begin to learn that in cases of judging guilt man must not be too easily condemned by man on a basis of rash credulity. What happened was this: he was walking about by himself, with his notebooks and pen, in front of the law court, and just then a young man, also a student, who was the real thief, with an ax hidden under his clothes, got in (though Alypius did not see him) as far as the leaden gratings over the silversmiths' shops and began to cut away the lead. But the silversmiths underneath

heard the sound of the ax, raised the alarm, and sent
people to catch whomever they could find. Hearing their
voices the thief ran away, leaving the ax behind for fear
that he might be caught with it. Alypius had not seen the
man coming in, but he noticed him going out and saw
that he was running away fast. Wanting to know the
reason for this, he went into the place, found the ax, and
stood in front of it, wondering what it was doing there.
At this moment the men who had been sent found him,
alone and with the weapon whose noise had alarmed them
and brought them there. They seized hold of him and
dragged him off, boasting to the shopkeepers in the forum,
who came crowding around, that they had caught the
thief red-handed. And so he was led away to be handed
over to justice. But his lesson stopped here. You, Lord,
now came to the aid of his innocence, of which you were
the only witness. For as he was being led off to prison or to
torture they were met by a man who was the chief architect in charge of the public buildings. Alypius' captors
were particularly glad to meet him because they themselves were often suspected by him of making off with
property that had disappeared from the market place;
now at last, they thought, they could show him who was
really guilty. But the architect had often seen Alypius in
the house of one of the senators at which he was in the
habit of calling. He recognized him at once, took him
by the hand, got him out of the way of the mob, and
asked him what all this trouble was about. He heard
what had happened and told the crowd, who were in
a most turbulent and threatening mood, to come with
him. They went to the house of the young man who
had actually committed the crime. By the door was a
boy who was too small to imagine that anything he
might say could injure his master and who was therefore likely to tell the whole story, for he had followed
his master into the market place. Alypius recognized him
and pointed him out to the architect, who showed him
the ax and asked him whom it belonged to. The boy
at once said: "It's ours," and, after further questioning,
revealed everything. So the crime was laid at the door
of that house, much to the confusion of the crowd, who

had already begun to treat Alypius as though he were their prisoner. He, who in the future would be a dispenser of your word and an investigator of many cases in your Church, went away a wiser and a more experienced man.

10   I FOUND ALYPIUS at Rome. We became very close friends, and he came with me to Milan, partly so as not to desert me and partly to practice the law which he had studied—though this was rather to please his parents than because he wanted to. He had already sat three times as an assessor and had shown an integrity which made others wonder at him, though he himself was more inclined to wonder at those others who could prefer gold to honesty. His character was also tested not only by the lure of gain but also by the threat of danger. At Rome he was assessor to the Count of the Italian Treasury. There was at the time an extremely powerful senator; many people were under obligations to him, and many people were afraid of him. This man, counting upon his usual influence, wanted to get something or other past the courts which was in fact illegal. Alypius stood out against it. Bribes were offered, which he treated with contempt; threats were made and he spurned them. Everyone wondered at so rare a spirit, which neither courted the friendship nor feared the enmity of a man who was so powerful and who was so well known for having countless means of helping people on or of doing them harm. The judge himself, in whose court Alypius sat, was also against making the concession, but he would not refuse it openly; instead he made Alypius responsible, saying that it was Alypius who was preventing him; and in fact, if he had given in, Alypius would have left the court.

One thing did tempt him, and that was his love of learning. He knew that he could have books copied for him at the cheap rate allowed to praetors. But when he considered the justice of the matter, he changed his mind for the better. Equity forbade, power allowed; he chose the former as being the more valuable. A small thing, perhaps. But *he that is faithful in little, is faithful also in much*. Nor can this be an empty word which came from the mouth of your truth: *If ye have not been faithful in the unrighteous Mammon, who will commit to your trust true riches? And if ye have not been faithful in that which is another man's, who shall give you that which is your own?*

This was the sort of person that Alypius was at that time. He was my great friend and together with me he was in a state of mental confusion as to what way of life we should take.

There was Nebridius too. He had left his native place near Carthage; he had left Carthage itself, where he usually lived; he had left his rich family estate in the country, left his home, and left his mother, since she was not prepared to follow him. He had come to Milan, and his one reason for doing so was to live with me in a most ardent search for truth and wisdom. Together with me he sighed and together with me he wavered. How he burned to discover the happy life! How keen and close was his scrutiny of the most difficult questions!

So there were together the mouths of three hungry people, sighing out their wants one to another, and *waiting upon Thee that Thou mightest give them their meat in due season*. And in all the bitterness which by your mercy followed all our worldly actions, as we looked toward the end and asked ourselves why should we suffer like this, darkness came down upon us, and we turned away in sorrow saying, *How long shall these things be?* This we said often enough, yet still we did not forsake these things, because there was no dawning gleam of a certainty to which we could hold once these things had been forsaken.

11   AND I, as I looked back over my life, was quite amazed to think of how long a time had passed since my nineteenth year, when I had first become inflamed with a passion for wisdom and had resolved that, when once I found it, I would leave behind me all the empty hopes and deceitful frenzies of vain desires. And now I was in my thirtieth year, still sticking in the same mud, still greedy for the enjoyment of things present, which fled from me and wasted me away, and all the time saying: "I shall find it tomorrow. See, it will become quite clear and I shall grasp it. Now Faustus will come and explain everything. What great men the Academics are! Is it true that no certainty can possibly be comprehended for the direction of our lives? No, it cannot be. We must look into things more carefully and not give up hope. And now see, those things in the Scriptures which used to seem absurd are not absurd; they can be understood in a different and perfectly good way. I shall take my stand where my parents placed me as a child until I can see the truth plainly. But where shall I look for it? And when shall I look for it? Ambrose has no spare time; nor have I time for reading. And where can I find the books? From where can I get them and when can I get them? Can I borrow them from anybody? I must arrange fixed periods of time and set aside certain hours for the health of my soul. A great hope has dawned. The Catholic faith does not teach the things I thought it did and vainly accused it of teaching. The learned men of that faith think it quite wrong to believe that God is bounded within the shape of a human body. Why then do I hesitate to knock, so that the rest may be laid open to me? My pupils take up all my time in the morning. But what do I do for the rest of the day? Why not do this? But, if I do, how shall I find time to call on influential friends whose support will be useful to me? When shall I prepare the lessons for which my pupils pay? When shall I have time to relax and to refresh my mind from all my preoccupations?

"But these are not the thoughts I should have. I must give up all this vanity and emptiness and devote myself entirely to the search for truth. Life is a misery, death an uncertainty. Suppose it steals suddenly upon me, in what state shall I leave this world? When can I learn what I have here neglected to learn? Shall I not be punished for my negligence? Or is it true that death will cut off and put an end to all care and all feeling? This too is something to be inquired into. But no, this cannot be true. It is not for nothing, it is not meaningless that all over the world is displayed the high and towering authority of the Christian faith. Such great and wonderful things would

never have been done for us by God, if the life of the
soul were to end with the death of the body. Why then
do I delay? Why do I not abandon my hopes of this
world and devote myself entirely to the search for God
and for the happy life?

"But wait. These worldly things too are sweet; the
pleasure they give is not inconsiderable; we must not be
too hasty about rejecting them, because it would be a
shame to go back to them again. Now think: it would
not be very difficult to get some high official appointment,
and then what more could I want? I have quite a number
of influential friends. Not to press on too fast, I could
easily get a governorship. Then I should marry a wife
with money, so that she would not increase my expenses.
And then I should have nothing more to desire. There
have been many great men, well worth imitating,
who have devoted themselves to the pursuit of wisdom
and have also been married."

So I used to speak and so the winds blew and shifted
and drove my heart this way and that, and time went by
and I was slow in turning to the Lord. My life in you I
kept on putting off from one day to the next, but I did not
put off the death that daily I was dying in myself. I was
in love with the idea of the happy life, but I feared to
find it in its true place, and I sought for it by running
away from it. I thought that I should be unbearably unhappy if I were deprived of the embraces of a woman, and
I never thought of your mercy as a medicine to cure
that weakness, because I had never tried it. I believed that
continency was something which depended on one's own
strength, and I knew that I had not enough strength for
it; for I was such a fool that I did not know that it is
written that no one can be continent unless you give the
power. And undoubtedly you would have given it to me
if with the groans of my heart I had beaten upon your
ears and if in settled faith I had cast my cares upon you.

12   ALYPIUS CERTAINLY kept me from marrying. He
      was always saying that, if I did marry, it would
be quite impossible for us to have the untroubled leisure

in which we could live together in the love of wisdom, as we had so long wanted to do. With regard to all this he himself was even then quite extraordinarily chaste. When he was an adolescent he had had the experience of sexual intercourse, but, so far from becoming addicted to it, he had regretted the experience and despised it and ever since had lived in the greatest continence. As to me, I countered his arguments by producing examples of men who, though married, had pursued wisdom and served God and kept their friends and loved them faithfully. In fact I myself fell far short of their grandeur of spirit; I was the prisoner of this disease of the flesh and of its deadly sweetness, and I dragged my chain about with me, dreading the idea of its being loosed, and I pushed aside the good advice of Alypius as I might push aside the hand of one coming to unchain me which had knocked against a wound.

Also it was by means of me that the serpent began to speak to Alypius himself. My tongue was used to weave sweet snares and scatter them in his path to trap his free and unsuspecting feet. He was much surprised to find that I, of whom he thought so highly, was so stuck in the glue of this kind of pleasure that I would assert, whenever we discussed the subject, that it was quite impossible for me to live a single life. I on my side, when I saw how surprised he was, would defend myself by saying that there was a great difference between that hurried and furtive experience of his—which he could now scarcely remember and could thus quite easily despise—and the delights of my normal state. If, I said, to these was added the honorable name of marriage, he could have no reason to be surprised that I was incapable of rejecting such a way of life. On hearing this Alypius began to want to get married himself, not because he lusted after that kind of pleasure, but simply for curiosity. He wanted to find out, he said, what this thing was without which my life, which seemed to him so pleasant, would be to me not worth living and indeed a torment. For his mind was free of my kind of bondage and was simply amazed at it. So from being amazed he went on to desire the experience of it. And he would have proceeded to the same experience and

next might well have fallen into the same slavery as that
which amazed him in me; since he wished to *make a
covenant with death*, and *he that loves danger shall fall
into it*. For neither of us had more than the faintest interest in the good and honorable side of marriage—the duty
of a controlled association and of having children. In my
case what chiefly enslaved me and kept me on tenterhooks
was the habit of sating a lust that could never be satisfied;
while he was being dragged into slavery simply by his
amazement at my behavior. So there we were until you,
most high, not forsaking our dust, but pitying our pitiful
state, came to our help in secret and wonderful ways.

13   THE MOVE TO get me married went on apace. I
      made my proposal and the girl was promised to
me. In all this my mother played a large part, for, once I
was married, she wanted me to be washed in the health-
giving water of baptism for which, to her joy, she saw
me becoming more fit every day, so that she now felt
that her own prayers and your promises were being fulfilled in my faith. It was at my request and also to satisfy
her own longing that at this time she begged you every
day, crying out to you from her heart, to show her in a
vision something about my future marriage; but you were
never willing to do so. She did have some visual experiences of a vain and fantastical nature (caused no doubt by
the eagerness of a human mind to be satisfied on this particular point), but when she told me of them, she spoke
slightingly of them and not with the confidence which she
always had when you were really showing her something.
She used to say that there was a kind of tone or savor,
impossible to define in words, by which she could tell
the difference between your revelations to her and the
dreams that came from her own spirit. Nevertheless, plans
for my marriage went ahead and the girl was asked for.
She was still about two years below the marriageable
age, but I liked her and was prepared to wait.

14   A GROUP OF US, all friends together, after much thought and conversation on how we hated the whole wearisome business of human life, had almost reached the conclusion that we would retire from the crowd and live a life of peace. In order to achieve this we planned to pool our resources and make one common property out of the property of all of us. So, in the sincerity of friendship, there would be no distinction between what belonged to one man or another; all our possessions should count as one piece of property, and the whole should belong to each individual and everything should belong to everybody. It appeared that there might be about ten of us in this society and among these ten were some very rich men—Romanianus in particular, who was a fellow townsman of ours and had been a great friend of mine from childhood. He had now come to the court at Milan because of some urgent business in connection with his own affairs. He was particularly enthusiastic about the project and his voice had much weight in persuading the rest of us, since his property was much greater than anybody else's. We had decided that two of us should be, like magistrates, appointed every year to deal with the necessary provisions for life, while the rest would be left in peace. Next, however, the question was raised as to whether our wives would put up with it—some of us having wives already and I being anxious to have one. And so the whole scheme, which had been so well worked out, fell to pieces in our hands and was abandoned as impracticable. We went back to our sighing and complaining and our steps continued to follow the broad and well-worn paths of the world; for we had many thoughts in our hearts, *but Thy counsel standeth forever*. And out of this counsel you laughed ours to scorn, and you were preparing for us your own things, being about *to give us meat in due season, and to open Thy hand, and to fill our souls with blessing*.

15   MEANWHILE MY SINS were being multiplied. The woman with whom I was in the habit of sleeping was torn from my side on the grounds of being an im-

pediment to my marriage, and my heart, which clung to
her, was broken and wounded and dropping blood. She
had returned to Africa after having made a vow to you
that she would never go to bed with another man, and
she had left with me the natural son I had had by her. But
I, in my misery, could not follow the example of a
woman. I had two years to wait until I could have the
girl to whom I was engaged, and I could not bear the
delay. So, since I was not so much a lover of marriage as
a slave to lust, I found another woman for myself—not,
of course, as a wife. In this way my soul's disease was fed
and kept alive so that it might reach the domination of
matrimony just as strong as before, or stronger, and still
the slave of an unbreakable habit. Nor was the wound
healed which had been made by the cutting off of my
previous mistress. It burned, it hurt intensely, and then it
festered, and if the pain became duller, it became more
desperate.

16 PRAISE TO YOU, glory to you, fountain of mercies!
    As I became more unhappy, so you drew closer
to me. Your right hand was ready, it was ready to drag
me out of the mud and to wash me; but I did not know.
And there was nothing to call me back from that deeper
gulf of carnal pleasure, except the fear of death and of
judgment to come, and this, whatever the opinions I
held from time to time, never left my mind. I used to
discuss the nature of good and evil with my friends
Alypius and Nebridius, and certainly in my judgment
Epicurus would have won the palm if I had not believed
(as he refused to believe) that there was a life for the
soul after death and treatment in accordance with its
deserts. And I would put the question: "Suppose we
were immortal and could live in perpetual bodily pleasure
without any fear of loss, why should we not be happy,
or what more could we want?" And I never realized that
it was just this that made me so miserable, that in my
drowned and sightless state I was unable to form an idea
of the light of honor and of a beauty that is embraced
for its own sake, which is invisible to the eye of flesh

and can only be seen by the inner soul. I was wretched enough not to consider why and from what source it was that I found it a pleasure to discuss these ideas (shabby though they were) in the company of friends and that I could not be happy, even in the way I then understood happiness, without friends, however great might be the amount of carnal pleasure I had in addition. For certainly I loved my friends for their own sake, and I knew that they too loved me for my own sake. What tortuous ways these were, and how hopeless was the plight of my fool-hardy soul which hoped to have something better if it went away from you! It has turned indeed, over and over, on back and side and front, and always the bed was hard and you alone are rest. And, see, you are close to us, and you rescue us from our unhappy errors, and you set our feet in your way and speak kindly to us and say: "Run and I will hold you and I will bring you through and there also I will hold you."

Book VII

1 Now MY EVIL abominable youth was a thing of the past. I was growing into manhood, and the older I was the more discreditable was the emptiness of my mind. I was unable to form an idea of any kind of substance other than what my eyes are accustomed to see. I did not think of you, God, in the shape of a human body. From the moment when I began to have any knowledge of wisdom I always avoided that idea, and I was glad that I had found the same view held in the faith of our spiritual mother, your Catholic Church. But how else I was to think of you, I did not know. And I, a man, and such a man too, was trying to think of you as the supreme, the only, the true God, and with all my heart I believed you to be beyond the reach of corruption and injury and change; because, though I did not know how or whence, I still saw quite plainly and with certainty that what can be corrupted is inferior to what cannot be corrupted, that what cannot be injured is undoubtedly to be preferred to what can be injured, and that what suffers no change is better than what is subject to change. My heart cried out passionately against all the phantoms I had believed in, and with this one blow I tried to beat away from the eye of my mind all those swarms of uncleanness which were buzzing around it. But they only disappeared for the flickering of an eyelid, and then they came straight back again in a mass, pressing on my sight and overclouding it, and the result was that, though I did not think of

you in the shape of a human body, I was still forced to think of you as a corporeal substance occupying space, whether infused into this world or diffused through the infinite space outside the world, and this substance too I regarded as being of that incorruptible, inviolable, and changeless nature which I saw as superior to the corruptible, the violable, and the mutable. And the reason was that if I tried to imagine something as not being in space it seemed to me to be nothing, and by "nothing" I mean absolutely nothing, not even a void. For if a body is taken out of its place and the place remains empty of any kind of body, whether of earth, water, air, or sky, it will still be an empty place, a "nothing" that is nevertheless in a spatial context.

So I with my gross mind (for I was not even clearly visible to myself) considered that whatever was not extended in space, whether diffused or condensed or swelling out or having some such qualities or being capable of having them, must be, in the full sense of the word, nothing. The images in my mind were like the shapes which I was used to seeing with my eyes, and I did not realize that this very act of the mind by which I formed these images was something of a different nature altogether; yet it would not be able to form the images unless it were itself something great. So, life of my life, I thought of you as an immensity through infinite space, interfused everywhere throughout the whole mass of the universe and extending beyond it in every direction for distances without end, so that the earth should have you, the sky should have you, all things should have you, and they should be bounded in you, but you should be boundless. For just as the body of the air which is above the earth does not resist the passage of the sun's light, which goes through it without breaking or cutting it, but simply by filling it entirely, so I thought that the body not only of the heaven and the air and the sea, but also of the earth, was permeable to you and, in its greatest parts as in its least, able to be penetrated so as to receive your presence and that thus a hidden kind of inspiration from within and from without governed all things which you had created.

This was the idea I formed, because I could not think

in any other way. But it was false. For according to this view a greater or a lesser part of the earth would contain a greater or a lesser part of you; all things would be full of you, but in such a way that the body of an elephant would contain more of you than the body of a sparrow to the extent that it is larger and occupies more space, and thus you would be imparting your presence piecemeal to different parts of the world—small portions of you to small parts, big portions to big parts. But this is not so. However, you had not yet enlightened my darkness.

2   As to those deceived deceivers, those dumb talkers (dumb because they never uttered your Word), I had a perfectly good argument to oppose to them, and I had had it ever since the time when we were in Carthage. It was put forward by Nebridius, and all of us who heard it were much taken aback by it. There is in the Manichaean creed a sort of nation of darkness which is set up as a counter substance to you; now what, Nebridius asked, would this nation of darkness have done to you, if you had been unwilling to fight against it? If the reply was: "it would have done you some harm," then it would follow that you were capable of suffering injury and corruption. If, on the other hand, it was admitted that it could have done you no harm, then no reason could be produced why you should fight with it. Particularly when the fighting was of this kind: some portion or member of you or offspring of your own substance was supposed to become mixed with opposite powers and natures not created by you; it was then so corrupted by them and so changed for the worse as to fall from beatitude into misery and to require help so as to be delivered and cleansed; this portion of your substance was the soul, and in its state of slavery and contamination and corruption it was to receive the aid of your Word, which was free, pure, and entire. But that Word was itself corruptible because it was the offspring of one and the same substance as the soul. And so if they say that you, in your real nature—that is, in your substance by which you are—are incorruptible, then all these

theories of theirs must be false and execrable, and if they say that you are corruptible, that very statement in itself, as is immediately obvious, must be false and must be abominated. This argument of Nebridius was therefore all I needed against the Manichees, whom I ought to have wholly vomited up from a stomach overcharged with them; for they had no possible answer and could not defend the way in which they thought and spoke about you without the most dreadful blasphemy of heart and tongue.

3   As TO ME, I would certainly say and I firmly believed that you—our Lord, the true God, who made not only our souls but our bodies, and not only our souls and bodies but all men and all things—were undefilable and unalterable and in no way to be changed, and yet I still could not understand clearly and distinctly what was the cause of evil. Whatever it might be, however, I did realize that my inquiry must not be carried out along lines which would lead me to believe that the immutable God was mutable; if I did that, I should become myself the very evil which I was looking for. And so I pursued the inquiry without anxiety, being quite certain that what the Manichees said was not true. I had turned against them with my whole heart, because I saw that in their inquiries into the origin of evil they were full of evil themselves; for they preferred to believe that your substance could suffer evil rather than that their substance could do evil.

And I made an effort to understand what I had heard, that free will is the cause of our doing evil and your just judgment the cause of our suffering it; but I could not grasp this clearly. And so, though I tried to raise the eyes of my mind from the pit, I fell back into it again and as often as I tried so often did I fall back. But I was a little raised up toward your light by the fact that I was just as certain that I had a will as that I had a life. So, when I willed to do or not to do something, I was perfectly certain that the act of willing was mine and not anybody else's, and I was now getting near to the conclusion that here was the cause of my sin.

But with regard to things which I did unwillingly, it seemed to me that I was suffering rather than doing, and I considered such things to be my punishment rather than my fault; though, as I thought of you as just, I was quick to admit that I was not being punished unjustly. But then I asked: "Who made me? Was it not my God, who is not only good but goodness itself? How then could it be that I should will evil and refuse my assent to good, so that it would be just for me to be punished? Who was it who set and ingrafted in me this plant of bitterness, seeing that I was wholly made by my most sweet God? If the devil is responsible, then where did the devil come from? And if it was by his own perverse will that the devil himself, after having been a good angel, became a devil, then what was the origin in him of the evil will by which he became a devil, seeing that he was made all angel by the all-good creator?" By these thoughts I was thrust down again and choked; but I was not brought down so low as to that hell of error where no one confesses to you and where it is believed that you suffer evil rather than that man does evil.

4   So I STRUGGLED ON to find out the rest in the same way as I had already discovered that the incorruptible is better than the corruptible, and therefore I was ready to confess that, whatever your nature might be, you must be incorruptible. For no soul ever has been or ever will be able to conceive of anything better than you, who are the supreme and the best good. And, since in all truth and certainty the view which I now held—that the incorruptible is to be preferred to the corruptible— was right, I should have been able, if you had not been incorruptible, to have reached in imagination something better than my God. It was here, therefore—in my knowledge that the incorruptible was better than the corruptible—that I ought to have been looking for you, and I should have gone on from here to discover where evil is, that is to say, what is the origin of that corruption by which your own substance cannot possibly be affected. For there is absolutely no way in which corruption can

affect our God, neither by will nor by necessity nor by accident; because He Himself is God and what He wills is good and He Himself is goodness; but to be corrupted is not good. Nor are you forced toward anything against your will, for your will is not greater than your power. But it would be greater, if you were greater than yourself. For the will and power of God is God Himself. And how could any accident surprise you, who know all things? There is nothing in existence except as a result of your knowing it. But what need is there of more words to show that the substance which is God is not corruptible? If it were, it would not be God.

5   I SEARCHED FOR the origin of evil, and I searched for it in an evil way, and I did not see the evil in the very method of my search. I put the whole creation in front of the eyes of my spirit, both what was visible—like earth, sea, air, stars, trees, and mortal creatures—and what was invisible—like the firmament of the heaven above and all the angels and spiritual beings there. Though even these spiritual beings I conceived of as bodies, each in its imagined place. And I thought of all your creation as one great mass, distinguished in accordance with the kinds of bodies of which it was made up, some being real bodies, others the kind of bodies which I imagined instead of spirits. I thought of this mass as being of an enormous size, not the size which it actually was (which I could not know), but the size which seemed to me convenient; though I conceived of it as being finite on every side. And I thought of you, Lord, as surrounding it on every side and penetrating it, but being in all directions infinite. It was as though there were a sea, which everywhere and on all sides through immensity was just one infinite sea, but which had inside it a sponge which, though very big, was still bounded. This sponge of course would in all its parts be completely filled with the immeasurable sea. So I thought of your creation as finite and as filled with you, who were infinite. And I said: "Here is God, and here is what God has created; and God is good and is most mightily and incomparably better

than all these. Yet He, being good, created them good, and see how He surrounds them and fills them. Where, then, is evil? Where did it come from and how did it creep in here? What is its root and seed? Or does it simply not exist? In that case why do we fear and take precautions against something that does not exist? Or if there is no point in our fears, then our fears themselves are an evil which goads and tortures the heart for no good reason—and all the worse an evil if there is nothing to be afraid of and we are still afraid. Therefore, either there is evil which we fear or else the fact that we do fear is evil. Where then does evil come from, seeing that God is good and made all things good? Certainly it was the greater and supreme Good who made these lesser goods, yet still all are good, both the creator and his creation. Where then did evil come from? Or was there some evil element in the material of creation, and did God shape and form it, yet still leave in it something which He did not change into good? But why? Being omnipotent, did He lack the power to change and transform the whole so that no trace of evil should remain? Indeed why should He choose to use such material for making anything? Would He not rather, with this same omnipotence, cause it not to exist at all? Could it exist against His will? Or, supposing it was eternal, why for so long through all the infinite spaces of time past did He allow it to exist and then so much later decide to make something out of it? Or, if He did suddenly decide on some action, would not the omnipotent prefer to act in such a way that this evil material should cease to exist, and that He alone should be, the whole, true, supreme, and infinite Good? Or, since it was not good that He who was good should frame and create something not good, then why did He not take away and reduce to nothing the material that was evil and then Himself provide good material from which to create all things? For He would not be omnipotent if He could not create something good without having to rely on material which He had not Himself created."

These were the kind of thoughts which I turned over and over in my unhappy heart, a heart overburdened with those biting cares that came from my fear of death and my failure to discover the truth. Yet the faith of your Christ, our Lord and Saviour, professed in the Catholic Church, remained steadfastly fixed in my heart, even though it was on many points still unformed and swerving from the right rule of doctrine. But, nevertheless, my mind did not abandon it, but rather drank more and more deeply of it every day.

6   BY THIS TIME TOO I had rejected the fallacious forecasts and impious ravings of the astrologers. Here also, my God, let your own mercies make confession to you from the very depths of my soul. For this was entirely due to you. Who else is it who calls us back from the death of error, except the life that does not know death, and the wisdom which, needing no light, enlightens minds which are in darkness, that wisdom by which the whole world, even to the leaves of trees drifting in the wind, is governed? So it was you who dealt with that obstinate state of mind in which I was when I argued with that sharp-witted old man Vindicianus and with the young Nebridius, with his fine spiritual qualities. Vindicianus used to maintain most energetically, and Nebridius, though with rather more hesitation, often used to say too that the supposed art of foretelling the future was no art at all; it was rather the case that the guesses people made had the luck of a lottery; those who made a number of predictions would make some that turned out true, though in making them no knowledge was shown; it was simply a question of saying so many things that in the course of it one was bound to stumble on something true. And then, again by your provision, I had a friend who was a very keen follower of the astrologers. He had no great knowledge of their literature but was, as I said, one who showed considerable curiosity about them. He did know something, however, which he said had been told him by his father; but he did not know how useful this information was for the overthrowing of any belief one might have in astrology. The man's name was Firminus; he had had a good education and was thoroughly trained in rhetoric. As he considered me a great friend he asked

me to give him my advice about some affairs of his which
greatly concerned his worldly ambitions, and he wanted
to know what I thought about his so-called "constella-
tions" in the matter. By this time I was beginning to come
around to the views of Nebridius about astrology, but I
did not refuse to make my conjectures and to tell
Firminus how (uncertain as I was) things seemed to me.
I added however that I was now practically certain that
all these inquiries were a ridiculous waste of time. He
then told me about his father, who had been a great student of astrology and had had a friend who was equally
enthusiastic and had joined him in his studies. They
studied zealously and compared notes and their hearts became so much on fire with this nonsense that they used to
make careful observations of the exact times when even
the dumb animals in their houses gave birth and they
noted the position of the heavens at these times—all in
order to collect experimental evidence for this presumed
art. Firminus said that his father had told him that at the
time when his mother was pregnant with him a female
slave belonging to this friend of his father's was also about
to have a child. This of course was known to the woman's
master, who, even when one of his bitches was having
puppies, would be most meticulously careful to find out
all about it. So now in the case of this slave of his he was
taking the most careful and thorough notes with regard to
days, hours, and the smallest fractions of hours, while
Firminus' father was doing just the same thing with regard to his wife. It happened that the two women had
their babies at the same moment, so that for each newborn
child the men were forced to cast exactly the same
horoscope down to the last detail, one for his son, the
other for the little slave. For as soon as the women's labor
began each friend had let the other know what was going
on in his house and they had messengers ready to send to
each other as soon as it was known that one or other of the
children had been born—and, since the births were taking
place in their own households, they would know at once.
Firminus said that the messengers sent by each met exactly
halfway between the two houses, so that it was impossible
for either of the men to have made any different observa-

tions from the other one with regard to the position of the stars or the precise moment of time. Yet Firminus, born to wealth in his parents' house, had one of the brighter careers in life; his riches increased and he held distinguished positions; whereas the slave had no alleviation in the burden of his condition; he continued to serve his masters. So Firminus, who knew him, told me.

After hearing this story and (since Firminus was a perfectly reliable witness) believing it, all my previous resistance gave way and collapsed. First I attempted to induce Firminus himself to give up this form of curiosity by telling him that if I had had to consult his stars in order to give him a true forecast of the future, I certainly ought to have seen in them that his parents were people of distinction, that his family was a noble one in his own city, that he was born free, and that he had had a good and liberal education. But if that slave had asked me for my opinion and I had consulted his stars, which were exactly the same as those under which Firminus was born, then I ought to have seen in them that his family was of the very lowest, that he was a slave, and that in every other respect he had a completely different lot in life from that of Firminus. It followed, therefore, that, after inspecting the same stars, I must, if I were to tell the truth, say different things in the two cases, for if I were to say the same things, it would be a falsehood, and from this it appeared to me quite certain that anything true which may be said after casting a horoscope is true by luck and not by skill, and anything false is false not because of any lack of skill in the art but simply because the luck has gone the other way.

With this approach to the subject I began to look more deeply into the same kind of argument in case one of those fools who make money out of astrology, and whom I was already longing to challenge and to make laughingstocks of, was to object by saying that what Firminus had told me or what his father had told him was untrue. So I considered the cases of those who are born twins. Most of them come from the womb very close to each other, and the small interval of time between the two births (whatever influence these people may pretend it has in reality) simply cannot be noted by any human method of observation so as to be put down in the tables which the astrologer must look at in order to foretell the truth. And of course it will not be the truth. After looking at the same figures an astrologer would have had to predict the same futures for Esau and for Jacob; but in fact the same things did not happen to them. Either, then, he would have to have made a false prediction, or else, if his prediction was true, it would have to have been different in each case; yet each case was based on the same figures. So, if he did tell the truth, it would be by luck and not by skill. For you, Lord, the most just controller of the universe, act in your own secret way so that, while neither he who consults nor he who is consulted knows what is being done, still when a man consults he is told out of the abyss of your just judgment what, in accordance with the secret deservings of souls, he ought to be told. Let no man say to you "What is this?" or "Why is this?" He must not, he must not say such things. For he is a man.

7 AND SO, MY HELPER, you had set me free from those chains. But still I asked: "What is the origin of evil?" and I could find no answer. Yet in all the fluctuations of my thought you did not allow me to be carried away from the faith in which I believed that you existed, that your substance was unchangeable, that you had care for men, and that you would judge them; also that in Christ your Son our Lord and in the Holy Scriptures approved by the authority of your Catholic Church you had laid down the way of man's salvation to the life which is to come after death. With these beliefs firmly and irrevocably rooted in my mind I sought, in a kind of passion, the answer to the question: "What is the origin of evil?" What agonies I suffered, what groans, my God, came from my heart in its labor! And you were listening, though I did not know it. When in silence I strongly urged my question, the quiet contrition of my soul was a great cry to your mercy. You knew what I was suffering, and no man knew it. For how little there

was of it which I could put into words even for the hearing of my most intimate friends! How could they hear the tumult of my soul when I had neither time nor language sufficient to express it? Yet all of it reached your hearing, all the roarings and groanings of my heart, and my desire was in front of you and the light of my eyes was not with me. For that light was within and I was out of doors; that was not in space, but my mind was intent on things which were in space, and I could find no place there to rest, and the things of space did not welcome me so that I could say: "It is enough, it is well," nor did they let me go back to where it would have been well enough with me. For I was superior to them, but inferior to you. You are my true joy and I am subject to you, and you have subjected to me the things in your creation which are below me. And this was the correct admixture, the middle way for my salvation—that I should remain in your image and, by serving you, be master of the body. But when I arrogantly rose up against you and *ran upon my Lord with my neck, with the thick bosses of my buckler*, even these inferior things became above me and kept me under, and there was no loosening of their hold and no chance of breathing. When I opened my eyes they swarmed around me from all sides in clouds, and when I tried to think, these corporeal images stood in my way and prevented me from returning to you. It was as though they were saying: "Where are you going to, you unworthy and unclean creature?" All this had grown out of my wound; for you humble the proud like one who is wounded, and I was separated from you by the swelling of my pride. It was as though my cheeks had swollen up so that I could not see out of my eyes.

8   But you, Lord, abide forever, and you are not angry with us forever because you have pity on our dust and ashes, and it was pleasing in your sight to reform my deformity. Inside me your good was working on me to make me restless until you should become clear and certain to my inward sight. Through the hidden hand

of your healing art my swelling abated and from day to day the troubled and clouded sight of my mind grew better through the stinging ointment of a healthy sorrow.

9   FIRST YOU WISHED to show me how *Thou resistest the proud but givest grace to the humble* and how great was your mercy in showing to men the way of humility in that the Word was made flesh and dwelt among men. And so by means of a man I knew (he was an extraordinarily conceited person) you brought to my notice some books written by the Platonists, which had been translated from Greek into Latin. In these books I found it stated, not of course in the same words but to precisely the same effect and with a number of different sorts of reasons, that: *In the beginning was the Word, and the Word was with God, and the Word was God: the Same was in the beginning with God: all things were made by Him, and without Him was nothing made: that which was made by Him is life, and the life was the light of men, and the light shineth in the darkness, and the darkness comprehended it not.* Also that the soul of man, though it bears witness to the light, yet itself *is not that light;* but the Word, God Himself, *is that true light that lighteth every man that cometh into the world.* Also that *He was in the world, and the world was made by Him, and the world knew Him not.* But I did not find in the books of the Platonists that: *He came unto His own, and His own received Him not; but as many as received Him, to them gave He power to become the sons of God, as many as believed in His name.*

I also read in these books that God the Word was *born not of flesh nor of blood, nor of the will of man, nor of the will of the flesh, but of God.* But I did not find then that *the Word was made flesh and dwelt among us.* I did discover, as I examined these books, that it was stated in a number of different ways that *the Son was in the form of the Father, and thought it not robbery to be equal with God,* because by nature He was God. But one will not find in the writings of the Platonists that *He emptied Himself, taking the form of a servant, being made in the likeness of men, and found in fashion as a man, humbled Himself, and became obedient unto death, even the death of the cross: wherefore God exalted Him from the dead, and gave Him a name above every name, that at the name of Jesus every knee should bow, of things in heaven, and things in earth, and things under the earth; and that every tongue should confess that the Lord Jesus is in the glory of God the Father.*

I did find there that your only-begotten Son was before all times and beyond all times and remains unchangeable, coeternal with you, and that *of His fullness souls receive,* that they may be blessed; also that by participation of the wisdom that abides in them they are renewed so as to become wise. But I did not find that *in due time He died for the ungodly,* or that *Thou sparedst not Thine only Son, but deliveredst Him for us all.* For *Thou hiddest these things from the wise, and revealedst them to babes;* so that they *that labor and are heavy laden might come unto Him and He refresh them,* because *He is meek and lowly in heart, and the meek He directeth in judgment, and the gentle He teacheth His ways, beholding our lowliness and trouble, and forgiving all our sins.* But those who, like actors on the stage, are raised up above the general level in their supposedly superior learning do not hear him saying: *Learn of Me, for I am meek and lowly in heart, and ye shall find rest to your souls.* Although they knew God, *yet they glorify Him not as God, nor are thankful, but wax vain in their thoughts, and their foolish heart is darkened; professing that they were wise, they became fools.*

I read there too that they had *changed the glory of Thy incorruptible nature* into idols and images of various kinds, *into the likeness of the image of corruptible man, and birds and beasts and creeping things,* indeed into that Egyptian food for which Esau lost his birthright, since that people which was your firstborn worshiped the head of a four-footed beast instead of you, turning in their hearts back to Egypt, and bowing down their soul, your image, in front of the image of a *calf that eateth hay.* I found these things here, but I did not feed on them. For it pleased you, Lord, to take away the reproach of inferiority from Jacob and to cause the elder to serve the younger, and you have called the Gentiles into your inheritance. I myself had come to you from the Gentiles, and I thought of the gold which you willed that your people should carry away from Egypt, since it was yours wherever it was. And you had said to the Athenians by your apostle that *in Thee we live and move and have our being, as certain of their own poets had said,* and for sure these books that I was reading came from Athens. But I did not set my mind on the idols of the Egyptians *which they served with the gold that was yours, changing the truth of God into a lie and worshiping and serving the creature more than the creator.*

10 I WAS ADMONISHED by all this to return to my own self, and, with you to guide me, I entered into the innermost part of myself, and I was able to do this because you were my helper. I entered and I saw with my soul's eye (such as it was) an unchangeable light shining above this eye of my soul and above my mind. It was not the ordinary light which is visible to all flesh, nor something of the same sort, only bigger, as though it might be our ordinary light shining much much more brightly and filling everything with its greatness. No, it was not like that; it was different, entirely different from anything of the kind. Nor was it above my mind as oil floats on water or as the heaven is above the earth. It was higher than I, because it made me, and I was lower because I was made by it. He who knows truth knows that light, and he who knows that light knows eternity. Love knows it. O eternal truth and true love and beloved eternity! You are my God; to you I sigh by day and by night. And when I first knew you, you raised me up so that I could see that there was something to see and that I still lacked the ability to see it. And you beat back the weakness of my sight, blazing upon me with your rays, and I trembled in love and in dread, and I found that I was far distant from you, in a region of total unlikeness, as if I were hearing your voice from on high saying: "I am the food of grown men. Grow and you shall feed upon me. And you will not, as with

the food of the body, change me into yourself, but you will be changed into me." And I learned that *Thou, for iniquity, chastenest man and Thou madest my soul to consume away like a spider*. And I said: "Is truth therefore nothing because it is not extended through any kind of space, whether finite or infinite?" And from far away you cried out to me: "I am that I am." And I heard, as one hears things in the heart, and there was no longer any reason at all for me to doubt. I would sooner doubt my own existence than the existence of that truth *which is clearly seen being understood by those things which are made*.

11 AND I CONSIDERED the other things which are below you, and I saw that, in a complete sense, they neither are nor are not in existence. They are, since they are from you; they are not, since they are not what you are. For that which truly is, is that which remains unchangeably. *It is good then for me to hold fast unto God;* because if I do not remain in Him, I shall not be able to remain in myself. But He, remaining in Himself, renews all things. And *Thou art my Lord, since Thou standest not in need of my goodness*.

12 AND IT BECAME clear to me that things which are subject to corruption are good. They would not be subject to corruption if they were either supremely good or not good at all; for, if they were supremely good, they would be incorruptible, and, if there was nothing good in them, there would be nothing which could be corrupted. For corruption does harm, and, unless what is good in a thing is diminished, no harm could be done. Therefore, either corruption does no harm (which is impossible), or (which is quite certain) all things which suffer corruption are deprived of something good in them. Supposing them to be deprived of all good, they will cease to exist altogether. For, if they continue to exist and can no longer be corrupted, they will be better than before, because they will be permanently beyond the reach of

corruption. What indeed could be more monstrous than to assert that things could become better by losing all their goodness? So if they are deprived of all good, they will cease to exist altogether. Therefore, so long as they exist, they are good. Therefore, all things that are, are good, and as to that evil, the origin of which I was seeking for, it is not a substance, since, if it were a substance, it would be good. For it would either have to be an incorruptible substance (which is the highest form of goodness) or else a corruptible substance (which, unless it had good in it, could not be corruptible). So I saw plainly and clearly that you have made all things good, nor are there any substances at all which you have not made. And because you did not make all things equal, therefore they each and all have their existence; because they are good individually, and at the same time they are altogether very good, because our God *made all things very good.*

13   To you, THEN, there is no such thing at all as evil. And the same is true not only of you but of your whole creation, since there is nothing outside it to break in and corrupt the order which you have imposed on it. But in some of its parts there are some things which are considered evil because they do not harmonize with other parts; yet with still other parts they do harmonize and are good and they are good in themselves. And all these things which do not fit in with each other do fit in with that lower part of creation which we call the earth, which has its own cloudy and windy sky which again is fitting to it. Far be it that I should say: "I wish these things did not exist," because even if these were the only things I saw, though certainly I should long for something better yet, still for these things alone I ought to praise you; for things from the earth show that you are to be praised—*dragons, and all deeps, fire, hail, snow, ice, and stormy wind, which fulfill Thy Word; mountains, and all hills, fruitful trees and all cedars; beasts and all cattle, creeping things and flying fowls; kings of the earth, and all people, princes and all judges of the earth; young men and maidens, old men and young, praise Thy name.* And since from the

heavens these *praise Thee, praise Thee, our God, in the heights, all Thy angels, all Thy hosts, sun and moon, all the stars and light, the heaven of heavens, and the waters that be above the heavens, praise Thy name*. So I no longer desired better things. I had envisaged all things in their totality, and, with a sounder judgment, I realized that, while higher things are certainly better than lower things, all things together are better than the higher things by themselves.

14   IT IS THE MARK of an unsound mind to be displeased with any single thing in your creation, and so it was with me, when I was displeased with many of the things which you made. And because my soul did not dare to be displeased with my God, I refused to admit that whatever did displease it was yours. And from this point it had gone on to hold the view that there are two substances, and here it found no rest and only talked perversely. And next it had gone back again and made for itself a God to fill the infinite distances of all space, and it had imagined this God to be you and had placed it in its own heart, thus again becoming the temple of its own idol, a temple abominable to you. But you, though I was not aware of it, laid your kindly hand upon my head and covered up my eyes so that they should not see vanity, and then I relaxed a little from myself, and sleep fell upon my madness. And I woke up in you and saw you infinite in a different way, and that sight was not from the eyes of the flesh.

15   AND I LOOKED AT other things and saw that they owe their existence to you and are all bounded in you, not in a spatial sense, but because your being contains everything in the hand of your truth, and all things are true insofar as they exist, and the only meaning of falsehood is when something is thought to exist when it does not. And I saw that all things fitted in not only with their places but with their times, and that you, who alone are eternal, did not begin to work after the passage of in-

numerable spaces of time, since all spaces of time, both past and future, could neither go nor come without your permanent presence and operation.

16   I KNEW FROM my own experience that there is nothing strange in the fact that a sick person will find uneatable the same bread which a healthy person enjoys, or that good eyes love the light and bad eyes hate it. Your justice too displeases the wicked, and even more displeasing are vipers and reptiles, though you created them good and well fitted to the lower parts of your creation, and to these lower parts of creation the wicked themselves are well fitted and become the better fitted the more they are unlike you, although in becoming more like you they will become better fitted to the higher parts of your creation. And I asked: "What is wickedness?" and found that it is not a substance but a perversity of the will turning away from you, God, the supreme substance, toward lower things—casting away, as it were, its own insides, and swelling with desire for what is outside it.

17   AND I FELT wonder at the thought that now I loved you and not a phantom instead of you. But I did not stay in the enjoyment of my God; I was swept away to you by your own beauty, and then I was torn away from you by my own weight and fell back groaning toward these lower things. Carnal habit was this weight. But there remained with me the memory of you; I knew with certainty that it was to you that I must cling, but I knew too that I was not yet capable of doing so; because *the body which is corrupted, presseth down the soul, and the earthly tabernacle weigheth down the mind that museth upon many things.* I was perfectly sure of this, *that Thy invisible works from the creation of the world are clearly seen, being understood by the things that are made, even Thy eternal power and Godhead.* For I considered how it was that I recognized the beauty of bodies, whether in the heaven or on earth, and what criterion I had to make a correct judgment of changing things and to

say: "This is as it should be, this is not." So, as I considered how it was that I came to make these judgments which I did make, I had discovered that above my changing mind was the unchangeable and true eternity of truth. And so I went on by stages from bodies to the soul which perceives by means of the bodily senses, and from this to the inner power of the soul to which the bodily senses present external things. The faculties of animals extend as far as this, and from this point I went on to the faculty of reason to which sense data are referred for judgment. This also found itself in me to be something subject to change. It then, as it were, raised itself up to the level of its own understanding, freed my thought from the power of habit, and withdrew itself from those crowds of contradictory phantasms, so that it might discover what was that light with which it was illumined when, without the least hesitation, it cried out that the unchangeable is to be preferred to the changeable, and how it was that it had knowledge of the unchangeable itself: for unless it had knowledge in some way of the unchangeable, it could in no way prefer it with certainty to the changeable. And then, in the flash of a trembling glance, my mind arrived at That Which Is. Now indeed I saw your *invisible things understood by the things which are made*, but I had not the power to keep my eye steadily fixed; in my weakness I felt myself falling back and returning again to my habitual ways, carrying nothing with me except a loving memory of it and a longing for something which may be described as a kind of food of which I had perceived the fragrance but which I was not yet able to eat.

18   AND I TRIED to find a way of gaining the strength necessary for enjoying you, and I could not find it until I embraced that *Mediator betwixt God and men, the Man Christ Jesus, who is over all, God blessed for evermore*, calling to me and saying, *I am the way, the truth and the life*, and mingling with our flesh that food which I lacked strength to take; for *the Word was made flesh*, so that your wisdom, by which you created all things, might give its milk to our infancy.

I was not humble enough to possess Jesus in His humility as my God, nor did I know what lesson was taught by His weakness. For your Word, the eternal truth, high above the highest parts of your creation, raises up to Itself those who are subdued; but in this lower world He built for Himself a humble dwelling out of our clay, by means of which He might detach from themselves those who were to be subdued and bring them over to Himself, healing the swelling of their pride and fostering their love, so that instead of going further in their own self-confidence they should put on weakness, seeing at their feet divinity in the weakness that it had put on by wearing our "coat of skin"; and then, weary, they should cast themselves down upon that divinity which, rising, would bear them up aloft.

19 BUT THIS WAS NOT the way I thought then. I thought of my Lord Christ simply as a man of the very highest wisdom, whom no one could equal; and in particular it seemed to me that His miraculous birth from a virgin—as an example of how temporal things should be despised for the sake of obtaining immortality—showed such divine care for us that He deserved full authority over us as a master. But I had not the faintest notion of the mystery contained in "The Word was made flesh." All that I had gathered from the written tradition about Him (accounts of how He ate, drank, slept, walked, was glad, was sad, preached) led me to believe that His flesh had only become united with your Word by means of a human soul and a human mind. This must be known to everyone who knows the immutability of your Word, and I, within the limits of my capacity, did now know this without having any doubt about it at all. For to be now moving and now not moving the limbs of the body by an act of will, to be now feeling some emotion and now not feeling it, to be at one moment uttering wisdom by means of the signs of speech and at the next moment to be silent— these are all marks of a soul and a mind which are mutable. And if the written tradition about Him were false on these points, all the rest too would come under suspicion of

falsehood, and there would be no sure faith in Scripture left for mankind. And so, since what is written in Scripture is true, I recognized in Christ a complete man; not merely with a man's body or with the body and soul of a man and not a man's mind, but altogether a man, and I thought that He was to be preferred to others, not because He was Truth in person, but because of the exceptional qualities of His human nature and His more perfect participation in wisdom.

Alypius, on the other hand, thought that the Catholic belief in a God clothed in flesh meant that in Christ there were God and the flesh, but not the soul; he did not think that they ascribed to Him a human mind. And since he was convinced that the actions recorded of Christ could only have been done by a vital and rational creature, his way toward the Christian faith itself was all the more laborious. Later he realized that this was the error of the Apollinarian heretics and he came over joyfully to the Catholic faith. As to me, I must admit that it was only some time afterward that I learned how in the understanding of "The Word was made flesh" Catholic truth is distinguished from the false view of Photinus. Indeed by proving heretics to be wrong we bring into clearer light what your Church believes and what sound doctrine is. *For there must also be heresies, that the approved may be made manifest among the weak.*

20   BUT THEN, after reading these books of the Platonists which taught me to seek for a truth which was incorporeal, I came to see your *invisible things, understood by those things which are made*. I fell back again from this point, but still I had an apprehension of what, through the darkness of my mind, I was not able to contemplate; I was certain that you are and that you are infinite, yet not in the sense of being diffused through space whether infinite or finite: that you truly are, and are always the same, not in any part or by any motion different or otherwise: also that all other things are from you, as is proved most certainly by the mere fact that they exist. On all these points I was perfectly certain, but I was

still too weak to be able to enjoy you. I talked away as if I were a finished scholar; but, if I had not sought the way to you in Christ our Saviour, what would have been finished would have been my soul. For I had begun to want to have the reputation of a wise man; my punishment was within me, but I did not weep; I was merely puffed up with my knowledge. Where was that charity which builds from the foundation of humility, the foundation which is Christ Jesus? Humility was not a subject which those books would ever have taught me. Yet I believe that you wanted me to come upon these books before I made a study of your Scriptures. You wanted the impression made by them on me to be printed in my memory, so that when later I had become, as it were, tamed by your books (your fingers dressing my wounds), I should be able to see clearly what the difference is between presumption and confession, between those who see their goal without seeing how to get there and those who see the way which leads to that happy country which is there for us not only to perceive but to live in. For if I had been first trained in your Scriptures and by my familiarity with them had found you growing sweet to me, and had then afterward come upon these books of the Platonists, it is possible that they might have swept me away from the solid basis of piety; or, even if I had held firmly to that healthy disposition which I had imbibed, I might have thought that the same disposition could be acquired by someone who had read only the Platonic books.

as in description of

21 So I MOST GREEDILY seized upon the venerable writings of your spirit and in particular the works of the apostle Paul. In the past it had sometimes seemed to me that he contradicted himself and that what he said conflicted with the testimonies of the law and the prophets; but all these difficulties had now disappeared; I saw one and the same face of pure eloquence and learned *to rejoice with trembling*. Having begun, I discovered that everything in the Platonists which I had found true was expressed here, but it was expressed to the glory of your grace; so that whoever sees should not *so glory as if he*

had not received—received, indeed, not only what he sees but also the power to see it; for *what hath he, which he hath not received.* I found too that one is not only instructed so as to see you, who are the same forever, but also so as to grow strong enough to lay hold on you, and he who cannot see you for the distance, may yet walk along the road by which he will arrive and see you and lay hold on you. For, though a man *be delighted with the law of God after the inner man,* what shall he do about that *other law in his members which warreth against the law of his mind, and bringeth him into captivity to the law of sin, which is in his members?* For, *Thou art righteous, O Lord, but we have sinned and committed iniquity, and have done wickedly,* and your hand has grown heavy upon us, and we have justly been handed over to that ancient sinner, the president of death; because he persuaded our will to be like his will, whereby he did not stand in your truth. *What shall wretched man do? Who shall deliver him from the body of this death, but only Thy Grace,* through Jesus *Christ, our Lord,* whom you have begotten coeternal and *formedst in the beginning of Thy ways, in whom the prince of this world found nothing worthy of death,* yet killed him, and *the handwriting, which was contrary to us, was blotted out.*

None of this is to be found in the books of the Platonists. Their pages make no mention of the face and look of pity, the tears of confession, your *sacrifice—a troubled spirit, a broken and a contrite heart,* the salvation of the people, *the bridal city, the earnest of the Holy Ghost, the cup of our redemption.* No one sings there, *Shall not my soul be submitted unto God? For of Him cometh my salvation. For He is my God and my salvation, my guardian, I shall no more be moved.* No one there hears him call, *Come unto Me all ye that labor.* They are too proud to *learn of Him, because He is meek and lowly of heart; for these things hast Thou hid from the wise and prudent, and hast revealed them unto babes.* It is one thing to see from a mountaintop in the forests the land of peace in the distance and not to find the way to it and to struggle in vain along impassable tracks, ambushed and beset on all sides by fugitive deserters under their chief *the Lion and the Dragon,* and it is another thing to hold to the way that leads there, a road built and guarded by our heavenly General, where no banditry is committed by deserters from the celestial army; for they avoid it like the plague. In marvelous ways these things grew and fixed themselves in the depths of my being as I read that *least of Thy apostles,* and had meditated upon your works and had trembled.

Book VIII

1 MY GOD, let me remember with thanks and let me confess to you your mercies done to me. Let my bones be penetrated with your love and let them say: *Who is like unto Thee, O Lord? Thou hast broken my bonds in sunder, I will offer unto Thee the sacrifice of thanksgiving.* I will tell how it was that you broke my bonds, and all your worshipers who hear this will say: "Blessed be the Lord in heaven and in earth, great and wonderful is His name."

Your words had stuck in my heart and *I was hedged around about on all sides by Thee.* Of your eternal life I was now certain, although I had seen it in an enigma and *as through a glass.* But I had ceased to have any doubt that there was an incorruptible substance from which came every substance. I no longer desired to be more certain of you, only to stand more firmly in you.

In my own temporal life everything was unsettled and *my heart had to be purged from the old leaven.* The way—the Saviour Himself—pleased me; but I was still reluctant to enter its narrowness. It was you who put the idea into my mind (and the idea seemed good to me) to go to Simplicianus. He seemed to me a good servant of yours and your grace shone in him. I had heard too that from his youth he had lived a life devoted to you. He had now grown old, and it seemed to me that he must have experienced much and learned much as a result of having lived so long in so earnestly following your way, and so indeed he had. So, after telling him of my troubles, I wanted him to make use of his experience and learning in order to show me the best means by which someone feeling as I did could set his foot on your way.

For I saw the Church full, and one went this way, and another that way. But I was displeased with the worldly life which I was leading. It was a really great burden to me and to help me bear such a heavy form of slavery I no longer had the impulse and encouragement of my old hopes and desires for position and wealth. Compared with your sweetness and the beauty of your house, which I loved, these things no longer pleased me. But I was still closely bound by my need of woman. Not that the apostle forbade me to marry, although he might recommend something better, his great wish being that all men should be as he was. But I lacked the strength and was inclined to choose the softer place, and because of this one thing everything else with me was in confusion; I was tired out and wasted away with gnawing anxieties, because I was compelled to put up with all sorts of things which I did not want simply because they were inseparable from that state of living with a wife to which I was utterly and entirely bound. I had heard from the mouth of Truth that *there were some eunuchs, which had made themselves eunuchs for the Kingdom of heaven's sake; but*, he says, *let him who can receive it, receive it. Surely vain are all men who are ignorant of God, and could not out of the good things which are seen, find out Him who is good.* But I was no longer in that kind of vanity; I had gone beyond it, and, by the common witness of all creation, I had found you, our Creator, and your Word, God with you, and one God together with you, by whom you created all things. But there is also another kind of impiety, that of those *who knowing God, glorified Him not as God, neither were thankful.* I had fallen into this wickedness too, but your right hand upheld me, took me out of it, and placed me where I might recover. For you have said to man, *Behold, the fear of the Lord is wisdom*, and *Desire not to seem wise;* because they *who affirmed themselves to be wise, became fools.* And I had now found that pearl of great price, and I ought to have sold all that I had and bought it. But I hesitated.

2   So I WENT TO Simplicianus who, in the matter of receiving grace, had been the father of Ambrose, now bishop, and indeed Ambrose loved him as a father. I described to him the winding paths of my error. But when I told him that I had read some books of the Platonists which had been translated into Latin by Victorinus— once professor of rhetoric at Rome, who, so I had heard, had died a Christian—he congratulated me for not having fallen upon the writings of other philosophers full of *fallacies and deceits, after the rudiments of this world*, whereas in the Platonists God and His Word are everywhere implied. Then, in order to lead me toward the humility of Christ *(hidden from the wise, and revealed to little ones)*, he went on to speak of Victorinus himself, with whom he had been on very friendly terms when he was in Rome. I shall make no secret of what he told me about him, for it is a story which ought to be confessed to you, containing, as it does, great praise of your grace. For Victorinus was an extremely learned old man, an expert scholar in all the liberal sciences, one who had read and weighed very many of the works of the philosophers, one who had been the teacher of numbers of distinguished senators and who, because of the exceptional brilliance of his teaching, had earned and accepted the honor of having his statue set up in the Roman forum, a thing which the citizens of this world regard as something quite remarkable, and up to old age he worshiped idols and took part in those sacrilegious ceremonies which were the craze with nearly all the Roman nobility, who had inspired the people with their enthusiasm for Osiris and

> The dog Anubis and that monstrous brood
> Of deity which once took arms and fought
> In arms against Minerva, Neptune, Venus

—gods which Rome had conquered and to which she now prayed, and for all these years old Victorinus, with his thundering eloquence, had been the champion of these gods; yet he did not blush to become the child of your Christ, an infant at your font, bending his neck to the yoke of humility and submitting his forehead to the ignominy of the Cross.

O Lord, Lord, *Which has bowed the heavens and come down, touched the mountains and they did smoke*, by what means did you find your way into that man's heart? According to Simplicianus, he read the Holy Scripture and examined all Christian literature with the most thorough and exact attention. He then said to Simplicianus—not in public, but in a private friendly conversation—"I should like you to know that I am now a Christian." Simplicianus replied: "That I will not believe, and I shall not count you as a Christian until I see you in the Church of Christ." Victorinus smiled and said: "Is it the walls, then, that make Christians?" And he often repeated that he was a Christian, and Simplicianus often made the same reply which was again countered by the joke about the walls. For Victorinus was afraid of offending his friends, who were important people and worshipers of these devils; he feared a great torrent of ill will falling upon him from the height of their Babylonian dignity, as from the tops of the cedars of Lebanon which the Lord had not yet brought down. But from his reading and deep meditation he drew strength. He feared that, if he was afraid to confess Christ before men, Christ might deny him in front of the holy angels, and it seemed to him that he was guilty of a great crime in being ashamed of the sacraments of the humility of your Word, while not being ashamed of the sacrilegious rites of those proud demons, in which he, imitating their pride, had taken part. So he turned his pride against what was vain, and kept his humility for the truth. Quite suddenly and unexpectedly he said to Simplicianus, as Simplicianus himself told me, "Let us go to the Church. I want to be made a Christian." And Simplicianus, who could not contain himself for joy, went along with him. Soon after he had received instruction in the first mysteries, he gave in his name as one who wished to be regenerated by baptism. Rome wondered and the Church rejoiced. The proud *saw and were wroth; they gnashed*

with their teeth and melted away. But the Lord God was
the hope of your servant, and *he regarded not vanities and
lying* madness.

Finally the time came for him to make his profession of
faith. At Rome this was usually done by those who were
about to enter into your grace, and there was a fixed form
of words which was learned by heart and spoken from a
platform in the sight of the faithful. In the case of Victorinus, however, so Simplicianus told me, the priests gave
him the opportunity to make his profession in a less public
manner—as was often allowed to those who seemed likely
to be frightened or embarrassed by the ceremony. But
Victorinus preferred to declare openly his salvation in
front of the holy congregation. In the past he had taught
rhetoric and there had been no salvation in that; yet he had
publicly professed it. He had shown no nervousness when
using his own words in front of crowds of people who
could scarcely be described as sane; why, then, in front of
your meek flock, should he fear to pronounce your
Word? So, when he mounted the platform to make his
profession, all those who knew him (and who was there
who did not?) began to whisper his name one to another
in glad murmurs. From the lips of the whole rejoicing
people came the soft sound: "Victorinus, Victorinus."
Quickly the sound had arisen because of the exultation
they felt when they saw him, and now quickly they became silent again so as to hear him speak. With a fine
confidence he declared openly the true faith, and they
all wished that they could draw him into their very
hearts. And in their love and their rejoicing (for these
were the hands they used) they did take him into their
hearts.

3   O GOOD GOD, what is it in men that makes them
rejoice more when a soul that has been despaired
of and is in very great danger is saved than when there
has always been hope and the danger has not been so
serious? For you too, merciful father, dost *more rejoice
over one penitent than over ninety-nine just persons, that
need no repentance*. We too are filled with joy whenever

we hear the story of how the sheep which had strayed was brought back on the exultant shoulders of the shepherd and of how the coin was put back into your treasury with all the neighbors of the woman who found it rejoicing. And the joy we feel in the solemn service of your house brings tears to our eyes, when in your house we hear read the story of your *younger son, that he was dead and lived again; had been lost and is found*. Indeed you rejoice in us and you rejoice in your angels who are holy in holy charity. For you are always the same, and as to those things which do not always exist or do not always exist in the same way, you know all of them, always and in the same way.

What is it in the soul, then, which makes it take more pleasure in the finding or recovery of things it loves than in the continual possession of them? There are all sorts of other examples of this; indeed the evidence is everywhere, simply crying out: "It is so." The victorious general has his triumph; but he would not have been victorious if he had not fought a battle, and the more danger there was in the battle, the more joy there is in the triumph. Sailors are tossed by a storm and in danger of shipwreck; they all grow pale at the thought of approaching death; then sky and sea become calm and their joy is just as excessive as was their fear. A friend is ill and his pulse shows that he is in danger; all who want him to be well become sick in mind with him; then he recovers, though he cannot walk yet quite as easily as he used to do; but there is already more joy than there was before, when he was well and perfectly able to walk. Also with regard to the ordinary pleasures of life, men seek them by way of difficulty and discomfort which are voluntary and self-chosen and not the kind which comes upon them unexpectedly and against their wills. There is no pleasure in eating or drinking unless it is preceded by the discomfort of being hungry or thirsty. Drunkards eat various kinds of salty things in order to produce an uncomfortable dryness, and, when this is alleviated by drink, they feel pleasure. It is also customary for girls who are engaged not to be given over immediately to their bridegrooms, the idea being that the husband may hold a woman cheap unless, while engaged, he has sighed for the long time he has had to wait.

We notice this, then, in pleasures that are foul and disgraceful and also in pleasures which are lawful and permitted; we notice it in the pure sincerity of friendship, and also in the case of him who was dead and became alive again, who had been lost and was found. Everywhere we find that the more pain there is first, the more joy there is after. Why is this, my Lord God? For you are to yourself eternal joy, you yourself are joy, and those beings who are around you find their joy forever in you. Why is it that this part of the universe alternates between deprivation and fulfillment, between discord and harmony? Or is this its condition, the measure given to it by you when, from the heights of heaven to the depths of earth, from the beginning to the end of time, from the angel to the worm, from the first movement to the last, you settled all the varieties of good and all your just works each in its proper place, each to be in its appointed time? I am abashed when I think how high you are in what is highest, how deep in what is deepest. Nowhere do you depart from us, and hard it is for us to return to you.

4   COME, LORD, act upon us and rouse us up and call us back! Fire us, clutch us, let your sweet fragrance grow upon us! Let us love, let us run! Certainly there are many who from a deeper hell of blindness than Victorinus come back to you and approach you and are enlightened with that light which *those who receive, receive power from Thee to become Thy sons.* But if they are not so well known in the world there is not so much rejoicing even among those who do know them; for when many people rejoice together, the joy of each individual is all the richer, since each one inflames the other and the warmth spreads throughout them all. Then too by the mere fact of being well known they have a great influence on others, leading them to salvation; they go first and many will follow in their steps. Thus even those who have gone before them on the same way feel

great joy, and the joy is not only for them. Indeed we must certainly not think that in your tabernacle the persons of the rich should be more welcome than the poor, or the people of birth more welcome than the ordinary man. Since *Thou hast chosen the weak things of the world, to confound the strong, and the base things of this world, and the things despised hast Thou chosen, and those things which are not, that Thou mightest bring to nought things that are.* These words of yours were spoken by the tongue of *the least of your apostles.* Yet when, as the result of his good service, the pride of Paulus the proconsul was so beaten down that he came under the light yoke of your Christ and became a simple subject of the great king, the apostle, to mark the glory of such a victory, wished to be called Paul instead of Saul, as he was called previously. For the defeat of the enemy is all the more conspicuous when one wins over from him a man of whom he has a particular hold and through whom he can particularly influence others. And people of importance in the world satisfy both conditions; their nobility gives him a particular hold over them, and their authority enables him to use them as an influence over others. It was natural, therefore, for there to be a particular welcome for the heart of Victorinus, which the devil had held as an impregnable stronghold, and for the tongue of Victorinus, which the devil had made use of as a strong and keen weapon for the destruction of so many. And it was right for your sons to feel a particular joy because our King had bound the strong man, and they saw his *vessels taken from him and cleansed*, and *made meet for Thy honor, and become serviceable for the Lord, unto every good work.*

5   WHEN THIS MAN of yours, Simplicianus, told me all this about Victorinus, I was on fire to be like him, and this, of course, was why he had told me the story. He told me this too—that in the time of the Emperor Julian, when a law was passed forbidding Christians to teach literature and rhetoric, Victorinus had obeyed the law, preferring to give up his talking-shop rather

than your Word, by which you make even the tongues of infants eloquent. In this I thought that he was not only brave but lucky, because he had got the chance of giving all his time to you. This was just what I longed for myself, but I was held back, and I was held back not by fetters put on me by someone else, but by the iron bondage of my own will. The enemy held my will and made a chain out of it and bound me with it. From a perverse will came lust, and slavery to lust became a habit, and the habit, being constantly yielded to, became a necessity. These were like links, hanging each to each (which is why I called it a chain), and they held me fast in a hard slavery. And the new will which I was beginning to have and which urged me to worship you in freedom and to enjoy you, God, the only certain joy, was not yet strong enough to overpower the old will which by its oldness had grown hard in me. So my two wills, one old, one new, one carnal, one spiritual, were in conflict, and they wasted my soul by their discord.

In this way my personal experience enabled me to understand what I had read—that *the flesh lusteth against the spirit and the spirit against the flesh*. I, no doubt, was on both sides, but I was more myself when I was on the side which I approved of for myself than when I was on the side of which I disapproved. For it was no longer really I myself who was on this second side, since there to a great extent I was rather suffering things against my will than doing them voluntarily. Yet it was my own fault that habit fought back so strongly against me; for I had come willingly where I now did not will to be. And who has any right to complain when just punishment overtakes the sinner? Nor did I have any longer the excuse which I used to think I had when I said that the reason why I had not yet forsaken the world and given myself up to your service was because I could not see the truth clearly. Now I could see it perfectly clearly. But I was still tied down to earth and refused to take my place in your army. And I was just as frightened of being freed from all my hampering baggage as I ought to have been frightened of being hampered. The pack of this world was a kind of pleasant weight upon me, as happens in sleep, and the thoughts in which I meditated on you were like the efforts of someone who tries to get up but is so overcome with drowsiness that he sinks back again into sleep. Of course no one wants to sleep forever, and everyone in his senses would agree that it is better to be awake; yet all the same, when we feel a sort of lethargy in our limbs, we often put off the moment of shaking off sleep, and, even though it is time to get up, we gladly take a little longer in bed, conscious though we may be that we should not be doing so. In just the same way I was quite certain that it was better to give myself up to your charity rather than to give in to my own desires; but, though the former course was a conviction to which I gave my assent, the latter was a pleasure to which I gave my consent. For I had no answer to make to you when you called me: *Awake, thou that sleepest, and arise from the dead, and Christ shall give thee light.* And, while you showed me wherever I looked that what you said was true, I, convinced by the truth, could still find nothing at all to say except lazy words spoken half asleep: "A minute," "just a minute," "just a little time longer." But there was no limit to the minutes, and the little time longer went a long way. It was in vain that *I delighted in Thy law according to the inner man, when another law in my members rebelled against the law of my mind, and led me captive under the law of sin which was in my members.* For the law of sin is the strong force of habit, which drags the mind along and controls it even against its will— though deservedly, since the habit was voluntarily adopted. *Who then should deliver me thus wretched from the body of this death, but Thy grace only, through Jesus Christ our Lord?*

6   Now, LORD, my helper and my redeemer, I shall tell and confess to your name how it was that you freed me from the bondage of my desire for sex, in which I was so closely fettered, and from my slavery to the affairs of this world. I was leading my usual life; my anxiety was growing greater and greater, and every day I sighed to you. I went often to your Church, whenever

I had time to spare from all that business under the weight of which I was groaning. Alypius was with me. He was free from his official legal work after a third term as assessor and was now waiting to sell his legal advice to anyone who came along, just as I was selling the ability to make speeches—if such an ability can be imparted by teaching. Nebridius, as an act of friendship to us, had consented to teach under Verecundus, a great friend of us all, a citizen and elementary schoolmaster of Milan. He had been very eager to have Nebridius on his staff and indeed had claimed it as something due from our friendship that one of us should come and give him the help and support which he badly needed. Nebridius was not influenced by any desire for profit; he could have done better for himself by teaching literature, if he had wanted. But he was the kindest and best of friends, and, being always ready to help others, would not turn down our request. He conducted himself very carefully in his work, being unwilling to become known in what are regarded by the world as "distinguished circles," and avoiding everything which could disturb his peace of mind; for he wanted to have his mind free and at leisure for as many hours as possible so as to pursue wisdom, to read about it, or to hear about it.

One day, when Alypius and I were at home (Nebridius, for some reason which I cannot remember, was away) we were visited by a man called Ponticianus who, coming from Africa, was a fellow countryman of ours and who held an important appointment at the emperor's court. He had something or other which he wanted to ask us, and we sat down to talk. In front of us was a table for playing games on, and he happened to notice a book lying on the table. He took it, opened it, and found that it was the apostle Paul. He was quite surprised at this, since he had imagined it would be one of the books over which I wearied myself out in the course of my profession. Next he began to smile and, looking closely at me, told me that he was not only surprised but pleased at his unexpected discovery that I had this book and only this book at my side. For he was a Christian, and baptized. He often knelt before you, our God, in Church, praying long and frequently to you. I told him that I gave the greatest attention to these works of Scripture, and then, on his initiative, a conversation began about the Egyptian monk Antony, whose name was very well known among your servants, although Alypius and I up to this time had never heard of him. When Ponticianus discovered this he talked all the more about him, since he wanted us in our ignorance, at which he was much surprised, to learn more about such a great man. And we were amazed as we heard of these wonderful works of yours which had been witnessed by so many people, had been done in the true faith and the Catholic Church, and all so recently—indeed practically in our own times. All of us were full of wonder, Alypius and I at the importance of what we were hearing, Ponticianus at the fact that we had never heard the story before.

He went on to speak of the communities living in monasteries, of their way of life which was full of the sweet fragrance of you, and of the fruitful deserts in the wilderness, about which we knew nothing. There was actually a monastery in Milan outside the walls of the city. It was full of good brothers and was under the care of Ambrose, but we had not even heard of this. So Ponticianus went on speaking and we sat quiet, listening to him eagerly. In the course of his talk he told us how once, when the emperor was at Treves and busy with holding the chariot races in the Circus, he himself with three friends had gone for a walk in the afternoon through the gardens near the city walls. It happened that they walked in two groups, one of the three going one way with him, and the others going another way by themselves. These other two, as they strolled along, happened to come to a small house which was inhabited by some of your servants, *poor in spirit, of whom is the kingdom of heaven*, and there they found a book in which was written an account of the life of Antony. One of the two friends began to read it. He became full of wonder and excitement, and, as he read, he began to think of how he himself could lead a life like this and, abandoning his profession in this world, give his service to you. For these two men were both officials in the emperor's civil service. Suddenly, then, he was filled with a holy love; he felt a sober shame, and, angry with himself, he looked toward his friend and said: "Tell me now; in all this hard work which we do, what are we aiming at? What is it that we want? Why is it that we are state officials? Can we have any higher hope at court than to become friends of the emperor? And is not that a position difficult to hold and full of danger? Indeed does one not have to go through danger after danger simply to reach a place that is more dangerous still? And how long will it take to get there? But, if I want, I can be the friend of God now, this moment." After saying this, he turned back to the book, troubled and perplexed by the new life to which he was giving birth. So he read on, and his heart, where you saw it, was changed, and, as soon appeared, his mind shook off the burden of the world. While he was reading and the waves in his heart rose and fell, there were times when he cried out against himself, and then he distinguished the better course and chose it for his own. Now he was yours, and he said to his friend: "I have now broken away from all our hopes and ambitions and have decided to serve God, and I am entering on this service now, this moment, in this place. You may not like to imitate me in this, but you must not oppose me."

The other replied that he would stay with him and be his comrade in so great a service and for so great a reward. Both of them were now yours; they were building their own fortress at the right cost—namely, the forsaking of all that they had and the following of you.

At this point Ponticianus and his companion, who had been walking in a different part of the garden, looking for their friends, came and found them in this place. When they found them, they suggested that they should go back, as it was now nearly sunset. The others however told them of the decision which they had reached and what they proposed to do; they described how the whole thing had started and how their resolution was now fixed, and they begged their friends, if they would not join them, not to interfere with their purpose. Ponticianus and his friend, while not changing from their former ways, did (as Ponticianus told us) weep for themselves and, devoutly and sincerely congratulating the others, asked them to remember them in their prayers; then, with their own hearts still down on the earth, they went off to the palace. But the other two, with their hearts fixed on heaven, remained there in the cottage. Each of these two was engaged to be married, and when the girls to whom they were engaged heard what had happened, they also dedicated their virginity to you.

7   This was what Ponticianus told us. But you, Lord, while he was speaking, were turning me around so that I could see myself; you took me from behind my own back, which was where I had put myself during the time when I did not want to be observed by myself, and you set me in front of my own face so that I could see how foul a sight I was—crooked, filthy, spotted, and ulcerous. I saw and I was horrified, and I had nowhere to go to escape from myself. If I tried to look away from myself, Ponticianus still went on with his story, and again you were setting me in front of myself, forcing me to look into my own face, so that I might see my sin and hate it. I did know it, but I pretended that I did not. I had been pushing the whole idea away from me and forgetting it.

But now the more ardent was the love I felt for those two men of whom I was hearing and of how healthfully they had been moved to give themselves up entirely to you to be cured, the more bitter was the hatred I felt for myself when I compared myself with them. Many years (at least twelve) of my own life had gone by since the time when I was nineteen and was reading Cicero's *Hortensius* and had been fired with an enthusiasm for wisdom. Yet I was still putting off the moment when, despising this world's happiness, I should give all my time to the search for that of which not only the finding but merely the seeking must be preferred to the discovered treasures and kingdoms of men or to all the pleasures of the body easily and abundantly available. But I, wretched young man that I was—even more wretched at the beginning of my youth—had begged you for chastity and had said: "Make me chaste and continent, but not yet." I was afraid that you might hear me too soon and cure me too soon from the disease of a lust which I preferred to be satisfied rather than extinguished. And I had gone along evil ways, following a sacrilegious superstition—not because I was convinced by it, but simply preferring it to the other doctrines into which I never inquired in a religious spirit, but merely attacked them in a spirit of spite.

I had thought that the reason why I was putting off from day to day the time when I should despise all worldly hopes and follow you alone was because I could see no certainty toward which I could direct my course. But now the day had come when in my own eyes I was stripped naked and my conscience cried out against me: "Can you not hear me? Was it not this that you used to say, that you would not throw off the burden of vanity for a truth that was uncertain? Well, look. Now the truth is certain, and you are still weighed down by your burden. Yet these others, who have not been so worn out in the search and not been meditating the matter for ten years or more, have had the weight taken from their backs and have been given wings to fly."

So I was being gnawed at inside, and as Ponticianus went on with his story I was lost and overwhelmed in a terrible kind of shame. When the story was over and the business about which he had come had been settled he went away, and I retired into myself. Nor did I leave anything unsaid against myself. With every scourge of condemnation I lashed my soul on to follow me now that I was trying to follow you. And my soul hung back; it refused to follow, and it could give no excuse for its refusal. All the arguments had been used already and had been shown to be false. There remained a mute shrinking; for it feared like death to be restrained from the flux of a habit by which it was melting away into death.

8   AND NOW inside my house great indeed was the quarrel which I had started with my soul in that bedroom of my heart which we shared together. My

looks were as disordered as my mind as I turned on
Alypius and cried out to him: "What is wrong with us?
What is this which you have just heard? The unlearned
rise up and *take heaven by force*, while we (look at us!)
with all our learning are wallowing in flesh and blood.
Is it because they have gone ahead that we are ashamed
to follow? And do we feel no shame at not even following
at all?" Some such words as these I spoke, and then the
disturbance in my mind tore me away from him, while
he stared at me in silence and amazed. For I sounded
strange to him. My forehead, cheeks, eyes, color of face,
and inflection of voice expressed my mind better than the
words I used.

There was a garden attached to our lodging, and we
had the use of this as of the whole house; for our landlord, the owner of the house, did not live there. To this
garden the tumult in my heart had driven me, as to a
place where no one could intervene in this passionate
suit which I had brought against myself until it could be
settled—though how it would be settled you knew, not I.
As to me I was mad and dying; but there was sanity in
my madness, life in my death; I knew how evil I was;
I did not know how well I would be soon.

So I withdrew to the garden and Alypius followed
close after me. When he was there, I still felt myself in
privacy, and how could he leave me when I was in such
a state? We sat down as far as possible from the house.
My spirit was in a turmoil; I was boiling with indignation
against myself for not entering into your will and covenant, my God, where all my bones cried out that I should
enter and praised it to the skies. And the way there is not
by ship or chariot or on foot; the distance is not so great
as that which I had come from the house to the place
where we were sitting. All I had to do was to will to go
there, and I would not only go but would immediately
arrive; but it was necessary for the will to be resolute
and sincere, not the turning and twisting this way and
that of a will that was half maimed, struggling, with one
part rising and another part falling.

Then in the middle of this storm of mental hesitation
I made many movements with my body—the kind of

movements which people sometimes want to make, but
cannot make, either because they have not the limbs, or
because their limbs are bound or weakened by illness or
in some way or other prevented from action. But I, if I
tore my hair, beat my forehead, locked my fingers together, clasped my knee, was performing these actions
because I willed to do so. But I might have willed to do
so and still not done so if the power of motion in my
limbs had not followed the dictates of my will. So I
was performing all sorts of actions where the will to do
and the power to do are not the same thing, and I was
not doing something the idea of which pleased me incomparably more and which soon after, when I should
have the will, I should have the power to do, since when
I willed, I should will it thoroughly. For in this matter
the power was the same thing as the will, and merely
to will was already to perform. And yet this was not done.
It was easier for my body to obey the slightest intimation
of the soul's will that the limbs should be put immediately
in motion than it was for the soul to give obedience
to itself so as to carry out by the mere act of willing
what was its own great will.

9   WHAT CAN BE the explanation of such an absurdity? Enlighten me with your mercy, so that I
may ask the question, if perhaps an answer may be found
in the secret places of man's punishment and in those
darkest agonies of the sons of Adam. What can be the
explanation of such an absurdity? The mind gives an
order to the body, and the order is obeyed immediately:
the mind gives an order to itself, and there is resistance.
The mind orders the hand to move, and such readiness is
shown that you can hardly distinguish the command from
its execution. Yet the mind is mind, and the hand is body.
The mind orders the mind to will; it is the same mind,
yet it does not obey. What can be the explanation of such
an absurdity? The mind, I say, orders itself to will: it
would not give the order, unless it willed it, yet it does
not obey the order. The fact is that it does not will the
thing entirely; consequently it does not give the order

entirely. The force of the order is in the force of the will, and disobedience to the order results from insufficiency of the will. For the will orders that there should be a will—not a different will, but itself. But it is not entire in itself when it gives the order, and therefore its order is not obeyed. For if it were entire in itself, it would not give the order to will; the will would be there already. So it is not an absurdity partly to will and partly not to will; it is rather a sickness of the soul which is weighed down with habit so that it cannot rise up in its entirety, lifted aloft by truth. So the reason why there are two wills in us is because one of them is not entire, and one has what the other lacks.

10   LET THEM PERISH from your presence, God, as perish empty talkers and seducers of the soul, who, having observed that there are two wills in the act of deliberating, conclude from this that we have in us two minds of two different natures, one good and one evil. They themselves are truly evil, when they hold these evil opinions, and they are just as capable of becoming good if they will realize the truth and agree with the truth, so that your apostle may say to them: *Ye were sometimes darkness, but now light in the Lord.* But these people, by imagining that the nature of the soul is what God is, want to be light, not in the Lord, but in themselves, and the result is that they have become an even deeper darkness, since in their appalling arrogance they have gone further away from you—from you, *the true Light that enlighteneth every man that cometh into the world.* Take heed what you say, and blush for shame: *draw near unto Him and be enlightened, and your faces shall not be ashamed.*

As to me, when I was deliberating about entering the service of the Lord my God, as I had long intended to do, it was I who willed it, and it was I who was unwilling. It was the same "I" throughout. But neither my will nor my unwillingness was whole and entire. So I fought with myself and was torn apart by myself. It was against my will that this tearing apart took place, but this was not an indication that I had another mind of a different nature; it was simply the punishment which I was suffering in my own mind. It was not I, therefore, who caused it, but *the sin dwells in me*, and, being a son of Adam, I was suffering for his sin which was more freely committed.

For if there are as many contrary natures as there are conflicting wills, we shall find that there are not two only, but many more. Suppose a man is wondering whether to go to one of the Manichaean conventicles or to the theater; the Manichees will say: "Here is an example of the two natures, one good, leading in one direction, one bad, leading in another. How else can you explain the hesitation caused by two wills in opposition to each other?" But I should say that both wills are bad—the one that takes a man to the Manichees and the one which takes him to the theater instead. But they of course believe that the will which takes a man to them must necessarily be good. Very well, then. Suppose now the case of one of us who, also with two wills struggling inside him, is wondering whether to go to the theater or to our Church. Will not the Manichees also be in a state of indecision about what to say on this point? They will either have to make an admission which they would be most reluctant to make—namely, that it is a good will which takes a man to our Church, just as the will is good which leads men who have received and are bound by their sacraments to their church; or else they will have to assume that in one man there are two evil natures and two evil wills in conflict, and then what they are always saying will not be true—that there is one evil and one good will. Otherwise they will have to be converted to the truth and not deny that when one is making up one's mind there is just one soul which is pulled in different directions by different wills.

Therefore, they can no longer say, when they observe two conflicting wills in one man, that the conflict is between two opposing minds, of two opposing substances, from two opposing principles—one good, one evil. Their arguments are checked, overthrown, and put out of court by you, God of truth. Take the case, for example, when both wills are bad, as when a man deliberates whether to commit a murder by poison or by a dagger; whether to seize this or that part of another man's property, since he cannot seize both; whether to squander his money on pleasure or to hoard it up like a miser; whether to go to the races or to the theater, if they happen both to be on the same day; or, as a third possibility, this same man may be wondering whether to commit a theft from someone else's house, if he gets the chance; or, as a fourth possibility, whether to commit adultery, supposing that the opportunity occurs at the same time. Now if all these four possibilities become practicable at the same moment and all are equally desired, though they cannot all be done simultaneously, the mind will be torn apart by four conflicting wills; indeed, considering the multitude of things which can be desired, there may be even more than four wills in conflict. But the Manichees do not hold that there is a similar abundance of different substances.

The same principle holds with regard to wills that are good. Let me ask them this question: Is it good to take pleasure in reading the Apostle, and also good to take pleasure in a sober psalm, and also good to discuss the Gospel? In each case they will reply: "It is good." If then all these activities at one and the same time offer us equal pleasure, must it not be that different wills are pulling at a man's heart while he makes up his mind which activity in particular he should choose? All these wills are good, yet they conflict with one another until one particular choice has been made, toward which the whole will, which was previously divided, now turns entirely. So too when eternity offers us a higher pleasure and the delight in some temporal good holds us down below, it is the same soul which feels both impulses; only its will for one or the other course is not total and complete, and consequently it is torn apart and heavily distressed as truth puts one way first and habit will not allow the other way to be abandoned.

11   So I WAS SICK and in torture. I reproached myself much more bitterly than ever, and I turned and twisted in my chain till I could break quite free. Only a

little of it still held me, but it did still hold me. And you, Lord, in the secret places of my soul, stood above me in the severity of your mercy, redoubling the lashes of fear and shame, so that I should not give way once more and so that that small weak piece of chain which still remained should not instead of snapping grow strong again and tie me down more firmly than before. I was saying inside myself: "Now, now, let it be now!" and as I spoke the words I was already beginning to go in the direction I wanted to go. I nearly managed it, but I did not quite manage it. Yet I did not slip right back to the beginning; I was a stage above that, and I stood there to regain my breath. And I tried again and I was very nearly there; I was almost touching it and grasping it, and then I was not there, I was not touching it, I was not grasping it; I hesitated to die to death and to live to life; inveterate evil had more power over me than the novelty of good, and as that very moment of time in which I was to become something else drew nearer and nearer, it struck me with more and more horror. But I was not struck right back or turned aside; I was just held in suspense.

Toys and trifles, utter vanities had been my mistresses, and now they were holding me back, pulling me by the garment of my flesh and softly murmuring in my ear: "Are you getting rid of us?" and "From this moment shall we never be with you again for all eternity?" and "From this moment will you never for all eternity be allowed to do this or to do that?" My God, what was it, what was it that they suggested in those words "this" or "that" which I have just written? I pray you in your mercy to keep such things from the soul of your servant. How filthy, how shameful were these things they were suggesting! And now their voices were not half so loud in my ears; now they no longer came out boldly to contradict me face to face; it was more as though they were muttering behind my back, stealthily pulling at my sleeve as I was going away so that I should turn and look at them. Yet still they did hold me back as I hesitated to tear myself away and to shake them off and to take the great step in the direction where I was called. Violence of habit spoke the words: "Do you think that you can live without them?"

But by now it spoke very faintly. In the direction toward which I had turned my face and still trembled to take the last step, I could see the chaste dignity of Continence; she was calm and serene, cheerful without wantonness, and it was in truth and honor that she was enticing me to come to her without hesitation, stretching out to receive and to embrace me with those holy hands of hers, full of such multitudes of good examples. With her were so many boys and girls, so much of youth, so much of every age, grave widows and women grown old in virginity, and in them all was Continence herself, not barren, but *a fruitful mother of children,* her joys, by you, Lord, her husband. She smiled at me and there was encouragement in her smile, as though she were saying: "Can you not do what these men and these women have done? Or do you think that their ability is in themselves and not in the Lord their God? It was the Lord God who gave me to them. Why do you try and stand by yourself, and so not stand at all? Let him support you. Do not be afraid. He will not draw away and let you fall. Put yourself fearlessly in His hands. He will receive you and will make you well."

And I was blushing for shame, because I could still hear the dim voices of those vanities, and still I hung back in hesitation. And again she seemed to be speaking: "Stop your ears against those unclean members of yours, so that they may be mortified. They tell you of delights, but not of such delights as the law of the Lord your God tells."

So went the controversy in my heart—about self, and self against self. And Alypius stayed close by me, waiting silently to see how this strange agitation of mine would end.

12 AND NOW FROM my hidden depths my searching thought had dragged up and set before the sight of my heart the whole mass of my misery. Then a huge storm rose up within me bringing with it a huge downpour of tears. So that I might pour out all these tears and speak the words that came with them I rose up from Alypius (solitude seemed better for the business of weeping) and went further away so that I might not be embarrassed even by his presence. This was how I felt and he realized it. No doubt I had said something or other, and he could feel the weight of my tears in the sound of my voice. And so I rose to my feet, and he, in a state of utter amazement, remained in the place where we had been sitting. I flung myself down on the ground somehow under a fig tree and gave free rein to my tears; they streamed and flooded from my eyes, an *acceptable sacrifice to Thee*. And I kept saying to you, not perhaps in these words, but with this sense: "*And Thou, O Lord, how long? How long, Lord; wilt Thou be angry forever? Remember not our former iniquities.*" For I felt that it was these which were holding me fast. And in my misery I would exclaim: "How long, how long this 'tomorrow and tomorrow'? Why not now? Why not finish this very hour with my uncleanness?"

So I spoke, weeping in the bitter contrition of my heart. Suddenly a voice reaches my ears from a nearby house. It is the voice of a boy or a girl (I don't know which) and in a kind of singsong the words are constantly repeated: "Take it and read it. Take it and read it." At once my face changed, and I began to think carefully of whether the singing of words like these came into any kind of game which children play, and I could not remember that I had ever heard anything like it before. I checked the force of my tears and rose to my feet, being quite certain that I must interpret this as a divine command to me to open the book and read the first passage which I should come upon. For I had heard this about Antony: he had happened to come in when the Gospel was being read, and as though the words read were spoken directly to himself, had received the admonition: *Go, sell all that thou hast, and give to the poor, and thou shalt have treasure in heaven, and come and follow me.* And by such an oracle he had been immediately converted to you.

So I went eagerly back to the place where Alypius

was sitting, since it was there that I had left the book of the Apostle when I rose to my feet. I snatched up the book, opened it, and read in silence the passage upon which my eyes first fell: *Not in rioting and drunkenness, not in chambering and wantonness, not in strife and envying: but put ye on the Lord Jesus Christ, and make not provision for the flesh in concupiscence.* I had no wish to read further; there was no need to. For immediately I had reached the end of this sentence it was as though my heart was filled with a light of confidence and all the shadows of my doubt were swept away.

Before shutting the book I put my finger or some other marker in the place and told Alypius what had happened. By now my face was perfectly calm. And Alypius in his turn told me what had been going on in himself, and which I knew nothing about. He asked to see the passage which I had read. I showed him and he went on further than the part I had read, nor did I know the words which followed. They were these: *Him that is weak in the faith, receive.* He applied this to himself and told me so. He was strengthened by the admonition; calmly and unhesitatingly he joined me in a purpose and a resolution so good, and so right for his character, which had always been very much better than mine.

The next thing we do is to go inside and tell my mother. How happy she is! We describe to her how it all took place, and there is no limit to her joy and triumph. Now she was praising you, *Who art able to do above that which we ask or think;* for she saw that with regard to me you had given her so much more than she used to ask for when she wept so pitifully before you. For you converted me to you in such a way that I no longer sought a wife nor any other worldly hope. I was now standing on that rule of faith, just as you had shown me to her in a vision so many years before. And so you had changed her mourning into joy, a joy much richer than she had desired and much dearer and purer than that which she looked for by having grandchildren of my flesh.

Book IX

1   *O Lord, I am Thy servant; I am Thy servant and the son of Thy handmaid: Thou hast broken my bonds in sunder. I will offer to Thee the sacrifice of praise.* Let my heart and my tongue praise you, and let *all my bones say, O Lord, who is like unto Thee?* Let them speak, and then, Lord, answer me and *say unto my soul, I am thy salvation.*

Who am I and what am I? Is there any evil that I have not done in my acts, or, if not in my acts, in my words, or, if not in my words, in my will? But you, Lord, are good and merciful; your right hand had regard for the profundity of my death, and from the bottom of my heart you dragged up that abysmal load of corruption. And this was what you did: I was able totally to set my face against what I willed and to will what you willed. But where had this ability been for all those years? And from what profound and secret depth was my free will suddenly called forth in a moment so that I could bow my neck to your *easy yoke* and my shoulders to your *light burden, O Christ Jesus, my Helper and my Redeemer?* How sweet it suddenly became to me to be without the sweetness of those empty toys! How glad I was to give up the things I had been so afraid to lose! For you cast them out from me, you true and supreme sweetness; you cast them out and you entered in to me to take their place, sweeter than all pleasure, but not to flesh and blood; brighter than all light, but more inward than all hidden

184

depths; higher than all honor, but not to those who are high in themselves. Now my mind was free of those gnawing cares that came from ambition and the desire for gain and wallowing in filth and scratching the itching scab of lust. And now I was talking to you easily and simply, my brightness and my riches and my health, my Lord God.

2 And I decided in your sight that, without making any violent gesture, I would gently withdraw from a position where I was making use of my tongue in the talking-shop; no longer should my young students (who were not so much interested in your law and your peace as in absurd deceptions and legal battles) buy from my mouth material for arming their own madness. And luckily it happened that there were only a few days more before the Vintage Vacation, and I decided to endure them so that I might retire from the profession in a regular way. I had been bought by you and was not going to return again to put myself up for sale. So our plan was known to you, but not known to men—except to our own friends. We had agreed among ourselves not to let the news out at all, although, as we were making our way up from *the valley of tears* and singing that *song of degrees*, you had given us *sharp arrows* and *destroying coals* against the subtle tongues of people who, under a show of care for us, would try to thwart us and by loving us would eat us up, as men do with their food.

You had shot through our hearts with your charity, and we carried about with us your words like arrows fixed deep in our flesh; stored up in the recesses of our thought were the examples of your servants whose darkness you had turned to light and whose death to life, and so that heavy sluggishness of ours that might have dragged us down again to the depths was utterly burned up and consumed. So much on fire were we that all the blasts of *the subtle tongue* of contradiction, so far from extinguishing the fire, only made it burn more fiercely. However because of your name, which you have sanctified throughout the earth, there would no doubt also be people who would praise the resolution and vows which we had taken, and I thought it would look like ostentation if, instead of waiting for the vacation which was now so close, I should resign from a public position which everyone knew about. All eyes would be upon me and upon what I had done; it would be noticed that I had not wished to wait for the day of the Vintage, although it was so close, and there would be much talk of me to the effect that I wanted to make myself seem important. And what good would it do me to have people thinking and talking about my state of mind and to have *our good to be evil spoken of?*

There was also the fact that that summer my lungs had begun to give way as the result of overwork in teaching. I found it difficult to breathe deeply; pains in the chest were evidence of the injury and made it impossible for me to speak loudly or for long at a time. At first this had distressed me, since I was being almost forced and compelled to give up this burden of teaching—or, at any rate, if I were able to be cured and made well again, to give it up for the time being. But now my will in its entirety had arisen and was set on having leisure and on seeing *how that Thou art the Lord*, and from this moment I began actually to be pleased that in this illness also I had quite a genuine excuse to soften the injured feelings of those parents who, so that their children might be free to learn, wanted me never to be free at all. And so, filled with such joy as this, I put up with the interval of time—I think it was about twenty days—which still had to pass. But I needed some resolution to do this. What had helped me in the past to bear my hard labor had been the desire to make money. The desire had now gone, and, if its place had not been taken by patience, I should have been quite overwhelmed by staying on at my work. Some of your servants, my brothers, may say that I sinned in this, because, with my heart fully set on your service, I continued to hold even for one hour my professorship of lies. It may be so. But I know that you, most merciful Lord, have pardoned and remitted this sin too along with any other terrible and deadly sins in the holy water of Baptism.

3 VERECUNDUS WAS MAKING himself ill with worry because of the good which we had found. He saw that, because of his own chains in which he was so tightly bound, he was losing our companionship. He was not yet a Christian, though his wife was. However she was a fetter which clung to him more tightly than all the rest, preventing him from setting out on the journey on which we had started. For he said that he would not be a Christian in any other way except the way that was impossible to him. Nevertheless, he most kindly offered us the hospitality of his house so long as we should remain there. You, Lord, will reward him *in the resurrection of the just,* seeing that you have already given him the lot of the just. This happened when we were away; we were already at Rome when Verecundus became ill of a bodily sickness; in the course of his illness he became a baptized Christian and then departed from this life. So *hadst Thou mercy not on him only but on us also;* for otherwise we should have been tortured with intolerable pain whenever we thought of the wonderful kindness that our friend had shown to us and reflected that we could not count him as one of your flock. We thank you, our Lord. We are yours, as is shown by your exhortations and your consolations. You are true to your promises and you will repay Verecundus for that country estate of his at Cassiciacum where we rested in you far from the turmoil of the world, with the loveliness of your eternally green and fresh paradise; for you have forgiven him his sins on earth and have placed him in that mountain rich in milk, your own mountain, the mountain of abundance.

But at that time Verecundus was sad and worried. Nebridius however was full of joy. He too was not yet a Christian and in the past he had fallen into that pit of deadly error, believing that the flesh of your Son, of your truth, was a phantom. However, he had emerged from this error and his present state was that, though he had not yet received any of the sacraments of your Church, he was a most ardent searcher for truth. Not long after our conversion and regeneration by your baptism, you took him from this fleshly life; by then he too was a baptized Christian, serving you in perfect chastity and continence among his own people in Africa, and having converted his whole household to the Christian faith. And now he lives in the bosom of Abraham. Whatever is meant by that bosom, there my Nebridius lives, my sweet friend, your son by adoption and no longer merely a freedman. There he lives. For what other place could there be for such a soul? There he lives in a place about which he used often to ask questions of me, an ignorant weak man. Now he no longer turns his ear to my lips; he turns his own spiritual lips to your fountain and drinks his fill of all the wisdom that he can desire, happy without end. And I do not think that he is so inebriated with that wisdom as to forget me; since it is of you, Lord, that he drinks, and you are mindful of us.

This, then, was how it was with us. We comforted Verecundus in his sorrow (for our friendship was not impaired by our conversion) and we urged him to keep the faith of his own state, that of the married life. But we waited for Nebridius to follow us, and he was so close that he might well have done so; indeed he was just on the point of doing so when at last those days of waiting came to an end. Long and many they had seemed to me because I was longing for the peace and the liberty in which I could sing to you from the depths of my being: *My heart hath said unto Thee, I have sought Thy face: Thy face, Lord, will I seek.*

4   AND THE DAY CAME on which I was actually to be freed of this profession of rhetoric, from which in my mind I was already free. So it was done. You rescued my tongue as you had rescued my heart. I rejoiced and blessed you and with all my friends went off to the country house. My writing was now done in your service, though still, in this kind of breathing space, the breath it drew was from the school of pride. The books I wrote then will show what I did in the way of writing—debates with my friends who were present, and debates held with myself in your presence—and my letters to Nebridius will show what I discussed with him while he was away. But I shall never have time to tell of all your

great kindnesses to me, especially at this period, since I must hurry on to more important matters still. For my memory brings all this before me, and it is a pleasure to me, Lord, to confess to you by what inward goads and stings you utterly tamed me, and how you evened me down, *lowering the mountains and hills of my high imaginations, straightening my crookedness, and smoothing my rough ways*, and how you also subdued that brother of my heart, Alypius, to the name of your only-begotten Son, our Lord and Saviour Jesus Christ. At first he felt that this name was not grand enough to have a place in our writings since he wanted them to have the redolence of the cedars of the literary world (cedars which the Lord has now broken down) rather than of those health-giving herbs which your Church uses against serpents.

My God, how I poured out my heart to you as I read the Psalms of David, those faithful songs and sounding syllables of holiness, quite excluding the swelling boastfulness of the spirit! I, still untrained in your true love, a catechumen resting in that country house with Alypius, another catechumen, and having my mother constantly with us in her woman's clothing, but with her masculine faith, tranquil in her age, maternal in her love, Christian in her goodness. How I cried aloud to you in those psalms! How they fired me toward you! How I burned to utter them aloud, if I could, to the whole world against the pride of mankind! And yet they are sung through the whole world, nor can *any hide himself from Thy heat*. How strong and full of bitter grief was the indignation I felt against the Manichees! Yet I pitied them too for their ignorance of those medicinal sacraments and for raging in madness against the antidote which might have made them sane. I would have liked them to have been standing somewhere near me (without my knowing that they were there) and to have seen my face and heard what I said when in this time of quietness I read the fourth Psalm, and to have seen what effect those words of the Psalm had on me: *When I called, the God of my righteousness heard me; in tribulation Thou enlargedst me. Have mercy upon me, O Lord, and hear my prayer.* I should like them to have heard me without my knowing

whether they heard. Otherwise they might think that
what I was saying as I read these verses was being said
because of them. And in fact I should neither say the
same things nor speak in the same way, if I realized that
they were watching me and listening to me. And even
if I did say the same things, they would not have understood how I was speaking with myself and to myself in
front of you, out of the natural feelings of my soul.

I trembled with fear, and then again I was on fire with
hope and with exultation in your mercy, Father. And all
these emotions were shown in my eyes and in my voice
when your good Spirit turned to us and said: *O ye sons
of men, how long slow of heart? Why do ye love vanity
and seek after lying?* For I had loved vanity and had
sought after lying. *And Thou, O Lord,* hadst already
*magnified Thy Holy One, raising Him from the dead,
and setting Him at Thy right hand,* whence *from on
high* He should send His *promise, the Comforter, the
Spirit of Truth.* And He had sent Him already, though I
did not know it. He had sent Him because He was already
magnified, risen from the dead and ascended into heaven.
For till then, *the Spirit was not yet given, because Jesus
was not yet glorified.* And the prophet cries out, *How
long, slow of heart? Why do ye love vanity and seek
after lying?* He cries out, *How long?* He cries out, *Know
this.* And I so long, not knowing, loved vanity and sought
after lying. And so I listened and trembled, because these
words were spoken to such people as I remembered myself to have been. For there was both vanity and lying
in those phantasms which I had accepted as the truth,
and now in the grief I felt at the remembrance of it I
loaded myself with bitter and sincere reproaches. I wish
that those who still love vanity and seek after lying could
have heard me. Then perhaps they would have been
disturbed and would have vomited up their error. And
you would have heard them when they cried to you.
For it was by a true death in the flesh that He died for
us who now *intercedeth unto Thee for us.*

I read too: *Be angry and sin not.* How deeply, my
God, was I moved by this—I who had now learned to be
angry with myself for the past so that I might not sin in

the future! Yes, and to be justly angry with myself; for it was not the case of some other nature belonging to the race of darkness which committed the sin in me, as the Manichees believe, who are not angry with themselves and who *treasure up wrath against the day of wrath and of the revelation of Thy just judgment*.

And now my good things were not external and were not sought with the eyes of the flesh in this sun that we see. For those who find their joys in things outside easily become vain and waste themselves on things seen and temporal and, with their minds starving, go licking at shadows. Oh that they would grow tired of their lack of nourishment and would say: *Who will show us good things?* Then we should say and they would hear, *The light of Thy countenance is sealed upon us, Lord.* For we are not ourselves *that light which enlighteneth every man*, but we are enlightened by you, so that *having been sometimes darkness, we may be light in Thee.* If only they could see the eternal light inside themselves! I had tasted of it and I was in a rage because I could not show it to them so long as they brought me their hearts looking out of their eyes away from you, while saying: *Who will show us good things?* For it was there, there in the place where I had been angry with myself, inside, in my own room, there where I had been pierced, where I had made my sacrifice, offering up my old self, and starting on the purpose of a new life, with my hope set on you—there it was that you began to grow sweet to me and *hadst put gladness in my heart.* I cried out as I read this with my outward eye and inwardly recognized its truth. Nor did I wish for any multiplication of earthly goods; in these one wastes and is wasted by time. In the Eternal Simplicity I had other *corn and wine and oil*.

And in the next verse how my heart cried out from its depths! *O in peace, O for the Selfsame!* And then this, *I will lay me down and sleep*, for who shall stand against us when *cometh to pass that saying which is written, Death is swallowed up in Victory?* And you supremely are the Selfsame, you who do not change, and in you is the rest which is oblivious of all labors, since there is no other beside you, nor are we to seek for those many other things which are not what you are. But you, Lord, *alone*, have *made me dwell in hope*. As I read, my heart became on fire. What could be done, I wondered, with those deaf corpses, of whom I myself had been one? For I, like a disease, like a blind man, had raised my bitter barking voice against these writings which are so honey-sweet of heaven and brilliant with your own light. And now my heart boiled as I thought of the enemies of this Scripture.

I shall never be able to recall and write down the whole story of those days of quiet. But I have not forgotten, and I will not pass over in silence how bitter was the scourge with which you afflicted me, and how wonderfully quickly came your mercy. At that time you tortured me with toothache, and when the pain became so bad that I was unable to speak it came into my heart to ask all my friends who were present to pray for me to you, the God of all kinds of health. I wrote this down on wax and gave it to them to read. As soon as we had in our simple devotion gone down on our knees, the pain went away. But what pain was it? And how did it go? I was terrified, I admit, my Lord and my God; for in all my life I had never felt anything like it. And so in the depths of me I experienced the power of your nod and, rejoicing in faith, I praised your name. But this faith would not let me be at ease about my past sins, since these had not yet been forgiven me by means of your Baptism.

5   AT THE END OF the Vintage holiday I gave notice to the citizens of Milan that they must find someone else to sell words to their students, both because I had chosen to enter your service and because I was no longer able to continue in my profession because of the pain in my lungs and my difficulty in breathing. And in a letter which I wrote to your bishop, the holy Ambrose, I explained my former errors and my present resolution and asked him to advise me what parts of your Scripture in particular I should read in order to prepare myself and become better fitted to receive so great a grace. He told me to read the prophet Isaiah, his reason, I think, being that Isaiah foretells the Gospel and the calling of the

Gentiles more clearly than the other writers. I, however, could not understand the first part that I read and, thinking that all the rest would be like this, laid it by with the intention of taking it up again when I should be better trained in the Lord's style of speech.

6   THEN, WHEN THE TIME CAME for me to give in my name, we left the country and returned to Milan. Alypius had decided to be born again in you at the same time. He was already clothed in that humility which so befits your sacraments, and he had so tamed and mastered his own body that, showing the most extraordinary fortitude, he could go barefooted over the icy soil of Italy. We also had with us young Adeodatus, the son of my flesh, begotten by me in my sin. You had made him well. He was scarcely fifteen, but he showed more intelligence than many serious and learned men. Here it is your gifts that I acknowledge to you, Lord God, Creator of all things, abundantly powerful to reform our deformities; for I myself had no part in that boy except for the sin. As to the fact that we brought him up in your discipline, it was you and no one else who inspired us to do this. Yours are the gifts which I acknowledge to you. There is a book of mine called *The Master*; it is a dialogue between Adeodatus and me. You know that all the ideas put into the mouth of the person conversing with me were his own ideas, when he was sixteen. And there were other things too, even more remarkable, which I noticed in him. I found his intelligence really awe-inspiring. And who except you could be the maker of such wonders? Soon you took away his life from this earth and, as I think of him, I am perfectly at ease, for there is nothing in his boyhood or youth or indeed his whole personality to make one feel fear for him. We took him with us as a companion, of the same age as we in your grace, to be brought up in your discipline. And we were baptized and all anxiety for our past life vanished away. In those days I could never have enough of the wonderful sweetness of meditating upon the depth of your counsel for the salvation of the human race. What

tears I shed in your hymns and canticles! How deeply
was I moved by the voices of your sweet singing Church!
Those voices flowed into my ears and the truth was dis-
tilled into my heart, which overflowed with my passionate
devotion. Tears ran from my eyes and happy I was in
those tears.

7   THE CHURCH OF MILAN had only recently begun to practice this kind of consolation and exhortation, and there was great enthusiasm among the
brethren as they joined together both with heart and
voice in the singing. In fact it was only a year or not much
more than a year previously when Justina, the mother of
the boy emperor Valentinian, was persecuting your servant Ambrose in the interests of her own heresy (she had
been led astray by the Arians). Then the devout congregation stayed day and night in the church, ready to die
with their bishop, your servant. In all this anxious watching, my mother, your handmaiden, took a leading part
and lived in prayer. I myself had not yet been warmed by
the heat of your Spirit, but I was nevertheless stirred up
by the state of alarm and excitement in the city. It was
then that the practice began of singing hymns and psalms
in the manner of the Eastern Churches, so that the people
should not grow faint and tired in this time of their sorrow. The custom has been kept from that day to this
and has been imitated by many, indeed by almost all,
of your congregations in other parts of the world.

At that time you revealed to your bishop Ambrose in
a vision where the bodies of the martyrs Gervasius and
Protasius lay hid. These you had kept stored up uncor-
rupted for so many years in your secret treasury until the
right time should come for you to produce them in order
to restrain the mad rage of a woman who was also an
empress. For when the bodies had been found and dug
up and brought with due honor to Ambrose's basilica
people who were tormented by unclean spirits were cured
and the devils who had been tormenting them openly admitted what they were and what they had done. Also
there was the case of a citizen of Milan, well known to

everyone, who had been blind for many years. When this man inquired and was told what was the reason why the people were shouting with joy, he jumped up and asked his guide to lead him to the place. When he got there he begged to be allowed in so that he could touch with his handkerchief the bier on which were lying the *saints whose death is precious in Thy sight*. He did this, put the handkerchief to his eyes, and immediately his eyes were opened. Then the news spread abroad; then fervent and shining were your praises; then that enemy was at least checked in her fury of persecution, even though her mind was not brought back to the health of a true belief. Thanks be to you, my God! From where and to what point have you led my memory that I should confess to you these things also, which, though they are great, I had passed over in forgetfulness? Yet even then, when *the odor of Thy ointments was so fragrant*, I did not *run after Thee*. And so I wept all the more at the singing of your hymns; once I had sighed for you and now at last I was breathing you in, so far as this house of grass allows the breath of your presence.

8 You, WHO MAKE MEN of one mind to dwell in our house, led Euodius, a young man from our own town, to join company with us. He had been in the government service, had been converted to you and baptized before us, had resigned from his official post and set himself to serve you. We stayed together with the intention of finding a place to live together in the good life which we planned. We asked ourselves what would be the place where we could serve you most usefully, and, as the result of our discussions, we went back again to Africa. When we had got as far as Ostia on the Tiber, my mother died.

I am passing over much because I am in much haste. And I beg you, my God, to receive my confessions and my thanksgivings for innumerable things about which I am silent. But I shall not pass over whatever my soul can bring forth about that servant of yours who brought me forth, giving me birth in the flesh to this temporal light, and in her heart to light eternal. It is not her gifts that I shall tell of, but your gifts in her. For she did not make herself or bring herself up. It was you who created her, and neither her father nor her mother knew what kind of child would be born of them. It was the scepter of your Christ, the discipline of your only-begotten Son, that brought her up in your fear, in a faithful household which was a worthy member of your Church. Yet she used to talk not so much of her mother's care in training her as of the care of an old womanservant, who had carried my mother's father on her back when he was a baby, as small children are often carried about on the backs of the bigger maidservants. Because of this and because of her age and her excellent character this servant was greatly respected by her master and mistress in that Christian household and was given the care of her mistress' daughters. She carried out her responsibilities most thoroughly; in checking the children, when it was necessary to do so, she acted sternly and with a holy severity, and in teaching them she showed prudence and good sense. For instance, except during those hours when they were receiving their very frugal meals at their parents' table, she would not allow them to drink water, however parched with thirst they might be. In this way she was guarding against the formation of a bad habit, and she used to say very sensibly: "Now you are drinking water, because you are not allowed to have wine. But when you are married and become mistresses of your stores and cellars, water will not be good enough for you, but you will still have this strong desire to drink." By this kind of advice and by the authority which she was able to exercise she brought under control the greediness from which children suffer and succeeded in imposing a good and proper limit even on the little girls' thirst, so that they did not want to have more than they should.

And yet there did, there actually did (for so your servant told me, her son) steal over her an excessive fondness for wine. For when in the usual way she, as a good sober girl, was told by her parents to go and draw some wine from the barrel, she would hold the cup under the tap and then, before pouring the wine into the flagon, would take a little bit, just wetting her lips, since she did not like the taste and could not take more. Indeed she did not act in this way because of any desire for drunkenness; it was just an excess of high spirits which are natural at that age, which boil over on ridiculous impulses and which, when we are children, are usually kept under restraint by the sobering influence of our elders. And so to that daily drop of wine she added more and more drops day after day *(for whoso despiseth little things, shall fall by little and little)*, and she fell into such a habit of drinking that she would greedily drink down cups which were nearly full of wine. Where then was that wise old woman with her stern prohibitions? Could there be anything strong enough to deal with a hidden disease, if it were not for the fact that your healing powers, Lord, were watching over us? Mother, father, and nurses may not be there, but you are there, you who made us, you who call us, you can also use those who are set over us to do something for the salvation of our souls. And what did you do then, my God? How did you cure her? How did you bring her to her right mind? Was it not as follows? Out of another soul you produced a bitter sharp taunt, as though from your secret store you were bringing out a surgeon's knife, and with one touch of this you cut out the putrefied matter in her. For there was a maid who often used to go with my mother to the cellar and once when there were just the two of them alone, this maid, as might easily happen, had a quarrel with her small mistress and in the course of it made the most bitter and insulting accusation possible. "You drunkard," she said. My mother was struck to the quick by this taunt. She saw the foulness of her conduct, at once condemned it and gave up the bad habit. Indeed just as the flattery of friends often leads us astray, so the insults of enemies often do us good. But you do not reward people for what you accomplish through them, but only in accordance with their intentions. That maid, for instance, was in a temper and wanted to hurt her small mistress, not to make her better; she said what she said privately, either as a result of the time and place where the quarrel started or perhaps because she was afraid that she might get into trouble herself for

having kept silent about it for so long. But you, Lord,
director of all things in heaven and on earth, who turn to
your own purposes the very depths of running rivers,
shaping to order the wild flow of time, brought health
to one soul by means of the unhealthiness of another; thus
showing us that if someone is improved by any word of
ours, we must not attribute this to our own power, even
if we meant this result to take place.

9   SHE WAS BROUGHT UP, then, in a modest, sober
way. It was you who made her obedient to her
parents rather than her parents who made her obedient
to you. And when she reached marriageable age she was
given to a husband whom she served as her master. She
tried to win him to you, preaching you to him by the
beauty of the character which you had given her and by
which you made her able to provoke love and respect and
the admiration of her husband. So she endured his in-
fidelities and never had a single quarrel with him on this
subject. She was waiting for your mercy to be shown
upon him so that he might believe in you and be made
chaste. He, in fact, though an extremely kind man by
nature, was also very hot-tempered. But my mother knew
that an angry husband must not be contradicted, not in
deed nor even in word. Only when he had calmed down
and become quiet would she, when she saw her opportunity, explain to him the reasons for what she had done, if
he had happened to fly into a rage for no good reason.
Indeed there were many wives with husbands much mild-
er than hers who went about with their faces disfigured
by the marks of blows, and when they got together to
talk they would often complain of the way their husbands
behaved. But my mother, speaking lightly but giving serious advice, used to say that the fault was in their tongues.
They had all heard, she said, the marriage contract read
out to them and from that day they ought to regard it as
a legal instrument by which they were made servants; so
they should remember their station and not set themselves up against their masters. And they, knowing what
a violent husband she had to put up with, were amazed

that it had never been heard of nor had there been any
evidence to show that Patricius had ever beaten his wife
or that there had been a family quarrel that had lasted as
much as a single day. They asked her in confidence how
she managed it, and she told them her rule, which was as
I have described. Those who followed it found that they
had every reason to thank her for it; those who did not
were still bullied and kept under.

There was a time when her mother-in-law had been
angry with her. This had all started because of the whis-
pering of malicious servants. But my mother showed such
a respectful attitude to her and so won her over by her
constant patience and forbearance that she went herself
to her son, told him the names of those whose interfering
tongues were disturbing the domestic peace between her
and her daughter-in-law and demanded that those concerned should be punished. Then out of deference to his
mother, care for good order in the household, and consideration for peace in his own family he had the servants
whose names had been given to him beaten, as his mother
had asked, and she told them that this was the reward
that any of them else might expect from her if they
tried to please her by speaking ill of her daughter-in-law.
None of them ventured to do so after that, and they
lived together in future on the most remarkably happy
and kind terms.

And this was another great gift, my God and my mercy,
which you bestowed on that good servant of yours in
whose womb you created me: among people who were
quarreling or at discord she showed herself, whenever
she could, very much of a peacemaker. She might hear
many very bitter things said on both sides, and this kind
of outpouring of swelling and undigested malice is very
likely to take place when a woman talks to a friend who
is present about an enemy who is absent; on these occasions hatred is expressed in its real crudity and in the
bitterest terms possible. But my mother would never
report to one woman what had been said about her by
another except insofar as what had been said might help
to bring the two together again. I might consider this a
small virtue if I had not had the sad experience of know-

ing countless numbers of people who, through some kind of horrible spreading infection of sin, not only tell others who are angry what their enemies said about them in anger, but actually add things which never were said. And yet ordinary humanity ought to make us feel that we have not done enough if we merely refrain from increasing and exacerbating ill feeling among men by our evil tongues; we ought to go further and try to use our tongues well so as to put an end to ill feeling. This was what my mother was like, and you were the master who, deep in the school of her heart, taught her this lesson.

Finally, toward the very end of his earthly life, she won her husband over to you, and now that he was a believer she no longer lamented in him the things which she had put up with in him before he was converted. She was also the servant of your servants. All of them who knew her found in her good reason to praise and honor and love you, because on the evidence of the fruit of her holy conversation they could feel your presence in her heart. For she had been *the wife of one man*, had *requited her parents*, had *governed her house* piously, *was well reported of for good works*, had *brought up children*, as often *travailing in birth of them* as she saw them straying away from you. Finally, Lord—since it is by your gift that we are allowed to speak—with regard to all of us your servants who, before she went to sleep in you, were living together after receiving the grace of baptism, she gave to each one of us the care that a mother gives to her son and to each one of us the service which a daughter gives to her father.

10   Now THE DAY was approaching on which she was to leave this life (you knew when this day would be, but we did not), and it so happened (this, I believe, was by your secret ordering) that she and I were standing alone, leaning in a window which looked onto the garden inside the house where we were staying, at Ostia on the Tiber. There we were out of the crowds and after our long and weary journey by land were resting ourselves for the sea voyage. So we were alone and talking together

and very sweet our talk was, and *forgetting those things which are behind, and reaching forth unto those things which are before,* we were discussing between ourselves and in the presence of Truth, which you are, what the eternal life of the saints could be like, *which eye hath not seen, nor ear heard, nor hath it entered into the heart of man.* Yet with the mouth of our heart we panted for the heavenly streams of your fountain, the fountain of life, which is with you, so that, if some drops from that fountain—all that we could take—were to be scattered over us, we might in some way or other be able to think of such high matters.

Our talk had reached this point: that the greatest possible delights of our bodily senses, radiant as they might be with the brightest of corporeal light, could not be compared with the joys of that eternal life, could not, indeed, even deserve a mention. Then, with our affections burning still more strongly toward the Selfsame, we raised ourselves higher and step by step passed over all material things, even the heaven itself from which sun and moon and stars shine down upon the earth. And still we went upward, meditating and speaking and looking with wonder at your works, and we came to our own souls, and we went beyond our souls to reach that region of never-failing plenty where *Thou feedest Israel* forever with the food of truth and where life is that Wisdom by whom all these things are made, both what is past and what is to come; but Wisdom herself is not made; she is as she has been and will be forever; or rather, there is no place in her for 'to have been' or 'to be going to be'; one can only say 'to be,' since she is eternal and 'have been' and 'going to be' are not eternal. And as we talked, yearning toward this Wisdom, we did, with the whole strength of our hearts' impulse, just lightly come into touch with her, and we sighed and we left bound there *the first fruits of the Spirit,* and we returned to the sounds made by our mouths, where a word has a beginning and an ending. And how unlike is this to your Word, our Lord, you who abide in yourself forever, without becoming old, making all things new!

So we said: if to any man the tumult of the flesh were

to grow silent, silent the images of earth and water and air, and the poles of heaven silent also; if the soul herself were to be silent and, by not thinking of self, were to transcend self; if all dreams and imagined revelations were silent, and every tongue, every sign; if there was utter silence from everything which exists only to pass away (for, if one can hear them, these all say: We did not make ourselves. He made us that abideth forever) but suppose that, having said this and directed our attention to Him that made them, they too were to become hushed and He Himself alone were to speak, not by their voice but in His own, and we were to hear His word, not through any tongue of flesh or voice of an angel or sound of thunder or difficult allegory, but that we might hear Him whom in all these things we love, might hear Him in Himself without them, just as a moment ago we two had, as it were, gone beyond ourselves and in a flash of thought had made contact with that eternal wisdom which abides above all things—supposing that this state were to continue, that all other visions, visions of so different a kind, were to be withdrawn, leaving only this one to ravish and absorb and wrap the beholder in inward joys, so that his life might be forever like that moment of understanding which we had had and for which we now sighed—would not this be: *Enter into Thy Master's joy?* And when shall that be? Shall it be when *we shall all rise again*, though we *shall not all be changed?*

Something like this I said, though not precisely in this way and in these words. Yet, Lord, you know that on that day when we were talking together as I have described and when, as we talked, this world with all its delights seemed to us so worthless, my mother said: "My son, as to me, I no longer find any pleasure in this life. What more I have to do here and why I am still here I do not know, since I have no longer anything to hope for in this world. There was only one reason why I wanted to stay a little longer in this life, and that was that I should see you a Catholic Christian before I died. Now God has granted me this beyond my hopes; for I see that you have despised the pleasures of this world and are become his servant. So what am I doing here?"

11 WHAT REPLY I MADE to these words of hers I cannot clearly remember. Within five days, or not much more, she fell into a fever. And one day while she was ill she had a fainting fit and temporarily lost consciousness of her surroundings. We hurried to her side, but she soon regained consciousness, and, seeing my brother and me standing by her, she said to us, as though she were trying to find the answer to some question, "Where am I?" Then, as we stood dumb with grief, she looked in our faces and said: "Here you will bury your mother." I remained quiet and kept back my tears; but my brother said something to her to the effect that he hoped that she would have the good fortune to die in her own country and not abroad. On hearing this an anxious expression came over her face, and she gave him a reproachful look for still savoring of such earthly things. Then she looked into my face and said: "See what he is saying!" Soon afterward she said to both of us, "You may lay this body of mine anywhere. Do not worry at all about that. All I ask you is this, that wherever you may be you will remember me at the altar of the Lord." This was what she said, speaking with difficulty, and then she became silent as the force of her illness grew heavier upon her.

But as I considered your gifts, invisible God, which you put into the hearts of your faithful ones to be the seeds of wonderful fruit, I rejoiced and gave you thanks. I knew well and I remembered how worried and anxious she had always been about the question of her burial. She had already provided for herself and prepared a tomb close to that of her husband. Since they had lived together in such harmony, she also wished (so little is the human mind capable of grasping things divine) to have this happiness of hers added to and to have it spoken of among men that after her pilgrimage across the seas it had been granted to her that the earthly part of both man and wife should lie covered under the same earth. Now when it was that, in the fullness of your goodness, this vain and empty notion of hers began to cease to be in her heart, I did not know, and I felt both joy and surprise now that I knew that it had ceased to be—although in that conversation we had had together in the window, when she said: "What am I still doing here?" she had shown no desire to die in her own country. Also I heard afterward how at this time when we were at Ostia she was talking one day with all the confidence and trust of a mother to some of my friends when I was not there. She was speaking about how one must despise this life and look forward to death, and they were amazed at finding such fortitude in a woman (it was you who gave it to her) and asked whether she was not afraid to leave her body so far from her own city. "Nothing," she replied, "is far from God, and there is no reason to fear that, at the end of the world, He will not recognize the place from which to raise me up."

And so on the ninth day of her illness, in the fifty-sixth year of her age and the thirty-third of mine, that devout and holy soul was freed from the body.

12   I CLOSED HER EYES, and a great flood of sorrow swept into my heart and would have overflowed in tears. But my eyes obeyed the forcible dictate of my mind and seemed to drink that fountain dry. Terrible indeed was my state as I struggled so. And then, when she had breathed her last, the boy Adeodatus burst out into loud cries until all the rest of us checked him, and he became silent. In the same way something childish in me which was bringing me to the brink of tears was, when I heard the young man's voice, the voice of the heart, brought under control and silenced. For we did not think it right that a funeral such as hers should be celebrated with tears and groans and lamentations. These are ways in which people grieve for an utter wretchedness in death or a kind of total extinction. But she did not die in misery, nor was she altogether dead. Of this we had good reason to be certain from the evidence of her character and from a faith that was not feigned.

Why, then, did I feel such pain within me? It was because the wound was still fresh, the wound caused by the sudden breaking off of our old way of living together in such sweet affection. I was glad indeed to have the

testimony which she gave me in these very last days
of her illness when, as I was doing what service I could
for her, she spoke so affectionately to me, calling me her
good and dutiful son, and, with such great love, she told
me that she had never once heard me say a word to her
that was hard or bitter. And yet, my God who made us,
what comparison was there between the respect I paid to
her and the slavery she offered to me? And so, now that I
had lost that great comfort of her, my soul was wounded
and my life was, as it were, torn apart, since it had been
a life made up of hers and mine together.

So, when the boy had been quieted and had ceased to
weep, Euodius took up the Psalter and began to sing—
while the whole household joined in the responses—the
Psalm: *I will sing of mercy and judgment to Thee, O
Lord*. And when it became known what we were doing,
many of the brethren and many religious women came to
join us. Those whose duty it was began in the usual way to
make preparations for the funeral, and I, with some of my
friends who thought I ought not to be left alone, found
another part of the house where we could decently be,
and there I spoke to them on such subjects as I thought
right for the occasion. So I was using truth as a kind of
fomentation to dull my torture, a torture which was
known to you, though the others, who listened intently
to my words, did not know of it and thought that I had
no feeling of pain. But in your ears, where none of them
could hear me, I reproached myself for being so feeble,
and I kept back the flood of my sorrow. And it did give
way to me a little; then gathered strength and swept back
on me again, though not to the point of making me break
out into tears or change the expression of my face. But
I knew well enough what I was crushing down in my
heart. And I was deeply vexed that these human feelings
should have such power over me—though in the proper
order and lot of the human condition these things must
be—and I grieved at my grief with a new grief and so
was consumed with a double sorrow.

And now the body was carried to burial. I went and I
returned and I did not weep at all. We poured forth our
prayers to you when the sacrifice of our redemption was

offered for her and when, as the custom is there, the body
was laid down near the grave before being lowered down
into it, and during all these prayers I did not shed a tear.
But all that day my sorrow weighed heavily on me in
secret, and in the disturbance of my mind I begged you,
as well as I could, to heal my sorrow; but you did not,
and I think this was because you were impressing on my
memory, by this one instance, how strong is the bond of
all habit, even upon a soul which is no longer nourished
by deceiving words. It even seemed to me a good idea
to go to the baths, because I had heard that the word for
bath (*balneum*) was derived from the Greek βαλανεῖον,
meaning something that drives sadness from the mind.
And I confess this also to your mercy, Father of the
fatherless: I went to the baths and I came back just the
same as I was before. For the bitterness of my sorrow did
not sweat itself out of my heart. Then I went to sleep
and woke up again to find that my grief was much relieved. And as I was alone in my bed I remembered those
true verses written by your servant Ambrose. For it is
you who are

> Creator Thou of everything,
> Director of the circling poles,
> Clothing the day in lovely light
> And giving night the grace of sleep,
>
> That peace may fall on loosened limbs
> To make them strong for work again,
> To raise and soothe the tired mind
> And free the anxious from their care.

And then little by little my former thoughts of your
handmaid returned. I remembered how devoutly and with
what holiness she conducted herself in your sight, how
kind and considerate she was to us. And now suddenly I
had lost all this. With you seeing me I found solace in
weeping for her and for myself, on her behalf and on my
own. So I allowed the tears which I had been holding
back to fall, and I let them flow as they would, making
them a pillow for my heart, and my heart rested on them,

for only your ears could hear my lament and not the ears of some man who might have given a wrong or contemptuous interpretation of it. And now, Lord, I am confessing this to you in writing and anyone who cares can read what I have written and interpret it as he likes, and if he finds that I did wrong in weeping during this small portion of an hour for my mother—a mother who for the time was dead to my eyes and who for so many years had wept for me, that I might live in your eyes— let him not despise me; let him rather, if he is a man of great charity, himself weep for my sins to you, the Father of all the brethren of your Christ.

13 BUT NOW THAT my heart is healed from that wound (in which later I blamed myself for a too carnal affection), I pour forth to you, our God, tears of a very different sort for your handmaid—tears that well up from a spirit shaken by the thoughts of the dangers that threaten every soul *that dieth in Adam.* Certainly she, after having been made alive in Christ and when still not freed from the flesh, lived such a life that in her faith and in her character your name was praised; yet even so I would not venture to say that from the time of her regeneration by you in baptism she never let fall a single word that was contrary to your commandment. Your son, the Truth, has said: *Whosoever shall say unto his brother, Thou fool, shall be in danger of hell-fire,* and it would go badly indeed with any man, however praiseworthy his life, if you were to lay aside your mercy before examining it. But because you do not look too rigorously into our sins, we confidently hope to find some place with you. But if a man recounts to you all the real merits he has, he is only telling you of your gifts to him. If only men would recognize that they are men, *and that he that glorieth, would glory in the Lord.*

And so, my praise and my life, God of my heart, I shall leave aside for the moment those good deeds of hers for which I joyfully thank you, and I shall now beg your mercy for my mother's sins. Hear me, I pray, in the name of that Medicine of our wounds, who hung upon the

cross, and now *sitting at Thy right hand maketh intercession to Thee for us.* I know that she dealt mercifully
and from her heart *forgave her debtors their debts; do
thou also forgive her debts,* whatever she has contracted
in all the years since the water of salvation. Forgive her,
Lord, forgive her, I beg you; *enter not into judgment
with her. Let Thy mercy be exalted above Thy justice,*
because your words are true, and *Thou hast promised
mercy unto the merciful.* And that they should be merciful was your gift, *who wilt have mercy on whom Thou
wilt have mercy, and compassion on whom Thou hast had
compassion.*

And I believe that you have already done what I am
asking; but *accept, O Lord, the free-will offerings of my
mouth.* For on that day when her death was so close, she
gave no thought to having her body richly adorned for
burial or embalmed in spices; she had no desire for any
special monument, nor was she anxious about being buried
in her own country. She gave us no instructions about any
of these things. All she desired was that she should be
remembered at your altar, which she had served without
ever missing a single day, and from which she knew was
dispensed that holy sacrifice by which *the handwriting
that was against us is blotted out,* by which the enemy was
triumphed over, who, reckoning up our sins and seeking
what there was to lay to our charge, *found nothing in
Him,* in whom we conquer. Who shall restore to Him His
innocent blood? Who shall give Him back the price for
which He bought us, and so take us from Him? To the
sacrament of this ransom of ours your handmaiden had
bound her soul by the bond of faith. Let none wrest her
from your protection; let neither *the lion nor the dragon*
interpose himself by force or by fraud. For she will not
reply that she has no debts, lest she should be convicted
and seized by that cunning accuser. She will reply that her
debts have been remitted to her by Him, to whom no one
can repay the price which He, who owed nothing, paid
for us.

So let her rest in peace with her husband, than whom
she had no other husband either before or after; whom
she obeyed, *with patience bringing forth fruit* for you, so

that she might win him for you also. And inspire, my Lord and my God, inspire your servants my brethren, your sons my masters, whom I serve with heart and voice and pen, that as many as shall read this may remember at your altar Monica, your servant, with Patricius, her husband, through whose flesh you brought me into this life, though how I do not know. May they with holy affection remember those two who were my parents in this transitory light, who are my brethren under you, Our Father, in our Catholic mother, and my fellow citizens in the eternal Jerusalem for which your people in their pilgrimage sigh from the beginning of their journey until their return home. And so by means of these Confessions of mine I pray that my mother may have her last request of me still more richly answered in the prayers of many others besides myself.

Book X

1 LET ME KNOW YOU, my known; *let me know Thee even as I am known.* Power of my soul, enter into it and fit it for yourself, so that you may have and hold it *without spot or wrinkle.* This is my hope, *therefore do I speak,* and in this hope is my joy, when my joy is healthy. As to the other things of this life, the more we weep for them the less they ought to be wept for, and the less we weep for them the more we ought to weep. For, see, you love the truth, and he that *doth the truth, cometh to the light.* This is what I want to do in my heart, in front of you, in my confession, and in my writing before many witnesses.

2 INDEED, LORD, to your eyes the very depths of man's conscience are exposed, and there is nothing in me that I could keep secret from you, even if I did not want to confess it. I should not be hiding myself from you, but you from myself. But now when my groaning bears evidence that I am displeased with myself, you shine out on me and are pleasing and loved and longed for, so that I am ashamed of myself and renounce myself and choose you and, except in you, can please neither you nor myself. Whatever I am, then, Lord, is open and evident to you. And what profit I have from confessing to you, I have already said. And I do not make my confession by means of the words and sounds of the flesh, but with

the words of the soul and the crying out of my thought
which your ear knows. For when I am wicked, confession to you is the same thing as being displeased with
myself; when I am good, confession to you is the same
thing as not attributing my goodness to myself. Since
Thou, Lord, *blessest the godly*, but first *Thou justifieth
him when ungodly*. So, my God, my confession in your
sight is made to you both silently and not silently; there
is no sound of words, but there is a clamor of feeling.
For if I say anything good to men, you have heard it
from me first, and if you hear any good from me, it was
you who first told it to me.

3   Why then do I bother to let men hear my confessions? It is not as though men are likely *to heal
all my infirmities*. Men are a race very inquisitive about
other people's lives, very lazy in improving their own.
Why should they want to hear from me what I am,
when they do not want to hear from you what they are?
And when they hear my own account of my own self,
how do they know that I am telling the truth, seeing
that *no man knows what is in man, but the spirit of man
which is in him?* But if they hear from you something
about their own selves they cannot say: "the Lord is
lying." For to hear from you about themselves is simply
to know themselves. And if one knows oneself and then
says: "it is false," one must be lying oneself. But *charity
believeth all things* (that is, among those whom it binds
together and makes one), and so, Lord, I make my confession to you in such a way that men may hear it, though
I cannot demonstrate to them that I am telling the truth;
yet those whose ears are opened to me by charity believe
what I say.

Yet still, my inmost Physician, I beg you to make clear
to me what advantage I get from doing this. You have
forgiven and covered up my past sins, blessing me in
you and changing my soul by faith and by your sacrament; yet when the confessions of these past sins are read
and heard, they rouse up the heart and prevent it from
sinking into the sleep of despair and saying "I cannot."

Instead they encourage it to be wakeful in the love of your mercy and the sweetness of your grace, through which the weak is made strong when, thanks to this grace of yours, he becomes conscious of his own weakness. Also good men are pleased when they hear of sins done in the past by people who are now free from them; they are pleased not because of the sins themselves, but because what were sins have now ceased to exist.

But, my Lord, to whom every day my conscience makes its confession, more secure in the hope of your mercy than in its own innocence, tell me, I beg you, of what advantage it is when, in front of you, I also by means of this book confess to men not what I once was, but what I now am. As to my confession of the past, I have already seen and mentioned the advantages of that. But as to what I now am, at the very moment of writing these confessions, there are many people who want to know about this—both those who know me personally and those who do not, but have heard something about me or from me; but their ear is not laid against my heart, where I am whatever I am. And so they want, as I make my confession, to hear what I am inside myself, beyond the possible reach of their eyes and ears and minds. And in wanting to hear, they are ready to believe; but will they know? For that charity, by which they are good, tells them that I am not lying about myself in my confessions, and it is the charity in them that believes me.

4   BUT WHAT ADVANTAGE do they wish to gain from this? Do they desire to rejoice with me when they hear how close I have come to you by your grace? And to pray for me, when they hear how I am kept back by my own weight? It is to people like this that I shall show myself. For it is no small advantage, my Lord God, that many people should give thanks to you for me and that many people should pray to you for me. I would wish that their brotherly minds should love in me what you teach them is to be loved, and should lament in me what you teach them is to be lamented. It is a brotherly mind that I would wish for, not the mind of strangers, not that

of the *strange children, whose mouth talketh of vanity, and their right hand is a right hand of iniquity;* but that brotherly mind which is glad for me when it sees good in me and sorry for me when it sees bad in me, because, whether it sees good or bad, it loves me. It is to people like this that I shall show myself, hoping that in my good deeds they will be glad and in my evil deeds they will be sad. My good deeds are your work and your gift, my evil deeds are my faults and your punishments. So I would wish there to be gladness for the one, sadness for the other, and that hymns and lamentations should rise up into your sight from those censers which are the hearts of my brethren. And I pray that you, Lord, pleased with the sweet incense of your holy temple, may *have mercy upon me according to Thy great mercy for Thine own name's sake,* and, in no way forsaking what you have begun, perfect my imperfections.

So in confessing not only what I have been but what I am the advantage is this: I make my confession not only in front of you, in a secret *exultation with trembling,* with a secret sorrow and with hope, but also in the ears of the believing sons of men, companions in my joy and sharers in my mortality, my fellow citizens and fellow pilgrims— those who have gone before and those who follow after and those who are on the road with me. These are your servants and my brothers; those whom you have willed to be your sons, my masters whom I am to serve if I wish to live with you and of you. And this word of yours to me would be a little thing if it only gave me a spoken command and did not also go in front of me in action. And so I do it both in deed and in word; I do it under your wings, and the danger would be too great if under your wings my soul were not subdued to you and my weakness known to you. I am only a little child, but my Father lives forever and my Protector is sufficient for me. For he is the same who begot me and who watches over me, and you yourself are all my good, you Almighty, who are with me even before I am with you. So it is to people like this, those whom you command me to serve, that I shall show not what I was, but what I now am and continue to be. *But neither do I judge myself*. It is in this way that I should like to be heard.

5   FOR *Thou, Lord, dost judge me*; because, although *no man knoweth the things of a man, but the spirit of a man which is in him*, yet there is still something of man which even the spirit of man that is in him does not know. But you, Lord, know all of him, you who made him. And as to me, though in your sight I despise myself and consider myself dust and ashes, yet still I know something of you which I do not know of myself. *Certainly now we see through a glass darkly*, and not yet *face to face*, and so, as long as I am on pilgrimage away from you, I am more present to myself than to you; yet I know that you are not in any way subject to violence, whereas I do not know in my case what temptations I can and what I cannot resist. And there is hope, because *Thou art faithful, Who wilt not suffer us to be tempted above that we are able; but wilt with the temptation also make a way to escape, that we may be able to bear it*. So I will confess what I know of myself, and I will also confess what I do not know of myself; because what I know of myself I know by means of your light shining upon me, and what I do not know remains unknown to me until *my darkness be made as the noonday* in your countenance.

6   THERE IS NO DOUBT in my mind, Lord, that I love you. I feel it with certainty. You struck my heart with your word, and I loved you. But, see, *heaven and earth and all that therein is* on every side are telling me to love you, and they never stop saying it to all men, *that they may be without excuse*. But more deeply *wilt Thou have mercy on whom Thou wilt have mercy, and wilt have compassion on whom Thou hast had compassion;* otherwise heaven and earth are telling your praises to deaf ears.

But what do I love when I love you? Not the beauty of the body nor the glory of time, not the brightness of light shining so friendly to the eye, not the sweet and various

melodies of singing, not the fragrance of flowers and un-
guents and spices, not manna and honey, not limbs welcome to the embraces of the flesh: it is not these that I love
when I love my God. And yet I do love a kind of light,
melody, fragrance, food, embracement when I love my
God; for He is the light, the melody, the fragrance, the
food, the embracement of my inner self—there where is a
brilliance that space cannot contain, a sound that time
cannot carry away, a perfume that no breeze disperses, a
taste undiminished by eating, a clinging together that no
satiety will sunder. This is what I love when I love my
God.

And what is this God? I asked the earth and it
answered: "I am not he," and all things that are on the
earth confessed the same. I asked the sea and the deeps
and the creeping things with living souls, and they replied: "We are not your God. Look above us." I asked
the blowing breezes, and the universal air with all its in-
habitants answered: "Anaximenes was wrong. I am not
God." I asked the heaven, the sun, the moon, the stars,
and "No," they said, "we are not the God for whom you
are looking." And I said to all those things which stand
about the gates of my senses: "Tell me about my God,
you who are not He. Tell me something about Him."
And they cried out in a loud voice: "He made us." My
question was in my contemplation of them, and their
answer was in their beauty. And I turned my attention on
myself and said to myself: "And you, who are you?" And
I replied: "A man." Now I find evidently in myself a
body and a soul, the one exterior, the other interior.
Which of these should I have employed in seeking for
my God? I had already looked for Him by means of the
body, searching from earth to heaven, as far as I could
send the beams of my eyes as messengers. But the interior
part of me is the better. It was to this part that all the messengers from my body gave in their reports and this part
sat in judgment weighing the replies of heaven and earth
and all things within them when they said: "We are not
God," and when they said: "He made us." The inner
man knew these things by means of the ministry of the
outer man. I, the inner man, knew them, I, the soul, knew

them through the senses of my body. I asked the whole mass and frame of the universe about my God, and it replied: "I am not he, but He made me."

Is not this appearance of the universe evident to all whose senses are not deranged? Then why does it not give the same answer to all? Animals, small and great, see it, but cannot ask the question. They are not gifted with reason to sit in judgment on the evidence brought in by the senses. But men can ask the question, so that *the invisible things of God are clearly seen, being understood by the things that are made;* but by loving these things, they become subject to them, and subjects cannot judge. And these things will only answer the questions of those who are prepared to judge. Not that they alter their speech—that is, their appearance. If one man merely looks at them and another not only looks but asks his question, they do not appear one thing to one man, and a different thing to the other. They look just the same to both, but to one man they say nothing and to the other they speak. Or it would be truer to say that they speak to everyone, but are only understood by those who compare the voice which comes to them from outside with the truth that is within. For truth says to me: "Your God is not heaven or earth or any other body." Their very nature declared this. Obviously there is less bulk in a part than in the whole. And now, my soul, I say to you that you are my better part; you animate the whole bulk of the body, giving it life—a thing which no body can do for another body. But your God is for you too the life of your life.

7 WHAT, THEN, do I love when I love God? Who is He that is above the summit of my soul? It is by my soul herself that I shall ascend to Him. I shall go past that force in me by which I cling to the body and fill its frame with life. It is not by that force that I can find my God; if it were so, the *horse and mule that have no understanding* might find Him, since their bodies too live by this same force. But there is another force—not the one by which I give life, but the one by which I give perception to my flesh. The Lord created this power in me, com-

manding the eye not to hear and the ear not to see, but giving me the eye to see by and the ear to hear by, and so allotting to each of the other senses its own particular duty and function, and through these senses, with all their diverse functions, I act, retaining my identity as one soul. But I shall go past this force too; for the horse and the mule have it too; they also perceive by means of the body.

8   I SHALL PASS ON, then, beyond this faculty in my nature as I ascend by degrees toward Him who made me. And I come to the fields and spacious palaces of memory, where lie the treasures of innumerable images of all kinds of things that have been brought in by the senses. There too are our thoughts stored up, if by thought we have increased or diminished or in any way altered those things with which our senses have been in contact, and there too is everything else that has been brought in and deposited and has not yet been swallowed up and buried in forgetfulness. When I am in this treasure house, I ask for whatever I like to be brought out to me, and then some things are produced at once, some things take longer and have, as it were, to be fetched from a more remote part of the store, and some things come pouring out all together and, when in fact we want and are looking for something quite different, they thrust themselves forward as though they were saying: "Surely you must be looking for me." With the hand of my heart I brush them away from the face of my memory, until the thing that I want is discovered and brought out from its hidden place into my sight. And some things are produced easily and in perfect order, just as they are required; what comes first gives place to what comes next, and, as it gives place, it is stored up ready to be brought out when I need it again. All this happens when I repeat anything by heart.

Here are kept distinct and in their proper classifications all sensations which come to us, each by its own route: for instance, light, color, and the shapes of bodies reach us through the eyes; all kinds of sound through the ears; all smells by the nostrils; all tastes by the mouth, and by the sensation of the whole body we derive our impression of what is hard or soft, hot or cold, rough or smooth, heavy or light, whether from outside or inside the body itself. And the great harbor of memory, with its secret, numberless, and indefinable recesses, takes in all these things so that they may be reproduced and brought back again when the need arises. They all enter the memory by their various ways and are all stored up in the memory. Or rather it is not the things themselves that enter; what happens is that the images of things perceived are there ready at hand for thought to recall.

Precisely how these images are formed who can tell? Though it is clear enough which sense was responsible for seizing hold of them and storing them up inside us. For even when I am surrounded by darkness and silence, I can, if I wish, summon up colors in my memory and tell the difference between black and white and any other colors I like, and while I am considering the images drawn in by my eyes, sounds do not come running in to disturb it, though they too are in my memory, stored up, as it were, in a separate compartment. For I can call for sounds also, if I wish, and they are present immediately; with no movement of tongue or vocal chords I sing as much as I like, and those images of color, which are still there in the memory, do not break in and interrupt when I call for something from that other storehouse which contains impressions brought in by the ear. In the same way I call up at pleasure all those other things which have been brought in and stored up by means of the other senses. I can tell the difference between the smell of lilies and of violets, though at the time I am smelling nothing; I prefer honey to sweet wine, something smooth to something rough, simply by memory and without using the sense either of taste or touch.

All this I do inside me, in the huge court of my memory. There I have by me the sky, the earth, the sea, and all things in them which I have been able to perceive—apart from what I have forgotten. There too I encounter myself; I recall myself—what I have done, when and where I did it, and in what state of mind I was at the time. There are all the things I remember to have experienced myself or to have heard from others. From the same store too I can take out pictures of things which have either happened to me or are believed on the basis of experience; I can myself weave them into the context of the past, and from them I can infer future actions, events, hopes, and then I can contemplate all these as though they were in the present. "I shall do this," or "I shall do that," I say to myself in this deep recess of my mind, full of the images of so many and of such great things, "and this or that follows." "Oh if only this or that could happen!" or "May God prevent this or that!" So I speak to myself, and, while I am speaking, the images of all the things that I am saying are present to my mind, all from this same treasury of my memory; indeed I would not be able to speak of these things at all if the images were not there.

How great, my God, is this force of memory, how exceedingly great! It is like a vast and boundless subterranean shrine. Who has ever reached the bottom of it? Yet this is a faculty of my mind and belongs to my nature; nor can I myself grasp all that I am. Therefore, the mind is not large enough to contain itself. But where can that uncontained part of it be? Is it outside itself and not inside? In that case, how can it fail to contain itself? At this thought great wonder comes over me; I am struck dumb with astonishment. And men go abroad to wonder at the heights of mountains, the huge waves of the sea, the broad streams of rivers, the vastness of the ocean, the turnings of the stars—and they do not notice themselves and they see nothing marvelous in the fact that when I was mentioning all these things I was not seeing them with my eyes, yet I would not have been able to speak of them unless these mountains and waves and rivers and stars (which I have seen) and the ocean (which I have heard about) had been visible to me inside, in my memory, and with just the same great spatial intervals and proportions as if I were really seeing them outside myself. Yet, when I saw them with my eyes, I did not by the act of seeing draw them into myself; it is not they but their images that are in me, and I know by what bodily sense each impression has come to me.

9 YET MORE STILL is contained in this immense capacity of my memory. Here too is everything that I have learned in the liberal sciences and not forgotten—removed somehow to an inner place, which is yet no place. And here I have with me not the images but the things themselves. What grammar is, or the art of disputation, or how many types of question there are—everything of this sort that I know is in my memory in a different way. Here it is not the case that I retain the image and leave the thing itself outside me. It is not the case of the sound of words which has ceased to sound, like a voice which has left a fixed impression on the ear by which it can be recalled as though it were sounding, when in fact it is not sounding; or like a smell which, while it is passing and vanishing into air, affects the sense of smell and so carries into the memory an image of itself which we can recall by the act of recollection; or like food, which certainly has no taste when it is in the stomach, but still has a kind of taste in our memory; or like something which is perceived by the sense of bodily touch and can still be imagined in our memory when it is no longer in contact with us. In all these cases it is not the things themselves that are brought into our memory; it is only their images which are seized upon with such amazing speed and are then, as it were, stored up in wonderful secret hiding places, from which by the act of remembering they can wonderfully be brought out again.

10 BUT WHEN I HEAR that there are three types of question—"Does the thing exist? What is it? Of what kind is it?"—I certainly hold in my mind the images of the sounds of which these words are compared, and I know that they passed through the air, making a particular kind of noise, and have now ceased to be. But as to the things themselves that are signified by these sounds, I never approached them by any bodily sense; my only means of discerning them was through the mind, and in my memory I have stored up, not their images, but the things themselves. How they got into me, let them say if they can. For as I go over all the gateways of my body,

I cannot find by which one they gained entrance. The eyes say: "If these images were colored, it was we who gave notice of them." The ears say: "If they made a sound, it was by us that they were reported." The nostrils say: "If they had a smell, they came in by way of us." And the sense of taste says: "Unless one could taste them, it is no use asking me." Touch says: "If the thing is not a body I did not handle it, and if I did not handle it, I gave no information about it." From where, then, and how did they enter into my memory? I do not know. For when I learned them, I was not taking them on trust from some other mind; I was recognizing them in my own mind; I accepted them as true and committed them to my mind as though I were depositing them in some place where I could find them again whenever I wanted. So they were in my mind, even before I learned them, but they were not in my memory. Then where were they? Or how was it that, when I heard them spoken, I recognized them and said: "That is right. That is true," unless in fact they were in my memory already, but so far back and so buried, as it were, in the furthest recesses that, if they had not been dragged out by the suggestion of someone else, I should perhaps not have been able to conceive of them?

11   WE FIND, THEREFORE, that to learn those things which we do not draw into us as images by means of our senses, but which we perceive inside ourselves as they actually are without the aid of images means simply this: by the act of thought we are, as it were, collecting together things which the memory did contain, though in a disorganized and scattered way, and by giving them our close attention we are arranging for them to be as it were stored up ready to hand in that same memory where previously they lay hidden, neglected, and dispersed, so that now they will readily come forward to the mind that has become familiar with them. My memory carries a very great number of things of this sort, which have been discovered and, as I said, placed as it were ready to hand. These are the things which we are said to have learned and to know. Yet if I cease, even for quite a short space

of time, to bring them up into my mind, down they sink again and slip away into some sort of distant hidden place, so that I have to think them out afresh from that same place (for there is nowhere else where they can have gone) and once again gather them together so that they may be known. In fact what one is doing is collecting them from their dispersal. Hence the derivation of the word "to cogitate." For *cogo* (collect) and *cogito* (re-collect) are in the same relation to each other as *ago* and *agito*, *facio* and *factito*. But the mind has appropriated to itself this word ("cogitation"), so that it is only correct to say "cogitated" of things which are "re-collected" in the mind, not of things re-collected elsewhere.

12   THE MEMORY also contains the innumerable principles and laws of numbers and dimensions. None of these has been imprinted on it by any bodily sense, since none of these is colored or can be heard, smelled, tasted, or touched. I have heard the sounds of the words by which these principles are signified when we discuss them, but the sounds and the principle are different things. The sounds will be different if the words used are Greek or Latin, but the principles are neither Greek nor Latin nor any other language. I have seen the lines drawn by architects, lines barely visible, like spiders' webs. But the principles involved are something different; they are not images of those things which are reported to me by my bodily eye, and the man who knows these principles recognizes them inside him without having to think of any kind of material body. Again, with all my bodily senses I have perceived the numbers which we use in counting; but the numbers by which we are able to count at all are not the same as these, nor are they images of these; they have a real existence of their own. Anyone who cannot see them may laugh at me for talking of them, and, while he laughs, I shall be sorry for him.

13 ALL THESE THINGS I hold in my memory, and I also hold in my memory how I learned them. And there are many completely false arguments which I have heard advanced against these things; these also I hold in my memory. And though they are false, it is not false to say that I remember them. I also remember that I have distinguished between the truths and the false objections made to those truths. And I see that for me to make the distinction between them now is a different thing from remembering how I often did make the distinction in the past, when I was thinking on these subjects. Therefore I remember that I often did understand them and also I store up in my memory what I see and understand now, so that later I may remember what I did understand at this moment. So I remember that I have remembered, and if in the future I recall that I have now been able to remember these things, it will be by the force of my memory that I shall recall it.

14 THIS SAME MEMORY also contains the feelings of my mind. It does not contain them in the same way as the mind itself has them when it is experiencing them, but in a very different way, appropriate to the nature of memory. For I remember that I was happy when I am not happy now, and I recall my past sadness when I am not sad now; when I am not frightened, I can remember that I once was frightened, and I can recall a desire I had once, when I have it no longer. Sometimes it works the other way: when I am happy I remember my past sadness, and when I am sad I remember my past happiness. There is nothing surprising in this, so far as the body is concerned; for the mind is one thing and the body another. So if I remember with joy some past pain of the body, there is nothing strange in that. But memory itself is mind. For example, when we tell someone to remember something we say: "Be sure to keep it in mind," and when we forget something we say: "It was not in my mind," or "It slipped out of my mind." So we call memory itself mind. Now since this is so, how is it that when I, being happy, remember my past sadness—so that the mind contains happiness and the memory contains sadness—the mind is happy because of the happiness in it, but the memory is not sad because of the sadness in it? Is it that the memory has no connection with the mind? Obviously one cannot say that. Therefore the memory must be, as it were, the stomach of the mind, and happiness and sadness like sweet and bitter food, and when they are committed to the memory it is as though they passed into the stomach where they can be stored up but cannot taste. A ridiculous comparison, perhaps, and yet there is some truth in it.

Observe too that it comes from my memory when I say that there are four types of disturbance in the mind—desire, joy, fear, sorrow—and in any statements that I may be able to make on these subjects by means of definition or classification under genus and species, it is in my memory that I find what to say and it is from my memory that I bring it out. Yet in calling back to mind by the act of recollection disturbances of this sort, I myself feel no disturbance, and they were there, in the memory, before I recalled them and brought them back; indeed it was only because they were there that I was able to recollect them. May one say, then, that just as food is brought up from the stomach by chewing the cud, so these things are brought up from the memory by recollection? But why then is the actual sweetness of joy or bitterness of sorrow not tasted in the cogitational mouth of the man who makes statements about, i.e., remembers, these things? Or is this the point where the comparison between rumination and recollection is incomplete? For we would be reluctant to talk about these subjects if, whenever we used the words "sorrow" or "fear," we had actually to feel sorrow or fear. Yet we could not talk about them at all, unless we could find within our memory not only the sounds of the words (according to images impressed upon it by the senses of the body) but also concepts of the things themselves, and we did not receive these concepts by the gateway of any bodily sense; it was the mind itself which, by the experience of its own passions, felt them and entrusted them to the memory; or else the memory retained them, even if they were not entrusted to it.

15 BUT IT IS NOT easy to say whether this takes place by means of images or not. I pronounce the word "stone" or "sun" when the things themselves are not present to my senses; images of them however are in front of my memory. I pronounce the word for some physical pain; this pain is not present to me, since I am not in pain; but unless the image of it was in my memory, I should not know how to speak of it and, in any discussion, I should be unable to draw a distinction between it and pleasure. I mention physical health, when I myself am in good health; the thing signified by the words is actually present in me, yet unless its image also was in my memory, it would be impossible for me to recall what is meant by the sound of the words denoting it; nor, when the word "health" was mentioned, would sick people recognize the meaning of what was said, unless, in spite of the fact that health itself was not in their bodies, they still retained through the force of memory an image of health. I name the numbers that we use in counting; it is the numbers themselves and not their images that are in my memory. I name the image of the sun, and this image is in my memory—not the image of its image, but the image itself; that is what is before me when I recall it. I say "memory" and I recognize what I mean by it; but where do I recognize it except in my memory itself? Can memory itself be present to itself by means of its image rather than by its reality?

16 Now SUPPOSE I say "forgetfulness" and once again recognize what I mean by the word, how do I recognize the thing itself unless it were that I remembered it? I am not speaking of the sound of the word, but the thing which the word signifies; for if I had forgotten the thing, I should certainly not be able to recognize what the word meant. When I remember memory, memory itself is, through itself, present to itself; but when I remember forgetfulness, there are present both memory and forgetfulness—memory by which I remember, forgetfulness which I remember. But what is forgetfulness except privation of memory? How then can it be present for me to remember it, when I am not able to remember it when it is present? But if we retain in our memory what we remember, and if, unless we remembered forgetfulness, we should be quite unable to recognize what was meant by the word when we heard it, then forgetfulness must be retained in the memory. Therefore, what, when present, we forget is present in order that we should not forget. Must we understand from this that forgetfulness, when we remember it, is not present to the memory in itself, but by its image, because if it were present in itself, it would cause us, not to remember, but to forget? Who can possibly find the answer to this or understand how it comes about?

For me, Lord, certainly this is hard labor, hard labor inside myself, and I have become to myself a piece of difficult ground, not to be worked over without much sweat. For we are not now examining the regions of the heaven or measuring the distances of the stars or inquiring into how the earth is balanced in space. It is I myself who remember, I, the mind. There is nothing remarkable in the fact that something other than myself is far away from me; but what can be nearer to me than my own self? Yet this force of my memory is incomprehensible to me, even though, without it, I should not be able to call myself myself. What am I to say, when I see so clearly that I remember forgetfulness? Shall I say that what I remember is not in my memory? Or that forgetfulness is in my memory in order that I should not forget? Both answers are absurd. Is the third possibility any better? Could I say that it is the image of forgetfulness, not forgetfulness itself, which is held by my memory when I remember it? No, I could not; since when the image of a thing is impressed on the memory, it is first of all necessary that the thing itself should be present from which the impression can be derived. In this way I remember Carthage, or any other place where I have been; in this way I remember the faces of people I have seen and all things reported to me by the other senses; so too I remember the health or sickness of the body. When these things were present, the memory received their images from them and these images remained present for me to contemplate and bring back to mind when I recollected the objects themselves, which were absent. If, therefore, forgetfulness is retained in the memory by means of an image, and not in itself, then undoubtedly forgetfulness must at some time have been present so that its image could be received. But how, when it was present, could it inscribe its image on the memory, when its presence means the destruction even of all records that are already there? Nevertheless, however it may be, however incomprehensible and inexplicable, I am quite sure that I do remember this forgetfulness by which what we remember is effaced.

17 GREAT INDEED is the power of memory! It is something terrifying, my God, a profound and infinite multiplicity; and this thing is the mind, and this thing is I myself. What then am I, my God? What is my nature? A life various, manifold, and quite immeasurable. Imagine the plains, caverns, and abysses of my memory; they are innumerable and are innumerably full of innumerable kinds of things, present either in their images, as in the case of all bodies, or in themselves, as with the arts, or in the form of some kind of notion or consciousness, as with the affections of the mind, which, even when the mind is not experiencing them, are still retained by the memory (though whatever is in the memory is also in the mind). Through all this I range; I fly here and I fly there; I dive down deep as I can, and I can find no end. So great is the force of memory, so great is the force of life in man who lives to die.

What shall I do, you true life of mine, my God? I will go past this force of mine called memory; I will go beyond it so that I may draw nearer to you, sweet light. What is it that you are saying to me? I mount up through my mind toward you who dwell above me, and now I shall go beyond this force of mine called memory, for I desire to reach you at the point from which you may be reached, to cling to you at the point from which it is possible for me to cling to you. For even beasts and birds have memory; otherwise they would not be able to find their ways back to their dens and nests or do any of the other things they are used to doing; indeed without memory they could not become used to doing anything. So I will pass beyond memory also, so that I may reach him who separated me from the four-footed beasts and made me wiser than the birds of the air. I will pass beyond memory to find you—Oh where, where, shall I find you, my truly good, my certain loveliness? If I find you beyond my memory, I can have no memory of you. And how shall I find you if I do not remember you?

18 THE WOMAN who had lost her groat sought for it with a light; but unless she had remembered it, she would not have found it. For when it was discovered, how could she have known whether it was the right one or not, if she had not remembered it? I remember many occasions when I have looked for and found something which I had lost, and from these experiences I know that when I was looking for the thing and people asked me: "Is this it?" or "Is that it?" I would go on saying: "No, it is not," until the thing that I really was looking for was produced. But unless I had remembered it, whatever it was, I would not have found it even if it were produced in front of me, since I would not have recognized it. And this is always the case when we look for and find something that was lost. If something happens to disappear from the eyes and not from the memory (as any visible body), its image is retained within us and is looked for until it is restored to sight, and when found, it is recognized by the image that is within. We do not say that we have found what was lost unless we recognize it, and we cannot recognize it unless we remember it. It was certainly lost to the eyes, but it was still held in the memory.

19 BUT WHEN THE MEMORY itself loses something, as happens when we forget a thing and try to recollect it, where can we possibly look for it except in the memory? And there if something other than what we are looking for is presented to us, we reject it until the thing that we are looking for turns up. And when it does turn

up we say: "This is it." We would not say this unless we recognized it, and we would not recognize it unless we remembered it. Yet certainly we had forgotten it.

Or could this be the solution: the whole thing had not slipped from our memory; part of it was retained and by means of this part the other part was sought for, because the memory realized that it was not carrying along with it the totality which it was used to and, going unevenly, as it were, through the loss of something to which it was accustomed, eagerly demanded the restoration of what was lacking. For instance if we see or think of some man who is known to us, but have forgotten his name and are trying to recall it, any name that occurs to us other than his will not fit in, because we are not in the habit of thinking of that name and that person together. Consequently we go on rejecting names until the name presents itself with which our knowledge can rest satisfied, since it is the name with which it was accustomed to make the appropriate connection. And that name cannot come from any other source except the memory. Even when we recognize it after being reminded of it by someone else, the recognition still comes from the memory. We do not accept it as though it were something new; instead we agree that this was what it was because we remember it to be so. If it were entirely blotted out of our mind, we should not remember it even when reminded of it. For if we can remember that we have forgotten something, this means that we have not entirely forgotten it. Whatever has been utterly forgotten cannot even be thought of as lost and cannot be sought for.

20 How, THEN, LORD, do I seek you? For when I seek you, my God, I am seeking the happy life. *I will seek Thee, that my soul may live.* For my body lives by my soul, and my soul lives by you. How, then, do I seek for the happy life? For I cannot find it until I can reach the place where I can truly say: "It is enough; it is there." How then, do I seek it? Is it by remembrance, as though I had forgotten it but can still remember that I have forgotten? Or is it through desire to learn something

unknown, something which either I never knew or which I have so completely forgotten that I cannot even remember that I have forgotten it? Is not the happy life the thing that all men desire, literally every single man without exception? But where did they get the knowledge of it, that they should desire it so? Where did they see it, that they should love it so? We have it, certainly; but how we have it, I do not know. In one sense a person may reach a certain degree of happiness and be called happy; others are happy in the hope of happiness. These latter do not have it in the same full sense as those who actually possess it; but they are better off than those who are neither happy in fact nor in hope. Though even these last must have it in some sense or other; otherwise they would not (as they certainly do) have such a wish to be happy. In some way or other they know of it and, therefore, may be said to possess it in some form of knowledge. Is this form of knowledge, I inquire, in the memory? If it is, then we must have experienced happiness at some time previously. I am not now asking whether this is an experience which we have all had individually, or whether the experience was in that man who first sinned, in whom we all died and of whom we are all born in misery. I am only asking whether the happy life is in our memory. For we could not love it, if we did not know it. We have heard the name "happiness" and all of us would agree that we desire the thing signified by the name; for it is not simply the sound of the word that pleases us. If a Greek hears the word in Latin, he derives no pleasure from it, since he does not know what has been said; but we are pleased, just in the same way as he would have been if he had heard the word in Greek. For the thing itself is neither Greek nor Latin, but it is something which Greeks, Latins, and men of all other languages long to attain. It is therefore known to all of them, and if they could all be asked with one voice: "Do you wish to be happy?" they would without any doubt reply, "We do." And this would not be so unless the thing itself, signified by the word, was contained in their memory.

21   But is this an example of the same kind of memory as when I, who have seen Carthage, remember Carthage? No, it is not; for the happy life, not being a body, is not visible to our eyes. Do we then remember it in the same way as we remember numbers? No, we do not; whoever has a knowledge of numbers is content with that and need seek no further; but we who have a knowledge of the happy life and therefore love it, do want to go further so that we may reach it and become happy. Is it, then, as we remember eloquence? No, it is not. Though it is true that on hearing the word "eloquence" many people, who have not yet become eloquent, call to mind the thing signified by the word and many people would like to be eloquent—all of which shows that the thing is in their knowledge; yet it is by means of the bodily senses that they have observed others who are eloquent, have been pleased by it, and have wanted to become eloquent themselves (though unless they had some interior notion, they would not be pleased, and, if they were not pleased, they would not want to possess this quality); however, there is no bodily sense which enables us to experience the happy life in others. Do we, then, remember it as we remember joy? This is possible. For I remember my joy even when I am sad, just as I remember the happy life even when I am unhappy. And never by any bodily sense did I see my joy, or hear it or smell it or taste it or touch it. I experienced it in my mind at the time when I was joyful, and the knowledge of it stuck in my memory so that I can call it back to mind, sometimes with contempt, sometimes with longing, according to the diversity of the things which I remember enjoying. For even base and disgraceful things have filled me with a kind of joy—things which now I detest and execrate when I recall them—and at other times I have had joy in good and worthy things which I remember with longing, though they may not be with me any more, so that I am sad when I recall the joy of the past.

Where, then, was it, and when was it that I experienced my happy life, so that I should remember it and love it and long for it? And not I alone, or I and a few others, but all of us; we all want to be happy. And unless we knew it with certain knowledge, we could not wish for it with so certain a will. But here is another point. Suppose two men are asked whether they want to join the army: it might happen that one would say "Yes" and the other would say "No." But if they are asked whether they want to be happy, both, without any doubt, would immediately say "Yes," and the only reason why one of them wanted to join the army and the other did not, was that they both wanted to be happy. Is it perhaps the case that different things make different people joyful and that so all agree that they want to be happy, just as they would agree, if they were asked, that they wanted to feel joy? And they think that joy itself is the same thing as the happy life? One may attain joy in one way, another in another way, but the end at which they are all aiming is one and the same, namely, a state of joy. And joy is something which no one can say he has no experience of; therefore, he finds it in his memory and recognizes it when he hears the words: "the happy life."

22   FAR BE IT, Lord, far be it from the heart of your servant who is confessing to you, far be it that I should think that any joy that I may experience makes me happy! For there is a joy that is not given to the ungodly, but only to those who love you for your own sake, and you yourself are their joy. And this is the happy life—to rejoice in you and to you and because of you. This is the happy life; there is no other. And those who think there is another, are in pursuit of another joy which is not the true joy. Yet all the same their will is still involved with some kind of an image of joy.

23   So IT IS NOT certain that all men want to be happy. Those who do not want to find their joy in you (which alone is the happy life) certainly do not want the happy life. Or do all men really desire it, but *because the flesh lusteth against the Spirit and the Spirit against the flesh, that they cannot do what they would*, they fall into

that state which is within their powers and are content with it because their will for a state which is beyond them is not strong enough to bring it within their reach? For if I ask anyone: "Would you rather have your joy in truth or in falsehood?" he would say: "In truth," with just as little hesitation as he would say that he wants to be happy. And certainly the happy life is joy in truth, which means joy in you, who are truth, God, *my light, health of my countenance, my God.* This is the happy life which all desire; this life which alone is happy all desire; joy in truth is what all desire. I have met many people who wanted to deceive, but no one who wanted to be deceived. But where did they gain their knowledge of this happy life except in the place where they also gained their knowledge of truth? For they love truth also (because they do not want to be deceived) and in loving the happy life (which simply means joy in truth) they must certainly love truth too, and they would not be able to love it, unless there were some knowledge of it in their memory. Why, then, do they not find their joy in it? Why are they not happy? Because they are more strongly taken up by other things which have more power to make them unhappy than that, which they so dimly remember, has to make them happy. For there is still only a little light in men, and they must walk, yes, they must *walk, that the darkness overtake them not.*

But why is it that "truth gives birth to hatred"? Why does your servant who preaches the truth incur enmity in spite of the fact that people love the happy life which simply is joy in truth? It is because truth is loved in such a way that those who love something else would like to believe that what they love is the truth, and because they would not like to be deceived, they object to being shown that in fact they are deceived. And so they hate truth for the sake of whatever it is they love instead of truth. They love the light of truth, but hate it when it shows them up as wrong. Because they do not want to be deceived and do want to deceive, they love truth when truth is giving evidence, but hate it when the evidence given is against themselves. And the retribution which will come to them is this: those who do not want to stand in the

light of truth, will have to stand in it, whether they like it
or not, but truth will not reveal her light to them. So it
is, yes, so indeed it is: this human mind of ours, so blind
and sick, so foul and ill-favored, wants to be hidden itself,
but hates to have anything hidden from it. But what
happens is just the contrary: it cannot hide from truth,
but truth can be out of its sight. Yet even so, wretched as
it is, it prefers to find joy in truth than in falsehoods. It
will be happy, therefore, when, with no distractions to
interpose themselves, it will find its joy in that only truth
by which all things are true.

24   SEE WHAT A DISTANCE I have covered searching
for you, Lord, in my memory! And I have not
found you outside it. Nor have I found anything about
you which I have not kept in my memory from the time
I first learned you. For from the time I learned you, I
have not forgotten you. For when I found truth, then I
found my God, truth itself, and from the time I learned
it I have not forgotten it. And so, since the time I learned
you, you stay in my memory, and there I find you whenever I call you to mind and delight in you. There are my
holy delights, which in your mercy you have given me,
having regard to my poverty.

25   BUT WHERE IS IT, Lord, in my memory that you
stay? In what part of it do you stay? What resting place have you framed for yourself? What sanctuary
have you built? You have given my memory the honor of
staying in it: but in what part of it do you stay? This is
what I now consider.

While I was calling you to mind, I went beyond those
parts of the memory which the beasts also have (because
I did not find you there among the images of material
things), and I came to those parts of it where I had stored
up the affections of my mind, but did not find you there
either. And I went into the seat of the mind itself (which
the mind has in my memory, since the mind remembers
itself), and you were not there. For, just as you are not a

material image, nor an affection of any living man (such as we feel when we are in a state of joy, sorrow, desire, fear, memory, forgetfulness, or anything else of this kind), so you are not the mind itself, because you are the Lord God of the mind, and all these things change, but you remain changeless over all things, and you have deigned to dwell in my memory, from the time I first learned of you. And why do I inquire in what place of my memory you dwell, as though there were any places there? Certainly you do dwell in my memory, because I remember you from the time I first learned of you, and I find you there when I call you to mind.

26 WHERE THEN did I find you, so that I could learn of you? For you were not in my memory before I learned of you. Where then did I find you, so that I could learn of you? I could only have found you in yourself, above me. Place there is none; we go *backward and forward*, and there is no place. Truth, you are everywhere in session, ready to listen to all who ask counsel of you, and at one and the same moment you give your answer to every diversity of question. You answer clearly, though everyone does not hear clearly. All ask what they wish, but they do not always hear what they want to hear. He serves you best who is not so anxious to hear from you what he wills as to will what he hears from you.

27 LATE IT WAS that I loved you, beauty so ancient and so new, late I loved you! And, look, you were within me and I was outside, and there I sought for you and in my ugliness I plunged into the beauties that you have made. You were with me, and I was not with you. Those outer beauties kept me far from you, yet if they had not been in you, they would not have existed at all. You called, you cried out, you shattered my deafness: you flashed, you shone, you scattered my blindness: you breathed perfume, and I drew in my breath and I pant for you: I tasted, and I am hungry and thirsty: you touched me, and I burned for your peace.

28   WHEN IN MY whole self I shall cling to you united, I shall find no sorrow anywhere, no labor; wholly alive will my life be all full of you. Those whom you fill, you raise up, and now, since I am not yet full of you, I am a burden to myself. Joys in which I should find sorrow conflict with sorrows in which I should find joy, and on which side stands the victory I do not know. I am sad for myself. Lord, have pity on me! My evil sorrows conflict with my good joys, and on which side stands the victory I do not know. I am sad for myself. Lord, have pity on me! I am sad for myself. Look, I am not hiding my wounds: you are the doctor and I am sick; you are merciful, I need mercy. *Is not the life of man upon earth all trial?* Does anyone want to be in trouble and difficulties? These you order us to endure, not to love. No one loves what he endures, even though he loves to endure. For however much he may rejoice in the fact of his endurance, he would still prefer that there were nothing to endure. In adversity I long for prosperity, in prosperity I fear adversity. What middle place is there between these two when the life of man is not all trial? All the prosperities of this world are cursed once and again —by the fear of adversity and by the corruption of joy. And the adversities of this world are cursed once, twice, and three times—by the longing for prosperity, by the very bitterness of adversity itself, and by the fear that it may break down our endurance. Is it not true, then, that the life of man upon earth is all trial without intermission?

29   AND ALL MY HOPE is nowhere except in your great mercy. Grant us what you command, and command us what you will. You demand that we should be continent. And *when I knew,* as it is said, *that no man can be continent, unless God give it, this also was a part of wisdom to know whose gift she is.* Certainly it is by continence that we are brought together and brought back to the One, after having dissipated ourselves among the Many. For he loves you insufficiently who loves something else with you which he does not love for your sake. O love, ever burning, and never extinguished, char-

ity, my God, set me on fire! You command continence. Grant what you command, and command what you will.

30 CERTAINLY you command me to restrain myself from the *lust of the flesh, the lust of the eyes, and the ambition of the world.* You commanded me to abstain from sleeping with a mistress, and with regard to marriage you advised me to take a better course than the one that was permitted me. And since you gave me the power, it was done, even before I became a dispenser of your Sacrament. But there still live in that memory of mine, of which I have spoken so much, images of the things which my habit has fixed there. These images come into my thoughts, and, though when I am awake they are strengthless, in sleep they not only cause pleasure but go so far as to obtain assent and something very like reality. These images, though real, have such an effect on my soul, in my flesh, that false visions in my sleep obtain from me what true visions cannot when I am awake. Surely, Lord my God, I am myself when I am asleep? And yet there is a very great difference between myself and myself in that moment of time when I pass from being awake to being asleep or come back again from sleep to wakefulness. Where then is my reason which, when I am awake, resists such suggestions and remains unshaken if the realities themselves were presented to it? Do reason's eyes close with the eyes of the body? Does reason go to sleep when the bodily senses sleep? If so, how does it happen that even in our sleep we do often resist and, remembering our purpose and most chastely abiding by it, give no assent to enticements of this kind? Nevertheless, there is a great difference, because, when it happens otherwise, we return on waking to a peace of conscience and, by the very remoteness of our state now and then, discover that it was not we who did something which was, to our regret, somehow or other done in us.

Almighty God, surely your hand is powerful enough to cure all the sicknesses of my soul and, with a more abundant measure of your grace, to quench even the lustful impulses of my sleep. Lord, you will increase your

gifts in me more and more, so that my soul, disentangled
from the birdlime of concupiscence, may follow me to
you; so that it may not be in revolt against itself and may
not, even in dreams, succumb to or even give the slightest
assent to those degrading corruptions which by means of
sensual images actually disturb and pollute the flesh. It is
not a hard thing for you, Almighty, who are *able to do
above all that we ask or think*, to prevent anything of this
sort, not even the very slightest inclination (so small that
a mere nod would check it), from affecting the chaste
mind of a sleeper—and to prevent it not only in this life
but at this age at which I am now. But now I have explained to my good Lord what is still my state in this
kind of evil, *rejoicing with trembling* in your gifts and
grieving for my imperfection and hoping that you will
perfect your mercies in me till I reach that fullness of
peace which both my inward and my outer self will have
with you when *death shall be swallowed up in victory*.

31 THERE IS ANOTHER *evil of the day*, and I wish that
it were *sufficient for it*. It is by eating and drinking that we repair the losses suffered by the body every
day until the time comes when you *destroy both belly
and meat*, when you kill all need with a wonderful fullness, and *clothe this corruptible* with an eternal *incorrup-
tion*. But now this necessity is sweet to me, and I fight
against this sweetness, so that I may not become its
prisoner; by fasting I carry on war every day, often
bringing my body into subjection, and the pain I suffer
in this way is driven out by pleasure. For hunger and
thirst are pains; they burn us up and kill us like a fever,
unless we are relieved by the medicine of nourishment.
And this nourishment is at hand by the consolation of
your gifts, in which earth and water and sky serve our
weakness, and so our calamity is called our delight.

This you have taught me, that I should have the same
attitude toward taking food as I have toward taking
medicine. But while I pass from the discomfort of hunger
to the satisfaction of sufficiency, in that very moment of
transition there is set for me a snare of concupiscence.

For the moment of transition is pleasurable, and we are forced to go through that moment; there is no other way. And while we eat and drink for the sake of health, there is a dangerous kind of pleasure which follows in attendance on health and very often tries to put itself first, so that what I say that I am doing, and mean to do, for the sake of my health is actually done for the sake of pleasure. Nor is there the same measure for both; what is enough for health is not enough for pleasure, and it is often hard to tell whether it is the necessary care of my body asking for sustenance or whether it is a deceitful voluptuousness of greed trying to seduce me. And because of this uncertainty the unhappy soul is delighted; it uses it as a cover and excuse for itself, and is glad that it is not clearly evident what is sufficient for a healthy moderation, so that under the cloak of health it may hide the business of pleasure. Every day I try to resist these temptations; I call upon your right hand to help me, and I refer my perplexities to you, since I have not yet found a settled plan in this matter.

I hear the voice of my God commanding: *Let not your hearts be overcharged with surfeiting and drunkenness.* I have no inclination to drunkenness, and in your mercy you will keep me far from it; but overeating has sometimes crept up on your servant. You will have mercy, so that it may be far from me. For *no one can be continent unless you give it.* You give us many things that we pray for, and everything good that we receive before we pray we receive at your hands. I have never been a drunkard, but I have known drunkards who have been made sober by you. Therefore, it is your doing that some men have never been drunkards; it is your doing that others who have been drunkards should not always remain so, and it is also your doing that both sorts of men should know that it is your doing.

I heard another voice of yours: *Go not after thy lusts, and from thy pleasure turn away.* This too, by your gift, I heard and I have greatly loved it: *Neither if we eat, shall we abound; neither if we eat not, shall we lack,* that is to say, the one will not make me rich and the other will not make me miserable. And I heard too: *For I have learned in whatever state I am, therewith to be content; I know how to abound, and how to suffer need. I can do all things through Christ that strengtheneth me.* There indeed speaks one who is a soldier of the heavenly army, not dust, as we are. But *remember*, Lord, *that we are dust, and that of dust Thou hast made man*, and *he was lost and is found.* Nor did he do it by his own power (since he was the same dust)—he, I mean, whom I loved so much when he said such things through the breath of your inspiration. *I can do all things*, he says, *through Him that strengtheneth me.* Strengthen me, so that I can. Give what you command, and command what you will. Paul confesses that he has received, and when he glories, it is in the Lord that he glories. I have heard another also begging that he might receive: *Take from me*, he says, *the desires of the belly.* From which, O holy God, it appears that it is your gift when what you command to be done is done.

Good Father, you have taught me that *to the pure all things are pure;* but that *it is evil unto the man that eateth with offense*, and, that *every creature of Thine is good, and nothing to be refused, which is received with thanksgiving*, and that *meat commendeth us not to God*, and, that *no man should judge as in meat or drink*, and that *he which eateth, let him not despise him that eateth not, and let not him that eateth not, judge him that eateth.* These things I have learned, thanks and praise to you, my God, my master, knocking at my ears, enlightening my heart; deliver me from all temptation. It is not any uncleanness in the meat that I fear; it is the uncleanness of gluttony. I know that Noah was allowed to eat all kinds of meat that are good for food; that Elijah was fed with meat; that John the Baptist, who was endowed with the most remarkable abstinence, was not polluted by the living creatures, locusts, which were given him for food. I know too that Esau was deceived because of his greediness for lentils; that David reproached himself for desiring some water, and that our King was tempted not with meat, but with bread. And the reason why the Israelites in the wilderness deserved to be blamed was not because they desired meat but because, in desiring food, they murmured against the Lord.

Placed as I am among these temptations, I strive every day against concupiscence in eating and drinking; for this is not the sort of thing that I can decide to give up once and for all and never touch again, as I was able to do with sex. Therefore, I must keep a hold which is neither too loose nor too tight on the bridle of my throat. And it is scarcely possible, Lord, not to be carried slightly beyond the bounds of necessity. Anyone who can keep exactly within them is a great man and greatly should he praise your name. But I am not he, since I am a sinful man. Yet I too magnify your name, and *He maketh intercession to Thee* for my sins who *hath overcome the world;* numbering me among the *weak members* of His *body;* because *Thine eyes have seen* that of Him which is *imperfect, and in Thy book shall all be written.*

32 As TO THE ENTICEMENTS which come to us from the sense of smell, I am not much concerned with them. I do not miss them when they are absent, or reject them when they are present, and I am quite prepared to be without them altogether. So it seems to me, though I may be deceiving myself. For here too there is a sad kind of darkness, the darkness in which the abilities that are in me are hidden from me, so that when my mind questions itself about its own powers, it cannot be certain that its replies are trustworthy, because what is inside the mind is mostly hidden and remains hidden until revealed by experience, and in this life, which is described as a continuous trial, no one ought to feel sure that, just as he has been worse and become better, he may not also, after having been better, become worse. Our one hope, our one confidence, our one firm promise is your mercy.

33 THE DELIGHTS of the sense of hearing had a stronger grip and a greater authority over me; but you loosed the bond and set me free. Yet now when I hear sung in a sweet and well-trained voice those melodies into which your words breathe life, I do, I admit, feel some pleasurable relaxation, though not of the kind

which would make it difficult for me to tear myself away, for I could get up and leave when I like. Nevertheless they do demand a place of some dignity in my heart so that they may be received into me together with the words that give them life, and it is not easy for me to give them exactly the right place. For sometimes it seems to me that I am giving them more honor than is right. I may feel that when these holy words themselves are well sung, our minds are stirred up more fervently and more religiously into a flame of devotion than if they are not so well sung, and I realize that the emotions of the spirit are various, each, by some secret kind of correspondence, capable of being excited by its own proper mode of voice or song. But I am often deceived by this pleasure of my flesh, to which the mind should not be given over to be enervated. The bodily sense only deserves to be admitted because of the reason; but often, instead of being content to follow behind reason, it tries to go ahead of reason and take the lead. So in these matters I sin without realizing it, only realizing afterward that I have sinned.

But at other times, when I am overanxious to avoid being deceived in this way, I fall into the error of being too severe—so much so that I would like banished both from my own ears and those of the Church as well the whole melody of sweet music that is used with David's Psalter—and the safer course seems to me that of Athanasius, bishop of Alexandria, who, as I have often been told, made the reader of the psalm employ so very small a modulation of the voice that the effect was more like speaking than singing. But then I remember the tears I shed at the singing in church at the time when I was beginning to recover my faith; I remember that now I am moved not by the singing but by the things that are sung, when they are sung with a clear voice and correct modulation, and once again I recognize the great utility of this institution. So I fluctuate between the danger of pleasure and my experience of the good that can be done. I am inclined on the whole (though I do not regard this opinion as irrevocable) to be in favor of the practice of singing in church, so that by means of the delight in hearing the weaker minds may be roused to a feeling of devotion. Nevertheless, whenever it happens to me that I am more moved by the singing than by what is sung, I confess that I am sinning grievously, and then I would prefer not to hear the music. See what a state I am in! I hope that you will weep with me and weep for me, all those of you who have inside you some of the good feeling from which good actions come. Those of you who have not, will not be moved by these things. And I pray that you, my Lord God, will hear me and look down upon me and see me and cure me. In your eyes I have become a problem to myself, and *that is my infirmity*.

34 THERE REMAINS the pleasure of these eyes of my flesh, and it is of this pleasure that I now make my confessions in the hearing of the ears of your temple— those brotherly and devout ears. With this I shall conclude the account of the temptations arising from *the lust of the flesh*, temptations which still beset me, *groaning earnestly, and desiring to be clothed with my house that is from heaven*.

The eyes love beautiful shapes of all kinds, glowing and delightful colors. These things must not take hold on my soul; that is for God to do. Certainly God made these things very good, but it is He Himself, not these things, who is my good. These things affect me during all the time every day that I am awake. I get no respite from them, as I get from the sounds of music and sometimes, in silence, from all sounds. For light is the queen of colors, and wherever I am in daytime she is suffused over everything visible; she glides up to me in shape after shape, cajoling me when I am doing something quite different and am paying no deliberate attention to her. But she makes her way so forcibly into my mind that, if light is suddenly withdrawn, I look for it again with longing, and if it is absent for long, my mind grows sad.

Let me think of that light which Tobias saw when, with these eyes shut, he showed his son the way of life and, with the feet of charity, went in front of him and never missed the path. Or the light which Isaac saw when, with his fleshly eyes heavy and dim with age, it was granted him to bless his sons without being able to see which was which, and yet in the act of blessing to gain the power of distinguishing between them. Or the light which Jacob saw when he also had become blind through great age; yet his heart was illumined and in the persons of his sons he shed light on the tribes of the future which were foreshadowed by them, and he laid his hands, mystically reversed, on his grandchildren, the sons of Joseph, not as their father, seeing from without, directed, but according to his own inner discernment. This is light itself; it is one, and all who see it and love it are one. As to that corporeal light, of which I was speaking, it is a tempting and dangerous sweetness, like a sauce spread over the life of this world for its blind lovers. Yet those who know how to praise you for this light, "Creator Thou of everything," carry it up to you in your hymn, and are not carried away by it into spiritual sleep. So I would like to be. I resist these seductions of the eyes, so that my feet with which I walk your way may not be ensnared, and to you I lift up my invisible eyes, so that you may *pluck my feet out of the snare*. Repeatedly you do pluck them out, for they are ensnared. You do not cease to pluck them out, while I so frequently entangle myself in the traps spread around me on all sides; because *Thou that keepest Israel shalt neither slumber nor sleep*.

And to the temptations of the eyes, men themselves in their various arts and manufactures have made innumerable additions: clothes, shoes, vases, products of craftsmanship; pictures too and all sorts of statues—far beyond what is necessary for use, moderate or with any religious meaning. So men go outside themselves to follow things of their own making, and inside themselves they are forsaking Him who made them and are destroying what they themselves were made to be. But I, my God and my glory, find here also something from which to make a hymn to you, and I offer my praise in sacrifice to Him who sanctifies me. Because all those beauties which pass through men's souls into their skillful hands come from that Beauty which is above souls and for which my soul is sighing day and night. From it artists and enthusiasts for external beauties derive the criterion by which to judge what is beautiful or not, but they do not find the rule for making the right use of these forms of beauty. Yet the rule is there, though they do not see it—a rule telling them not to go too far, and to keep their strength for you instead of dissipating it upon delights that end in lassitude. Yet I who am saying this and who see the truth of what I say still entangle my steps in these outer beauties. But you will pluck me out, Lord, you will pluck me out, *because Thy loving kindness is before my eyes.* For I am most pitifully caught up by them, but you will pity me and pluck me out, and sometimes, when I am only lightly caught in the trap, I scarcely realize what you are doing; sometimes, when I have become deeply implicated, I feel pain.

35   I MUST NOW mention another form of temptation which is in many ways more dangerous. Apart from the concupiscence of the flesh which is present in the delight we take in all the pleasures of the senses (and the slaves of it perish as they put themselves far from you), there is also present in the soul, by means of these same bodily senses, a kind of empty longing and curiosity which aims not at taking pleasure in the flesh but at acquiring experience through the flesh, and this empty curiosity is dignified by the names of learning and science. Since this is in the appetite for knowing, and since the eyes are the chief of our senses for acquiring knowledge, it is called in the divine language *the lust of the eyes.* For "to see" is used properly of the eyes; but we also use this word of the other senses when we are employing them for the purpose of gaining knowledge. We do not say: "Hear how it flashes" or "Smell how bright it is" or "Taste how it shines" or "Feel how it gleams"; in all these cases we use the verb "to see." But we not only say: "See how it shines," a thing which can only be perceived by the eyes; we also say "See how it sounds," "See how it smells," "See how it tastes," "See how hard it is." Therefore, the general experience of the senses is, as was said before, called "the lust of the eyes," because seeing, which belongs properly to the eyes, is used by analogy of the

other senses too when they are attempting to discover any kind of knowledge.

In this it is easy to see how pleasure and curiosity have different objects in their use of the senses. Pleasure goes after what is beautiful to us, sweet to hear, to smell, to taste, to touch; but curiosity, for the sake of experiment, may go after the exact opposites of these, not in order to suffer discomfort, but simply because of the lust to find out and to know. What pleasure can there be in looking at a mangled corpse, which must excite our horror? Yet if there is one near, people flock to see it, so as to grow sad and pale at the sight. They are actually frightened of seeing it in their sleep, as though anyone had forced them to see it when they were awake or as if they had been induced to look at it because it had the reputation of being a beautiful thing to see. The same is true of the other senses. There is no need to go to the length of producing examples. Because of this disease of curiosity monsters and anything out of the ordinary are put on show in our theaters. From the same motive men proceed to investigate the workings of nature which is beyond our ken—things which it does no good to know and which men only want to know for the sake of knowing. So too, and with this same end of perverted science, people make inquiries by means of magic. Even in religion we find the same thing: God is tempted when signs and portents are demanded and are not desired for any salutory purpose, but simply for the experience of seeing them.

In this enormous forest, so full of snares and dangers, many are the temptations which I have cut off and thrust away from my heart, as you, God of my salvation, have granted me the power. Yet since so many things of this kind are buzzing around our daily life in all directions, how can I dare to say, how can I ever dare to say that nothing of this sort can make me give my attention to it or fill me with the empty desire to possess it? True that I am no longer carried away by the theater; I am not interested in knowing about the courses of the stars; my soul has never made inquiries from the ghosts of the dead; I detest all sacrilegious mysteries. Yet, my Lord

God, to whom I owe my humble and pure service, there are all kinds of artifices of suggestion by which the enemy urges me to seek for some sign from you. But I beg you by our King and by our country Jerusalem, the chaste and pure, that just as up to now it has been far from me to give my assent to such suggestions, so the possibility of doing so may become more and more remote. But when I pray to you for the good of someone else my mind is directed to a quite different end; you do as you will, and you give and will give me the grace cheerfully to accept your will.

Nevertheless, there are very many occasions, small and contemptible enough, in which this curiosity of ours is tempted every day, and it is impossible to count the times when we slip. It often happens that people talk to us in some empty idle way, and we listen to them tolerantly at first, so as not to give offense to the weak; but then we gradually begin to take a serious interest in their gossip. I no longer go to the Games to see a dog coursing a hare; but if I happen to be going through the country and see this sport going on, it may attract my attention away from some serious meditation—not so much as to make me turn my horse's body out of the way, but enough to alter the inclination of my mind. And unless you showed me my infirmity and quickly admonished me either by some thought connected with the sight itself to rise up toward you, or else to pay no attention to the thing at all and to pass by, I should stand there empty-headed like a stock. And then there are all the occasions when I am sitting at home and my attention is attracted by a lizard catching flies or by a spider entangling them in his web. The animals may be small, but this does not make the thing any different. I go on from them to praise you, wonderful Creator and Director of all things; but it was not this that first drew my attention. It is one thing to get up quickly and another thing not to fall down. My life is full of such things and my only hope is in your great, great mercy. For when our heart is made the receptacle for things of this kind and becomes laden with pressing throngs of vanity, the result is that even our prayers are interrupted and disturbed, and when, in your presence, we are directing the voice of our heart to your ears, our great and serious purpose is broken off by an invasion of idle empty thoughts, coming from I know not where.

36 CERTAINLY WE CANNOT regard this as among things of little importance. And there is nothing to bring us back to hope except your known mercy, since you have begun to change us.

And you know how far you have already changed me, you who first cured me of my lust for asserting myself against others, so that you may be merciful also to the rest of my iniquities, *and heal all my infirmities, and redeem my life from corruption, and crown me with mercy and pity, and satisfy my desire with good things:* you who curbed my pride with your fear and tamed my neck to your yoke. And now I bear that yoke and I find it light. This was what you promised and this is what you have done. And indeed it always was light, though I did not know it in the time when I was afraid to take it upon me.

But tell me, Lord, you who alone are Lord without pride, because you are alone the true Lord, who has no other Lord, has this third kind of temptation disappeared from me, or can it ever entirely disappear in this life? I mean the wish to be feared and loved by men for no other reason but to get from it a joy, which is no true joy. It is a wretched way of life, a disgusting kind of ostentation. Here in particular we may find the reason why you are not purely loved or feared, and therefore *dost Thou resist the proud, and givest grace to the humble*, and you thunder down upon the ambitions of this world, and *the foundations of the mountains tremble*. And so, because there are certain positions in human society where the holder of office must be loved and feared by men, the enemy of our true happiness is always close upon us, setting his snares everywhere in the words "Well done, well done," and hoping that, while we greedily snatch at them, we shall be taken unawares, shall no longer plan our joy in your truth but shall entrust it to the deceitfulness of men, and shall want to be loved and feared not because of you but instead of you. In this way our enemy will make us become like him and will have us united to him not in the bonds of charity but in the bonds of punishment—he who decided to *set his throne in the north*, so that there, in cold and darkness, men might become his slaves as he attempts pervertedly and crookedly to imitate you. But as to us, Lord, see, we are your *little flock*. Keep us in your possession. Stretch out your wings so that we may take refuge beneath them. It is you who must be our glory; let us be loved for your sake, and let it be your word that is feared in us. The man who wishes to be praised by men regardless of your approval will not be defended by men when you judge him, nor delivered by men when you condemn him. It may not be the case of a *sinner being praised in the desires of his soul* or a man *blessed who doth ungodlily;* it may be that a man is praised for some gift which you have given him and takes more pleasure in hearing himself praised than in having that gift for which he is praised; this man too is praised by men, but blamed by you, and those who praise him are better than he who is praised; for what gives them pleasure is the gift of God in a man, but he takes more pleasure in what men give than in what God has given.

37   WE ARE TEMPTED, Lord, by these temptations every day; without intermission we are tempted. The tongue of man is the furnace in which we are tried every day. Here too you command us to be continent. Give what you command, and command what you will. You know how on this matter my heart groans to you and my eyes stream tears. For I cannot easily discover how far I have become cleaner from this disease, and I much fear my hidden sins which are visible to your eyes, though not to mine. For in other kinds of temptation I have at least some means of finding out about myself; but in this kind it is almost impossible. With regard to the pleasures of the flesh and the unnecessary curiosity for knowledge I can see how far I have advanced in the

ability to control my mind simply by observing myself
when I am without these things, either from choice or
when they are not available. For I can then ask myself how
much or how little I mind not having them. So too with
regard to riches, which are desired for the satisfaction of
one or two or all of those three concupiscences; if one is
not able to be quite sure in one's own mind whether or
not one despises them when one has them, it is possible
to get rid of them so as to put oneself to the test. But
how can we arrange things so as to be without praise and
make the same experiment with regard to it? Are we to
live a bad life, to live in such a wicked and abandoned way
that everyone who knows us will detest us? Nothing
could be madder than such a suggestion as that. On the
contrary, if praise both goes with and ought to go with
a good life and good works, we should no more part with
it than with the good life itself. Yet unless a thing is not
there I cannot tell whether it is difficult or easy for me to
be without it.

With regard to this kind of temptation then, what,
Lord, shall I confess? This I can say, that I take pleasure
in praise, but more pleasure in truth than in praise. For
if I were given the choice of either being out of my wits
and wrong on every subject, yet praised by everyone, or
being firm and sure in the truth, yet abused by everyone,
I know which I should choose. Yet I wish it were not
the case that when someone else praises me, my joy in
whatever good quality I may have is increased. It is increased however, I admit; not only that, but it is diminished by dispraise. And when I am troubled at this
wretched state of mine, an excuse occurs to me, whether
it is a good one or not, you, God, know; for it leaves me
uncertain. You demand from us not only continence—
that is, to restrain our love from certain things—but also
justice—that is, to direct our love upon certain things—
and it is your will not only that we should love you but
also that we should love our neighbor. So it often seems
to me that when I am pleased by intelligent praise I am
pleased because of the sound judgment or the promise
shown by my neighbor, and in the same way it is his
faults that make me sad when I hear him dispraise some-

thing which he does not understand or which is good. For there are also times when I feel sad to hear myself praised, either when people praise things in me which I dislike in myself or when some trifling and unimportant good qualities in me are rated at more than their proper value. But again I am in doubt: do I feel like this simply because I do not want a man who praises me to think about me differently from the way I think myself? And am I moved not so much by what is good for him as by the fact that those good qualities of mine which I approve of in myself are all the more pleasing to me when someone else approves of them too? For in a sense I am not being praised when my own opinion of myself is not praised, when, that is, qualities of mine are praised of which I myself do not approve, or when a high value is set on things in me which I regard as unimportant. It seems then that I am doubtful of myself in this matter.

Yes, Truth, in you I see that when I am praised the pleasure I feel should not be for my own sake but for the sake of the good of my neighbor. But whether this is really how I do feel I do not know. In this matter I know less of myself than of you. I beg you, my God, to show me myself, so that I may confess the fault that is in me to my brethren who will pray for me. Let me question myself again more carefully. If, when I hear myself praised, I am moved by thoughts of the good of my neighbor, why is it that I am less moved when someone else is unjustly blamed than when I myself am unjustly blamed? Why am I more wounded by a reproach leveled against me than by one which, with equal injustice, is, while I am present, leveled against someone else? Am I ignorant of this too? Or is not the fact simply this, that I deceive myself and in your presence fail to be truthful in heart and tongue? Put this madness far from me, Lord, lest my own mouth be to me the *sinner's oil to make fat my head*.

38 *I am poor and needy*, yet I am the better when, groaning secretly in my dissatisfaction with myself, I seek your mercy till the time comes when what is

defective in me will be made good and brought to perfection in that peace which is unknown to the eye of the proud. Words which come from the mouth and actions which are known to men carry with them a most dangerous temptation from the love of praise which goes around as it were canvassing and collecting votes for the advancement of one's personal distinction. It still tempts me even when I condemn it in myself; indeed it tempts me even in the very act of condemning it; often in our contempt of vainglory we are merely being all the more vainglorious, and so one cannot really say that one glories in the contempt of glory; for one does not feel contempt for something in which one glories.

39 INSIDE US TOO is another evil belonging to the same class of temptation. It is the vanity of those who are pleased with themselves, however much they may not please others, or may displease them, or may not care whether they please them or not. But those who are pleased with themselves certainly do not please you. Here it is not so much a case of taking pleasure in things that are not good as though they were good; the fault is in taking pleasure in good things which come from you as though they came from oneself; or, even if they are acknowledged as coming from you, in assuming that one deserves to have them; or, even if it is admitted that they are due to your grace, in not rejoicing with their brethren but envying your grace to others. In all these and other similar dangers and difficulties you see the trembling of my heart, and often as you heal my wounds I feel new wounds being inflicted upon me.

40 WHEN HAVE YOU not walked with me, O Truth, teaching me what to beware of and what to seek after, when I referred to you what I have been able to see here below and asked your advice? With my outward senses I surveyed, to the best of my ability, the world, and I observed both the life which my body has from me and these senses themselves. From these I entered into

the recesses of my memory, space folded upon huge space
and all miraculously full of innumerable abundance, and
I considered it and I was amazed; no one of all the things
there could I discover without you, and I did not find
any of them was you. Nor was I myself the discoverer,
though I went through them all and tried to distinguish
each from each, estimating them according to their proper
worth, taking some things on the report of my senses,
questioning others which I felt to be somehow parts of
myself, and I counted and distinguished between these
messengers, and now in the vast treasury of my memory
I would meditate on something stored there, or put something away or take something out. But it was not I myself
who did all this—that is to say, the power by which I
did it was not myself—nor were you that power, because
you are the permanent and abiding light which I consulted on all these things, asking whether they are, what
they are, and what they are worth. And I heard you
teaching me and commanding me. And I often do this.
I find a delight in it, and whenever I can relax from my
necessary duties I have recourse to this pleasure. And in
all these things over which I range as I am consulting you
I find no secure place for my soul except in you, and in
you I pray that what is scattered in me may be brought
together so that nothing of me may depart from you. And
sometimes working within me you open for me a door
into a state of feeling which is quite unlike anything to
which I am used—a kind of sweet delight which, if I
could only remain permanently in that state, would be
something not of this world, not of this life. But my sad
weight makes me fall back again; I am swallowed up by
normality; I am held fast and heavily do I weep, but
heavily I am held. So much are we weighed down by the
burden of custom! Here I have the power but not the
wish to stay; there I wish to be but cannot; both ways,
miserable.

41   So, UNDER THE HEADINGS of the three forms of
      concupiscence I have considered the sicknesses of
my sins, and I have called your right hand to my help.

For I have seen your splendor, but my own heart has been wounded; I have been beaten back and have said: Who can reach there? *I am cast away from the sight of Thine eyes.* You are Truth presiding over everything. But I in my covetousness, while not wanting to lose you, wanted at the same time to possess a lie; just as no man wants to speak so falsely that he himself ceases to be conscious of the truth. And this was why I lost you, because you will not be possessed together with a lie.

42   WHOM COULD I FIND to reconcile me to you? Was I to seek the help of angels? By what prayer, what sacraments? Many people in their attempts to return to you and not being able to do so by their own strength have, so I hear, tried this way and have fallen into a desire for strange visions and have become, rightly, the victims of delusions. For in seeking you they have drawn themselves up in the arrogance of their learning; they have thrown out their chests instead of beating their breasts, and so through likeness of heart they drew to themselves the *princes of the air* as their fellow-conspirators in pride and were deceived by them through magical powers. They were seeking a mediator through whom to become clean, but this was not he. It was the devil, *transforming himself into an angel of light*, and for proud flesh it proved a strong attraction that he himself had not a body of flesh. For they were mortal and sinners; you, Lord, to whom they wished to be reconciled, are immortal and without sin. So a mediator between God and men should have something in common with God and something in common with men. If he were in both respects like men, he would be far from God, and if he were in both respects like God, he would be far from men, and so neither way could he be a mediator. But that deceitful mediator, by whom, according to your secret judgment, pride deserves to be mocked, has one thing in common with men—namely, sin—and appears to have another thing in common with God—that is that, not being clothed in the mortality of flesh, he can pretend to be immortal.

But, since *the wages of sin is death*, he has this in common with men—that he, like them, is condemned to death.

43 But the true mediator whom in your secret mercy you have shown to men and have sent Him so that they, by His example, might learn humility, that *Mediator between God and man, the Man Christ Jesus*, appeared between mortal sinners and the immortal Just One: mortal with men, just with God; so that, because the wages of justice is life and peace, He might, by a justice conjoined with God, make void the death of those sinners who were justified by Him; for He was willing to let that death be common both to Him and to them. He was revealed to the holy men of old so that they might be saved through faith in His passion that was to come, just as we may be saved through faith in His passion now that it is in the past. For insofar as He is man, He is mediator; but insofar as He is the Word, He is not midway between God and man; for He is equal to God, both God with God, and together one God.

How greatly have you loved us, good Father, who *sparedst not Thine only Son, but deliveredst Him up for us ungodly!* How you have loved us, for whom, *He that thought it no robbery to be equal with Thee, was made subject even to the death of the cross*. He alone free among the dead, *having power to lay down His life, and power to take it again*: for us He was to you both victor and victim, and victor because victim: for us He was to you both priest and sacrifice, and priest because sacrifice: and He made us sons to you instead of slaves by being born of you and by becoming your slave. With reason, then, my hope in Him is strong, that *Thou wilt heal all my infirmities* by Him who *sitteth at Thy right hand and maketh intercession for us;* otherwise I should despair. For many and great are my infirmities, many they are and great; but your medicine has more power still. We might have thought that your Word was far from any union with man, and we might have despaired, unless it had been *made flesh and dwelt among us*.

Terrified by my sins and the mass and weight of my

misery, I had pondered in my heart a purpose of flight to the wilderness. But you forbade me and gave me strength by saying: *Therefore Christ died for all, that they which live may now no longer live unto themselves, but unto Him that died for them*. See, Lord, *I cast my care upon Thee*, that I may live and *consider wondrous things out of Thy law*. You know my unskillfulness and my weakness; teach me and heal me. He, your only Son, *in Whom are hid all the treasures of wisdom and knowledge*, has redeemed me with His blood. *Let not the proud speak evil of me*, for my thoughts are on the price of my redemption; I eat it and drink it and give it to others to eat and drink, and, being poor myself, I desire to be satisfied by it among those that *eat and are satisfied, and they shall praise the Lord who seek Him*.

Book XI

1 LORD, SINCE ETERNITY is yours, can you be ignorant of what I say to you? Or do you see what happens in time only at the moment when it is happening? Why then do I put before you in order the stories of so many things? Not, certainly, so that you may come to know them through me, but to stir up my own and my readers' devotion toward you, so that we may all say: *Great is the Lord, and greatly to be praised.* I have said this before and I shall say it again: I do this for the love of your love. For we pray also in spite of the fact that Truth has said: *Your Father knoweth what you have need of, before you ask.* What we do, therefore, is to lay open our feelings to you, confessing to you our own wretchedness and your acts of mercy to us, so that you may set us entirely free, as you have already begun to free us, and we may cease to be wretched in ourselves and may become happy in you; for you have called us to be *poor in spirit, and meek, and mourners, and hungering and athirst after righteousness, and merciful, and pure in heart, and peacemakers.*

See, I have told you many things, so far as I could and with the will that I had, because you, my Lord God, first willed that I should make my confession to you; *for Thou art good, for Thy mercy endureth forever.*

2   BUT MY PEN's tongue will never have strength
to declare all your exhortations and your terrors,
the consolations and the guidance by which you brought
me to become a preacher of your word to your people
and a dispenser of your sacrament. And suppose I have
the strength to declare all this in order, yet the drops of
my time are too precious, and for long I have been full
of a burning desire to *meditate in Thy law* and to confess
to you both my knowledge and my lack of skill in it,
the first beginnings of the light you shed on me and the
remnants of my darkness, until my weakness be swallowed
up in strength. And I am reluctant to spend on anything
else the hours that I can find free from the necessities of
refreshing my body, intellectual labor, and the services
which we owe to others or, even if we do not owe them,
which we give to others.

My Lord God, listen to my prayer and let your mercy
give ear to my desire; it does not burn for myself alone,
but wishes to be of use in the service of brotherly charity,
and you see in my heart that this is so. I want to sacrifice
to you the service of my thought and of my tongue, and
I beg you to give me what I may offer to you. For *I am
poor and needy, Thou rich to all that call upon Thee.*
You are free from care, yet care for us. From all rashness
and all lying *circumcise my lips* both within and without.
Let your Scriptures be my chaste delight. Let me neither
be deceived in them nor deceive others by them. Lord,
listen and have pity, my Lord God, light of the blind and
strength of the weak, light too of the seeing and strength
of the strong, listen to my soul and hear its cry from the
depths. For unless your ears are there to hear us even
in the depths, whither shall we go? To whom shall we
cry?

The day is Thine, and the night is Thine; at your nod
the moments fly past. Grant me from them a space for my
meditations on *the hidden things of Thy law,* and do not
close your law against me when I knock. For it was not
for nothing that you willed that so many pages should be
filled with the writing of such dark secrets; nor are those
forests without their stags which shelter there and range
and walk, feeding, lying down, and chewing the cud.

O Lord, perfect me and reveal those pages to me! See, your voice is my joy; your voice surpasses all abundance of pleasures. Give me what I love, for I do love it, and that love too was your gift. Do not forsake your own gifts; do not despise your grass that is thirsty for you. Let me confess to you whatever I shall find in these books of yours, let me *hear the voice of praise*, let me drink of you and consider the *wonderful things out of Thy land*, from the *beginning* in which *Thou madest the heaven and the earth* until the coming of the time when we are with you in the everlasting kingdom of your holy city.

Lord, have pity on me and give ear to my desire. For it is not, I think, a desire for earthly things, not for gold and silver and precious stones, or beautiful clothes or honors or power or pleasures of the flesh, or for things necessary for the body and for this life of our pilgrimage, *all which shall be added unto those that seek Thy kingdom and Thy righteousness.* See, my God, from what my desire springs! *The wicked have told me of delights, but not such as Thy law, O Lord.* That is the reason for my desire. See, Father, look well at it, see and approve, and I pray that it may be pleasing in the sight of your mercy that I may find grace before you so that the inner secrets of your words may be laid open to me when I knock. This I beg by our Lord Jesus Christ, Thy Son, *the Man of Thy right hand, the Son of man, whom Thou hast established for Thyself* as the mediator between you and us, through whom you sought for us when we were not seeking you—indeed you sought us so that we might seek you—your *Word, through whom Thou madest all things*—and me among them—your only-begotten through whom you have called to adoption the people of believers and me among them—in His name I make my prayer to you, in His name who *sitteth at Thy right hand, and intercedeth with Thee for us, in Whom are hidden all the treasures of wisdom and knowledge.* These are the treasures I seek in your books. *Of Him did Moses write;* this he says and this Truth says.

3   I want to hear and I want to understand how "in the beginning you made heaven and earth." This is what Moses wrote; he wrote and went his way, passing hence from you to you; he is not now here in front of me. If he were, I should hold onto him and ask him and beg him in your name to explain these things to me; I should lay the ears of my body open to the sounds that would burst from his mouth, and if he spoke in Hebrew he would merely beat upon my hearing in vain; nothing of what was said would reach my mind; but if he spoke in Latin, I should know what he was saying. But how should I know whether what he said was true? And if I did know it, would it be from him that I knew it? No it would not; it would be from inside me, from that inner house of my thought, that Truth, which is neither Hebrew nor Greek nor Latin nor Barbarian, and which speaks without the aid of mouth or tongue, without any sound of syllables, would say: "He is speaking the truth," and at once I would be sure and I would say with perfect confidence to that servant of yours: "You are speaking the truth." Since, then, I am not able to question Moses, it is you that I ask, you, Truth, full of whom Moses spoke truth, you, my God, you I ask to forgive my sins and, just as you gave Moses the power to speak these words, give me the power to understand them.

4   See, there are the heaven and the earth. They cry aloud that they were created; for they change and vary. Whereas anything which exists but was not created cannot have anything in it which was not there before, and this is just what is meant by change and variation. They cry aloud also that they did not create themselves: "We exist because we were created; therefore we did not exist before we were in existence, so as to be able to create ourselves." And the voice of the speakers is in the very fact that they are there to be seen.

It was you, Lord, who made them, you who are beautiful (for they are beautiful), you who are good (for they are good), you who are (for they are). But they have neither the beauty, nor the goodness, nor the existence which you, their creator, have; compared with you they are not beautiful, not good, not in existence. This, thanks to you, we know, and our knowledge compared with your knowledge is ignorance.

5   But how did you make heaven and earth? What instrument did you use for this tremendous work of yours? You were not like a craftsman who forms one body from another as the result of an act of choice made in his mind, which has the power somehow to impress on material the form which it perceives inside itself with its inner eye. And how could it have this power except because you made it? And it imposes the form on something which already exists and has a body—clay, for instance, or stone or wood or gold or something of the sort. And how could these things have come into existence except because you made them to be? It was you who made for the craftsman his body, you who made the mind that directs his limbs, the material out of which he makes anything, the intelligence by which he grasps the principles of his art and sees inwardly what he is to make outwardly; you made his bodily sense by which he translates what he is doing from the mind to the material and then reports back again to the mind what has been done, so that the mind may within itself consult the truth presiding over it as to whether the work has been well done or not. All these things praise you, the Creator of all. But how do you make them? How, God, did you make heaven and earth? Certainly it was not in the heaven or in the earth that you made heaven and earth; nor was it in the air or in water, since these too belong to heaven and earth; nor was it in the universe that you made the universe, because there was no place for it to be made in until it was made to exist. Nor did you hold anything in your hand from which to make heaven and earth. For how could you have got something which you had not made to use for making things? For nothing exists except because you exist. Therefore *Thou spakest and they were made*, and *in Thy Word Thou madest them.*

6 BUT HOW DID YOU SPEAK? Was it in the same way as when the voice came from the cloud, saying: *This is my beloved Son?* That voice came and passed, had a beginning and an end. The syllables were heard and then ceased to be heard, the second after the first, the third after the second, and so on in order until the last came after all the others, and after the last there was silence. From this it is plain and evident that the voice was uttered through the motion of something created, something itself temporal, though serving your eternal will. And these words of yours, created in time, were reported by the outer ear to the intelligent soul, whose inner ear listened to your eternal word. But the soul compared those words which were pronounced in time with your eternal word which is in silence, and said: "It is different, utterly different. These words are far beneath me, indeed they are not at all, because they pass away and disappear; but the word of my God is above me and abides forever."

If, then, in words that are pronounced and pass away you said: "Let heaven and earth be made" and so created heaven and earth, there must have been in existence before heaven and earth a corporeal creature by whose motion in time that voice could sound and end in time. But there was no bodily thing in existence before heaven and earth; or, if there was, certainly you had not brought it into existence by means of an utterance made in time which would produce the conditions for making, later, another utterance in time by which to say: "Let the heaven and the earth be made." For whatever may have been the source of such a voice, it must have been made by you; otherwise it would not have existed at all. What word, then, did you use in order to produce a bodily substance by means of which these words could be created?

7 AND SO YOU call us to understand the Word who is God and God with you, the Word which is spoken eternally and by which all things are spoken eternally. For here it is not a case of first one thing being said and finished, then another thing so that all can be said: no, all things are said together and eternal-

ly. Otherwise there would be already time and change, and not a true eternity nor a true immortality. I know this, my God, and I thank you. I know it, Lord God, and I confess it to you. And everyone else who is not ungrateful to assured truth knows it as I do and praises you. We know, Lord, we know it; for insofar as a thing either ceases to be what it was or begins to be what it was not, to that extent it is undergoing death or birth. Therefore nothing in your Word can pass away and then be replaced, because your Word is truly immortal and eternal. So it is by a word coeternal with you that you say, together and eternally, all that you say, and everything is made that you say is to be made. Yet all the things which you make by saying are not made together and eternally.

8 But why, I beseech you, my Lord God? I see it in a way, but I do not know how to express it, except that everything which begins to exist and ceases to exist begins at that moment and ceases at that moment when in the eternal reason it is known that it ought to begin and ought to cease, and in that Reason there is no beginning and no ending. This is your Word which is also *the Beginning because also It speaketh unto us*. He says this in the Gospel, speaking through the flesh, and this sound was heard outwardly by the ears of men so that it might be believed and sought for inwardly and found in the eternal Truth, which is where the good and only master teaches all his disciples. It is there, Lord, that I hear your voice as you speak to me; for it is our teacher who speaks to us, and he who is not our teacher, even if he speaks, is not speaking to us. And who is our teacher except the steadfast truth? For even when we learn something by means of a changing creature it is to this steadfast truth that we are led, and then we truly learn *while we stand and hear Him*, and *rejoice greatly because of the Bridegroom's voice*, giving ourselves back to that from which we are. And that, therefore, is the Beginning, because if it did not remain there would be nowhere to which, after going astray, we could return. But when we return from error, we return by realizing the Truth,

and it is by His teaching that we do realize the Truth, *because* He is *the Beginning and speaking unto us.*

9   IT WAS IN this beginning, God, that you made heaven and earth—speaking wonderfully, creating wonderfully in your Word, your Son, your power, your wisdom, your truth. Who shall understand this? Who shall put it into words? What is that light that shines through me and strikes my heart without hurting it? And I am both terrified and set on fire. Terrified insofar as I am unlike it, on fire insofar as I am akin to it. It is Wisdom, Wisdom herself that shines through me, splitting through the cloud in which I am wrapped and which, as I faint away from it, again enfolds me in the thick mist and weight of my punishment. For *my strength is brought down in need,* so that I cannot support my good, till you, Lord, who have been *gracious to all mine iniquities* shall *heal all my infirmities.* For *Thou shalt also redeem my life from corruption, and crown me with loving kindness and tender mercies, and shalt satisfy my desire with good things, because my youth shall be renewed like an eagle's.* For *in hope we are saved,* therefore *we through patience wait for* your promises. Let him that is able hear your discourse deep within him. I, in the words of your oracle, will confidently cry out: *How wonderful are Thy works, O Lord, in Wisdom hast Thou made them all,* and that Wisdom is "the Beginning," and in that Beginning you made heaven and earth.

10   CERTAINLY IT IS a mark of being full of the old error when people say to us: "What was God doing before He made heaven and earth?" Their argument is as follows: If God was unoccupied with the making of anything, why did He not go on forever remaining in the same state as that in which He had always been? For if there came into existence in God a new motion and a new will to make something which He had never made before, how can one call it a true eternity, when a will arises which was not previously in existence? For the will of God is not a creature; it is prior to all creation, because nothing could be created unless the will of the creator had come first. Therefore, God's will belongs to the very substance of God. But if something which was previously not there arose in God's substance, then one could not truly call that substance eternal. If, on the other hand, God's will that there should be a creation had been in existence from eternity, why is creation also not from eternity?

11 THOSE WHO SAY this do not yet understand you, O Wisdom of God, light of minds. They do not yet understand how these things are made which are made by you and in you, and they are trying to taste eternity while their mind is still fluttering about in the past and future movements of things, and so is still unstable.

Can we not hold the mind and fix it firm so that it may stand still for a moment and for a moment lay hold upon the splendor of eternity which stands forever, and compare it with the times that never stand, and see that no comparison is possible? Then it would see that a long time is long only because of the numbers of movements passing by in succession, which cannot have a simultaneous extension; but that in eternity nothing passes by; everything is present, whereas time cannot be present all at once. It would be seen too that all time past is driven on by time future, and all the future follows from the past, and that both past and future are created by and proceed from that which is perpetually present. Who can so hold the mind of man that it may stand and see how eternity, which stands still and is neither past nor future, dictates the times that are past and the times that are to come? Could my hand have strength enough, or could the hand of my mouth by speech achieve so great a thing?

12 AND NOW I HAVE my answer to the man who says: "What was God doing before He made heaven and earth?" Someone once, evading the force of this question, is said to have made the jesting reply: "God

was making hells for people who look too deeply into things." This is not my answer. To make a joke about something does not mean that one understands the subject. No, that is not my answer. Personally I would rather say: "I don't know," when I don't know, than make that kind of reply which brings ridicule on someone who has asked a deep question and wins praise for an inaccurate answer.

But I say that you, our God, are the creator of every creature, and if by "heaven and earth" we mean "every creature," I boldly declare that: "Before God made heaven and earth, He did not make anything." For if He did, it could have been nothing else except a creature. And I wish I knew all those good and useful things which I want to know as clearly as I know this, that before there was any creature in existence there was no creature in existence.

13   A MAN MAY LET his fluttering mind wander through images of times past and may feel surprise at the thought that you, God all-powerful, all-creating, and all-supporting, the maker of heaven and earth, abstained from so vast a work for all those countless ages before you brought it into existence. Anyone who thinks like this should wake up and reflect that his reasons for surprise are false ones. For how could countless ages pass by, when you, the author and creator of all ages, had not yet made them? What times could there have been which were not created by you? And how could they pass by, if they had never been in existence?

So, since it is by your work that all times are made, how can it be said, if there was a time before you made heaven and earth, that you were abstaining from your work? That time itself was of your creation, and no times could pass by before you made those times. If, on the other hand, there was no time before the creation of heaven and earth, the question "What were you doing then?" is meaningless. For when there was no time, there was no "then."

When we say that you are before times, we cannot

mean that you are before them in time; otherwise you would not be before all times. You are before all the past in the sublimity of your ever-present eternity, and you are above all future things because they are still to come, and when they have come they will be past; *but Thou art the Same*, and *Thy years fail not*. Your years neither go nor come; but these years of ours go and come, so that they may all come. Your years stand still all together, because they do stand still; the going years are not thrust out by the coming years, since there is no passing from one state to the other; but these years of ours will not all be until all will have ceased to be. Your years are one day, and your day does not come daily, but is today, because your today is followed by no tomorrow and comes after no yesterday. Your today is eternity, and so it was that you begot one who is coeternal with you to whom you said: *This day have I begotten Thee*. You made all times and before all times you are; nor was there ever a time in which there was no time.

14   THEREFORE, since you made time itself, one cannot say that there was any time in which you had not made anything. And no times are coeternal with you, because you are permanent, whereas, if they were permanent, they would not be times. What then is time? Who can find a quick and easy answer to that question? Whoever in his mind can grasp the subject well enough to be able to make a statement on it? Yet in our ordinary conversation we use the word "time" more often and more familiarly than any other. And certainly we understand what we mean by it, just as we understand what others mean by it when we hear the word from them.

What then is time? I know what it is if no one asks me what it is; but if I want to explain it to someone who has asked me, I find that I do not know. Nevertheless, I can confidently assert that I know this: that if nothing passed away there would be no past time, and if nothing were coming there would be no future time, and if nothing were now there would be no present time.

But in what sense can we say that those two times, the

past and the future, exist, when the past no longer is and the future is not yet? Yet if the present were always present and did not go by into the past, it would not be time at all, but eternity. If, therefore, the present (if it is to be time at all) only comes into existence because it is in transition toward the past, how can we say that even the present *is?* For the cause of its being is that it shall cease to be. So that it appears that we cannot truly say that time exists except in the sense that it is tending toward nonexistence.

15   NEVERTHELESS, we say " a long time" and "a short time," though we only use these expressions about the past and the future. A hundred years ago, for instance, we say is a long time past, and a hundred years from now a long time ahead; ten days ago a short time past, ten days from now a short time ahead. But how can we say that something which does not exist at all is either long or short? For the past no longer is, and the future has not yet come to be. Should we then not say: "It is long?" Should we instead say of the past: "It was long" and of the future: "It will be long"?

My Lord, my light, is it not so that here also man is mocked by your truth? For as to this time in the past that was long, when was it long? When it was already past or when it was still present? It could be long only while it was in existence to be long. But once past, it had ceased to exist. So, not being in existence at all, it could not be long.

Therefore we must not say: "the time past was long"; for we shall not find anything in it which could be long, since from the moment when it becomes past, it ceases to exist. Let us say instead: "that particular present time was long," because while it was present, it was long. For it had not yet passed away so as not to exist, and consequently there was something which could be long; though once it had passed away, it ceased to be long by also ceasing to exist.

Let us see, therefore, soul of man, whether present time can be long. For to you, soul of man, it has been granted to feel spaces of time and to measure them. Now what answer will you give me?

Is a present time of a hundred years a long time? But first let us see whether a hundred years can be present. If we are in the first of these years, it is present, but the ninety-nine other years are still to come and therefore do not yet exist. And if we are in the second year, one year is already past, one is present, and the rest are to come. In the same way, whatever year we may care to choose in the hundred-year series as being present, all the years before it will be past and all the years after it will be future. Therefore a hundred years cannot be present.

But let us at least see whether this one year itself which we have selected is present. Here too, if we are in the first month, the other months are still to come, and if we are in the second month, the first is already in the past and the others do not yet exist. For a year is twelve months, of which just that one month in which we are is present, all the rest being either past or future. Yet even the month in which we are is not present; only one day of it is. If that day is the first, the other days are still to come; if the last, all the other days are in the past; if any intermediate day, it is between days past and days to come.

So now we see that this "present time," which we discovered to be the only time that could be called "long," has contracted to the space of scarcely one day. But let us look into this one day too, because not even a single day is wholly present. It (including the hours of day and night) is made up of twenty-four hours; the first of these has all the other hours still to come; the last has them all in the past; any intermediate hour has those before it in the past, those after it in the future. And that very hour itself is made of fleeting moments; whatever part of these has fled away is in the past, whatever remains is in the future. If anything can be meant by a point of time so small that it cannot be divided into even the most minute particles of moments, that is the only time that can be called "present." And such a time must fly so rapidly from future to past that it has no duration and no extension. For if it does have any extension, it can be divided into past and future; whereas the present does not take up any space.

Where, then, is the time that we can call "long"? Is it in the future? But we cannot say of the future: "It is long," because it is not yet in existence to be long. We have to say: "It will be long." But when will it be long? If we are still imagining it in the future, it will not be long, because there will still not be anything in existence to be long. If, on the other hand, we say that it will be long at the moment when out of the future (which does not yet exist) it will begin to take on being and become present, so that there can be something in existence to be long, then the present cries aloud in the words which we have just heard that it cannot be long.

16   AND YET, LORD, we do perceive definite periods of time, and we compare them with each other and say that some are longer and others shorter. We even measure how much longer or shorter this time is than that, and we say that it is twice or three times as long, or equivalent—one time being of the same length as another. But when we measure time by our perception of it, it is time passing that we are measuring. For it is impossible to measure the past, which is no longer in existence, or the future which is not yet in existence, unless perhaps one is going to be rash enough to maintain that it is possible to measure something which does not exist. When, therefore, time is passing, it can be perceived and measured; but when it has passed, it cannot, because it does not exist.

17   I AM ASKING questions, Father, not making statements. My God, govern me and direct me. We learned at school and we teach at school that there are three times—past, present, and future. Am I now to be told that this is not so, that there is only the present, since the other two times do not exist? Or can we say that they do exist, but that there is some secret place from which time emerges when from the future the present comes

into existence, and again some secret place into which
it withdraws when the past comes out of the present? For
where can those who have prophesied the future see the
future, if the future is not yet in existence? For that which
does not exist cannot be seen. And those who tell us about
the past certainly could not tell us the truth unless they
saw it in their mind's eye, and if the past were nonexistent, it would be quite impossible for it to be perceived.
Therefore both the future and the past exist.

18 ALLOW ME, LORD, to push my questions further.
My hope, let me maintain this line of inquiry
without being distracted from it.

If the future and the past exist, I want to know where
they are. And if I still lack the strength to know this,
nevertheless one thing I do know, which is that, wherever
they are, they are not there as future and as past, but as
present. For if there too they are future, they are not yet
there, and if there too they are past, they are no longer
there. Thus, wherever they are, and whatever they are,
they cannot be anything except present. Although with
regard to the past, when this is reported correctly what
is brought out from the memory is not the events themselves (these are already past) but words conceived from
the images of those events, which, in passing through the
senses, have left as it were their footprints stamped upon
the mind. My boyhood, for instance, which no longer
exists, exists in time past, which no longer exists. But when
I recollect the image of my boyhood and tell others about
it, I am looking at this image in time present, because it
still exists in my memory. Whether a similar cause oper-
ates with regard to predictions of the future—namely,
that images of things which do not yet exist are felt in
advance as already existing—this, I confess, my God, I
do not know. But I do know this, that we often premedi-
tate our future actions, and this premeditation is present
while the action which we are premeditating, being in the
future, does not yet exist. But when we have embarked
on it and begun to do what we were premeditating, then

that action will exist, because then instead of being in the future, it will be in the present.

Whatever, then, may be the mode of this secret foreknowledge of the future, nothing can be seen which does not exist. And what is already in existence is not future, but present. Therefore, when we speak of seeing the future, what is seen is not the actual future itself (which, being future, does not yet exist), but the causes, or perhaps the signs of that future—causes and signs which are already in existence. And so to those who see them they are not future, but present, and from them future events are conceived in the mind and predicted. These concepts, again, are already in existence, and by those who make the predictions they are contemplated as being present in the mind.

Let me take one example out of the great number of possible examples. I am looking at the dawn sky and I foretell that the sun is going to rise. What I am looking at is present; what I foretell is future. What is future is not the sun, which is already in existence, but its rising, which has not yet taken place. Yet unless I could imagine in my mind this rising (as I do now in speaking of it), I should not be able to predict it. But the glow which I see in the sky is not the sunrise, although it comes before the sunrise; nor is the image in my mind the sunrise. Both those two are perceived in the present, so that the sunrise, which is in the future, can be foretold. The future, therefore, is not yet, and if it is not yet, it does not exist, and if it does not exist, it is quite impossible for it to be seen. But it can be predicted from the present which is already in existence and which can be seen.

19   RULER OF YOUR CREATION, tell me now how it is that you teach souls the things that are to come. For you have taught this to your prophets. To you nothing is future; how do you teach the future? Or rather, how do you give present indications of future events? For what does not exist cannot possibly be taught. Here your proceedings are beyond the reach of my sight; *it is too mighty for me, I cannot attain unto it.* But with your

help I shall be able, when you grant it to me, sweet light of my hidden eyes.

20 IT IS NOW, HOWEVER, perfectly clear that neither the future nor the past are in existence, and that it is incorrect to say that there are three times—past, present, and future. Though one might perhaps say: "There are three times—a present of things past, a present of things present, and a present of things future." For these three do exist in the mind, and I do not see them anywhere else: the present time of things past is memory; the present time of things present is sight; the present time of things future is expectation. If we are allowed to use words in this way, then I see that there are three times and I admit that there are. Let us go further and say: "There are three times—past, present, and future." It is an incorrect use of language, but it is customary. Let us follow the custom. See, I do not mind, I do not object, I find no fault, provided that we understand what is said —namely, that neither what is to come nor what is past is now in existence. It is not often that we use language correctly; usually we use it incorrectly, though we understand each other's meaning.

21 I SAID JUST NOW that we measure time as it passes, and in such a way that we are able to say that one period of time is twice as great as another, or of the same length, and so on of any other parts of time which are measurable. For this reason, as I said, we measure time as it is passing, and if I am asked how I know this, I should reply that I know it because we do measure time, and we cannot measure what does not exist, and the past and the future do not exist. But how do we measure the present, since it has no extent? It is measured while it is passing; when it has passed by it is not measured, for then there will be nothing there to measure.

But where does time come from, by what way does it pass, and where is it going to when we are measuring it? It can only come from the future, it can only pass by way

of the present, and it can only go into the past. Therefore it comes from something which is not yet in existence, it passes through something which has no extension,
and it goes in the direction of something which has ceased
to exist.

But how can we measure time except in some sort of
extension? When we say single and double and triple and
all the other expressions of this sort which we use about
time, we must be speaking of extensions or spaces of time.
In what kind of extension, then, do we measure time as it
is passing by? In the future, from which it comes? But we
cannot measure something which is not yet in existence.
In the present, through which it passes? But we cannot
measure something which has no extension. In the past,
toward which it is going? But we cannot measure something which no longer exists.

22 MY SOUL IS on fire to solve this very complicated
enigma. Do not shut the door on these things, my
Lord God, good Father, in the name of Christ I beg you,
do not shut the door in the face of my longing to know
these things which are so familiar and at the same time
so obscure; but let my longing penetrate into them and
let them shine out clearly in your enlightening mercy,
Lord. Whom shall I ask about them? And to whom shall
I confess my ignorance more profitably than to you, for
you do not look with distaste at my violent burning enthusiasm for your Scriptures? Grant me what I love;
for I do love and it was you who granted me to love.
Give, Father, *who truly knowest to give good gifts unto
Thy children.* Give, because I have *studied that I might
know and it is a labor in my sight,* until you open the
door to me. By Christ I beg you, in His name, the Holy
of Holies, let no one disturb me. *I believed and therefore
do I speak.* This is my hope and for this I live, that *I may
contemplate the delights of the Lord. Behold Thou hast
made my days old,* and they pass away, and how they do
this I do not know. We are constantly using the word
"time," both in the singular and the plural. We say: "How
long did he speak?" "How long was he in doing that?"

"For how long a time have I not seen that?" "This syllable is double the length of that short one." We use these expressions ourselves and we hear other people using them; we both understand and make ourselves understood; they are the commonest of expressions and the clearest, and yet on the other hand they are extraordinarily obscure and no one has yet discovered what they mean.

23   I ONCE HEARD a learned man say that what constitutes time is the motions of the sun and moon and stars. I did not agree. For one might equally well say that the motions of all bodies constitute time. Suppose that the lights of the heavenly bodies were to cease and a potter's wheel were to be turning around: would there be no time by which we could measure its rotations and say that these rotations were of equal duration, or, if it turned sometimes faster and sometimes slower, that in the one case the period taken by the turn was shorter and in the other case longer? And when we were saying these things, would not we too be speaking in time? In our words would there not be some syllables that are long and others that are short, simply because some take a longer and some a shorter time to pronounce? God, grant us men to see in a small thing principles which are common to things both small and great. There are stars and lights in the heavens to be *for signs, and for seasons, and for years and for days;* there certainly are; yet, just as I should not say that one turn of that little wooden wheel constituted a day, so that learned man should not say that it does not constitute any time at all.

What I want to know is the force and nature of time, by which we measure the motions of bodies and say, for example, that this motion is double the length of that one. And I put forward the following question: now what we mean by "a day" is not simply the time when the sun is above the earth (this merely distinguishes day from night), but the whole circuit of the sun from the east back to the east again (as, when we say "so many days have passed" we include the nights with the days and do not reckon up their spaces separately). Since, then, a day is constituted by the motion of the sun and its circuit from east to east, what I want to know is this: is it the motion itself which makes the day? Or is it the time taken by that motion? Or is it both?

If it were the movement of the sun that makes the day, then it would still be a day even if the sun completed its course in a time so small as to last only one hour. If it were the time now taken by the sun to complete its circuit that makes a day, then it would not be a day if there were only the space of one hour between one sunrise and the next; to make a day the sun would have to complete its circuit twenty-four times. If what makes a day is both the motion and the time taken, we could not call it "a day," if the sun stood still and a time passed which was equivalent to the time normally taken by the sun to go on its way from one dawn to the next.

So I shall not now inquire what it is which we call "a day." My question is: "what is time?" The time by which we measure the circuit of the sun and by which we should be able to say that the sun had gone around in half its normal time, if it went around in a time equal to twelve hours. The time by which we are able to compare the two periods and say that one is twice as long as the other, and this proportion of one to two would still hold good though the sun were, for its part, always doing its circuit from east to east; yet on some occasions it would be doing it in single, on others in double time.

Let no one tell me, then, that the motions of the heavenly bodies constitute time. When, at a man's prayer, the sun stood still so that he might fight and win a battle, the sun did indeed stand still but time went on; it went on for the space necessary for that battle to be fought and brought to its conclusion.

I see, therefore, that time is an extension of some sort. But do I see this? Or do I only seem to see it? You, light, you, truth, will show me.

24 Is IT YOUR WILL that I should agree if someone tells me that time is the motion of a body? It is not your will. That no body can move except in time is something which I understand; it is what you say to me. But that the motion of a body actually *is* time is something which I do not understand; you do not say this to me. For when a body is in motion, I measure the length of the motion in time from the moment when it begins to move until the moment when it ceases to move. And if I did not observe the moment when the movement began and if the movement continues to go on so that I cannot observe the moment when it ends, then I am incapable of measuring it—except in the sense of measuring from the moment when I began to look until the moment when I stopped looking. If I look at it for a long time, all I can say is: "It was a long time." I cannot say how long a time; because we can only say "how long" by means of comparison—as, "this is as long as that," "this is twice as long," and so on. But when we can observe the points in space from which the body in motion comes and to which it goes (or the parts of a body, if it is revolving on its axis), then we can say exactly how much time has been taken to complete the movement of the body (or of its part) from one place to another place.

It is clear, then, that the motion of a body is one thing and the means by which we measure the duration of that motion is another thing. Is it not obvious which of the two deserves the name of "time"? A body may sometimes be in motion, at varying speeds, and may sometimes be standing still; but by means of time we measure not only its motion but its rest. We say: "It was at rest for the same time as it was in motion," or "It was at rest twice or three times as long as it was in motion," or any other proportion which we have either exactly measured or else guessed ("more or less" as we say).

Time, therefore, is not the motion of a body.

25 AND I CONFESS to you, Lord, that I still do not know what time is, and then again I confess to you, Lord, that I do know that I am saying these things

in time, that I have been speaking of time for a long time and that this "long time" is only long because of the passage of time. But how do I know this, when I do not know what time is? Or by "not knowing" do I perhaps mean simply that I do not know how to express something which is in fact known to me? A bad state indeed to be in, not even to know what it is that I do not know! See, my God, I am in your presence and I do not lie. As I speak, so is my heart. *Thou shalt light my candle; Thou, O Lord my God, wilt enlighten my darkness.*

26   MY SOUL SPEAKS with truth when it confesses to you that I do measure time. Is it the case then, Lord my God, that I perform the act of measuring but do not know what I am measuring? I measure the motion of a body in time. Is it the case that I do not measure time itself? But could I measure the motion of a body—how long it lasts, how long it takes to go from one place to another—if I were not measuring the time in which the motion takes place? How, then, do I measure time itself? Do we measure a longer time by means of a shorter time, as, for instance, we measure a rood in terms of cubits? In this way, certainly, we seem to measure the quantity of syllables—the long by the short—and we say that a long syllable is double the length of a short. So we measure the length of poems by the lengths of the lines, and the lengths of the lines by the lengths of the feet, and the lengths of the feet by the lengths of the syllables, and the lengths of the long syllables by the lengths of the short ones. I do not mean measuring poems by pages; that is a spatial and not a temporal measurement. I mean the measurement of words as they are pronounced and pass away, and we say: "That is a long poem, for it is made up of so many lines; the lines are long, for they are composed of so many feet; the feet are long, for they extend into so many syllables; that syllable is long, for it is the double of a short one."

Yet all this still does not give us a fixed measure of time. It may happen that a short line, if recited slowly, may take up more time than a longer line, if spoken hurriedly. The same holds good of a poem, or a foot or a syllable. And so it seems to me that time can only be a kind of extension; but I do not know what it is an extension of. Could it not be, I wonder, an extension of the mind itself? What is it, I beseech you my God, that I measure when I say, either in an indefinite way: "This time is longer than that" or, with precision: "This is double that"? That I am measuring time, I know. But I am not measuring the future, because it is not yet in existence; I am not measuring the present, because the present has no extension in space; I am not measuring the past, because it no longer exists. What then am I measuring? Is it time passing, but not past? That was what I said previously.

27 Press on, my mind! Go forward with all your strength! *God is our helper. He made us and not we ourselves.* Go forward toward the place where truth begins to dawn.

Let us consider the case of a bodily voice. The voice begins to sound, it sounds, it continues to sound, and then it stops sounding. Now there is silence; the voice is past and is no longer a voice. Before it began to sound, it was in the future and could not be measured because it did not yet exist, and now it cannot be measured because it no longer exists. Therefore, it could only be measured while it was actually sounding, because only then was there something in existence which could be measured. But even then it was not static; it was going, and going away into the past. Was it this that made it the more measurable? For while it was in the process of going away it was extended through a certain space of time which made measurement possible; for the present occupies no space.

We grant, therefore, that then it was able to be measured. Now consider the case of another voice. This voice begins to sound; it still goes on sounding; it sounds at the same pitch continuously with no variation. Let us measure it while it is sounding; for when it has stopped sounding it will be in the past, and this will be nothing which can be measured. Obviously, then, we must measure it and say how long it is. But it is still sounding and measurement is only possible from the beginning, when it started to sound, to the end, when it ceased sounding. What we measure is the space between a beginning and an end. Therefore, a voice that has never ceased to sound cannot be measured; we cannot say how long or how short it is; it cannot be described as equal to another or single or double or anything of that sort. But when it has ceased to sound, it will no longer exist. How then shall we be able to measure it? And yet we do measure time. But the times we measure are not those which do not yet exist, not those which no longer exist, not those which are without duration, not those which are without beginning and end. Therefore, what we measure is neither the future nor the past nor the present nor what is passing. Yet nevertheless we do measure time.

"*Deus creator omnium*"—this line is composed of eight syllables, short and long alternately. Thus the four short syllables (the first, third, fifth, and seventh) are single in relation to the four long ones (the second, fourth, sixth, and eighth). Each long syllable has double the time of each short syllable—I pronounce them and I say that it is so, and, by the plain evidence of our senses, so it is. So far as sense can make things plain I measure a long syllable by a short, and I feel by means of my senses that it has twice the length. But when two syllables sound one after the other—the first short, the next long—how shall I keep hold of the short one? How, in my measurement, shall I apply it to the long one, so as to find that the long one has twice its length? The long one has not even begun to sound unless the short one has ceased to sound. And how can I measure the long syllable as something present? I cannot begin to measure it until it is finished. And when it is finished it has passed away.

What, then, is it that I measure? Where is that short syllable by which I measure? Where is that long syllable which I measure? Both have sounded, have fled away, have gone into the past, and no longer exist; and yet I do measure; I reply in all sincerity (my reply being based on the confidence one may have in a practiced sense) that one syllable is, so far as space of time is concerned, twice the length of the other. And I cannot make this judgment except when both the syllables have gone into the past and are finished. Therefore, what I am measuring is not the syllables themselves (they no longer exist) but something in my memory which remains there fixed.

It is in you, my mind, that I measure time. Do not interrupt me, or rather, do not allow yourself to be interrupted by the thronging of your impressions. It is in you, I say, that I measure time. As things pass by they leave an impression in you; this impression remains after the things have gone into the past, and it is this impression which I measure in the present, not the things which, in their passage, caused the impression. It is this impression which I measure when I measure time. Therefore, either this itself is time or else I do not measure time at all.

Now what happens when we measure periods of silence and say that this period of silence occupied the same amount of time as that period of speech? Is it not the case that we extend our thoughts up to what would have been the length of a speech if that speech were audible, and in this way are able to reach a conclusion about the intervals of silence in a given space of time? Without making any use of voice or tongue, we can go over in our mind poems, verses, speeches, and we can form our conclusions about the measurements of their movements and about the spaces of time taken up by one in relation to another just as well as if we were actually reading these passages aloud. If a man decides to utter a rather long sound and makes up his mind how long it is going to be, he has passed through that space of time in silence; then, committing it to memory, he begins to utter the sound and it goes on sounding until it reaches the limit which he set for it. Or it would be truer to say "it did sound" and "it will sound"; for the part of it which at any moment is completed *has* sounded, and the part of it which remains to be uttered *will* sound, and so it goes on, as the act of will, which is in the present, transfers the future into the past, the past growing as the future diminishes, until the future is consumed and it is all past.

28 BUT HOW CAN the future, which does not yet exist, be diminished or consumed? How can the past, which no longer exists, grow? Only because, in the mind, which performs all this, there are three things done. The mind looks forward to things, it looks at things, and it looks back on things. What it looks forward to passes on through what it looks at into what it looks back on. No one, of course, can deny that the future does not yet exist. But nevertheless there is in the mind already the expectation of the future. No one can deny that the past no longer exists. But nevertheless there is still in the mind the memory of the past. No one can deny that the present time has no extension, since it passes in a flash. But nevertheless our attention (our "looking at") is something constant and enduring, and through it what is to be proceeds into what has been. Thus it is not the future that is long, for the future does not exist; a long future is a long expectation of the future. Nor is the past long, since it does not exist; a long past is a long memory of the past.

Suppose I am about to recite a psalm which I know. Before I begin, my expectation (or "looking forward") is extended over the whole psalm. But once I have begun, whatever I pluck off from it and let fall into the past enters the province of my memory (or "looking back at"). So the life of this action of mine is extended in two directions—toward my memory, as regards what I have recited, and toward my expectation, as regards what I am about to recite. But all the time my attention (my "looking at") is present and through it what was future passes on its way to become past. And as I proceed further and further with my recitation, so the expectation grows shorter and the memory grows longer, until all the expectation is finished at the point when the whole of this action is over and has passed into the memory. And what is true of the whole psalm is also true of every part of the psalm and of every syllable in it. The same holds good for any longer action, of which the psalm may be only a part. It is true also of the whole of a man's life, of which all of his actions are parts. And it is true of the whole history of humanity, of which the lives of all men are parts.

29 BUT BECAUSE *Thy loving kindness is better than all lives,* see, my life is a kind of distraction and dispersal. And *Thy right hand upheld me* in my Lord, the *Son of Man, the Mediator betwixt Thee,* the One, and us, the many (many also in our many distractions over so many things), so that *through Him I may apprehend in Whom I have been apprehended* and that I may be gathered up from my former days to follow the One, *forgetting what is behind,* not wasted and scattered on things which are to come and things which will pass away, but intent and *stretching forth to those things which are before*—no longer distracted, but concentrated as *I follow on for the prize of my heavenly calling,* where *I may hear the voice of Thy praise,* and contemplate Thy delight which is neither coming nor passing. But now *are my years spent in mourning,* and you, my comfort, my Lord, my Father, are eternal. But I have been spilled and scattered among times whose order I do not know; my thoughts, the innermost bowels of my soul, are torn apart with the crowding tumults of variety, and so it will be until all together I can flow into you, purified and molten by the fire of your love.

30 AND I SHALL STAND and become set in you, in my mold, in your truth. And I shall not endure the questions of men who, victims of a disease which is its own punishment, want to drink more than their stomachs can hold and who ask: "What was God doing before He made heaven and earth?" or: "Why did the idea of making something occur to Him, when previously He had never made anything?" Grant them, Lord, to think carefully what they are saying and to realize that when there is no time, one cannot use the word "never." To say, therefore, that God "never" made anything can only mean that God did not make anything "in any time." Let them see, then, that without created being, time cannot exist and let them cease to *speak* that *vanity.* I pray that they too may be *stretched out to those things which are before,* so that they may understand that before all times you are the eternal creator of all times, that no times are

coeternal with you, nor is any other creature, even if there were a creature before all times.

31   LORD MY GOD, how deep are the inner recesses of your secrets, and how far from them have I been thrown by the consequences of my sins! Heal my eyes and let me share the joy of your light! Certainly if there were a mind gifted with such vast knowledge and foreknowledge as to know all the past and all the future as well as I know one well-known psalm, that mind is wonderful beyond belief, stupendous, and awe-inspiring. To that mind everything that is past and done, everything that is to come in future ages, is as clear as, when I was singing that psalm, it was clear to me how much and what I had sung from the beginning of it, how much and what remained to be sung before I reached the end. But far be it from me to say that it is in this way that you, the creator of the universe, creator of souls and bodies, know all the future and the past. No; your knowledge is far more wonderful, far more mysterious than this. When a man is singing or hearing a song that he knows, his feelings vary and his sense is distracted as the result of his expectation of the words to come and his memory of the words that are past. But nothing of this kind happens to you, the immutably eternal—that is, the truly eternal creator of minds. Therefore, just as *in the Beginning* you knew *the heaven and the earth* without any variation in your knowledge, so *in the Beginning* you created *the heaven and the earth* without any alteration of your action. Let him who understands confess to you, and let him who does not understand confess to you. How high you are! And the humble in heart are the house in which you dwell. For *Thou raisest up those that are bowed down;* you are their height and from that height they do not fall.

Book XII

1 LORD, IN THIS neediness of my life, my heart, at which the words of your Holy Scripture are knocking, is busily enough employed. And it is chiefly for this reason that the poverty of human understanding shows an exuberance of words, since inquiry has more to say than discovery, asking takes longer than obtaining, and the hand that knocks does more work than the hand that receives. We have the promise; no one can alter or distort it: *If God be for us, who can be against us? Ask, and ye shall have; seek, and ye shall find; knock, and it shall be opened unto you. For every one that asketh, receiveth, and he that seeketh, findeth, and to him that knocketh, it shall be opened.* These promises are yours, and when truth makes the promise, who can fear deception?

2 IN THE LOWLINESS of my language I confess to your highness that you made heaven and earth—this heaven, which I see; this earth, on which I tread and from which comes the earthly body which I wear. You made them. But where is that heaven of heavens, Lord, of which we hear in the words of the psalm, *The heaven of heavens is the Lord's; but the earth hath He given to the children of men?* Where is that heaven which we do not see, the heaven compared with which all that we do see is mere earth? For the entire corporeal universe, which is not present everywhere in its entirety, has received its beauty right down to its lowest parts of which this earth of ours is the lowest; but compared to that heaven of heaven even the heaven above our earth is only earth, and so it is reasonable to call both these great bodies "earth" in comparison with that unknown heaven which is for the Lord and not for the children of men.

3   Now THIS EARTH WAS *invisible and without form*, a kind of depth of abyss over which there was no light, because it had no shape or form. Therefore you commanded it to be written that *darkness was upon the face of the deep*. What else can that mean but absence of light? For if there had been light, it could only have been from above, an illumination from on high. But since there was no light, the presence of darkness simply means the absence of light. *Darkness was upon* it, therefore, because light was not upon it—in the same way as when there is no sound there is silence. For the presence of silence simply means the absence of sound.

Was it not you, Lord, who taught this soul of mine which now makes its confession to you? Was it not you, Lord, who taught me that, before you gave shape and variety to this formless matter, there was nothing—no color, no outline, no body, no spirit? And yet not absolutely nothing; there was a kind of formlessness, lacking all definition.

4   WHAT NAME, THEN, can we give to this formlessness? How can we convey an idea of it to minds that are not very quick, unless we employ some word which is already familiar? And in the whole of the world what seems to come closest to utter formlessness are "earth" and "deep." They occupy the lowest position and are correspondingly less beautiful than the other higher things which are all transparent and shining. I may, therefore, accept that under the name of *earth invisible and without form* a sufficiently accurate intimation is given to men of that formless matter which you had

created without beauty and from which you were to make this beautiful world.

5   Here our thoughts may lead us to inquire what there is in this concept that can be grasped by sense. We may say: "It is not an intellectual form—as life, or justice—because it is the matter of which bodies are made; nor is it a sensible form, because there is nothing to be seen or apprehended by the senses in what is invisible and formless." When the mind of man questions itself in this way, it must aim either at knowledge through ignorance or at ignorance through knowledge.

6   As to me, Lord—if by tongue and pen I may confess to you everything you have taught me about this formless matter—the fact is that previously I heard the name without understanding it, being told of it by others who did not understand it either. I thought of it as having an enormous variety of different forms, and consequently I was not thinking of it at all. I turned over in my mind the notions of forms which were hideous and horrible and disjointed from all order; but they were forms all the same, and this I called "the formless." By this I meant not something which was without form, but something which had a form of such a kind that, if it were to appear, my senses would recoil from it as from something utterly strange and incongruous and upsetting to the weakness of one's human nature. So what I was thinking of was "formless" not in the sense of being without form, but only in the sense of being less well formed in comparison with forms that were more beautiful. Right reason certainly led me to believe that I should strip away entirely every kind of remnant of form, if I wanted truly to conceive of "the formless"; but this I could not do. I found it easier to think that what was deprived of all form was nonexistent, than to conceive of something which was between form and nothingness, something which lacked form yet was not nothing, something formless and almost nothing.

And my mind ceased to question my spirit on this, my spirit being full of images of formed bodies which it changed and varied at its will. Instead I turned my attention to the bodies themselves; I looked more deeply into their mutability, considering how they cease to be what they have been and begin to be what they were not. And I suspected that this transition from one form to another happened through something that was formless but was not absolutely nothing. But I wanted to know, not merely to suspect. And if my tongue and pen were to confess to you the whole story, all the knots that you untied for me on this question, which of my readers could hold out to take it all in? Nevertheless, my heart shall not cease to give you honor and to sing your praises for those things which it lacks power to express.

For it is just this mutability of changeable things which is itself capable of receiving all those forms into which mutable things are changed. And what is this mutability? Is it soul? Is it body? Is it any species of soul or of body? If one could speak of a nothing that was something or an existence which is nonexistent, that would be the expression I would use for it. Yet even then it must certainly have had some kind of existence in order to receive those visible and composite forms.

7   AND IN ANY CASE, whence could it have been except from you, from whom all things, insofar as they exist, derive their existence? But the more a thing is unlike you, the further it is from you (though not, of course, in any spatial sense). So, Lord, you, who do not change with time or circumstance, you who are the Selfsame and the Selfsame and the Selfsame, *Holy, Holy, Holy, Lord God Almighty*—you, *in the Beginning*, which is from you, in your Wisdom, which is born of your substance, made something and made it out of nothing.

You *created heaven and earth;* but you did not create them out of yourself. If you had, they would be equal to your only-begotten Son and therefore to yourself too, and it could not possibly be right that something not proceeding from you should be equal to you. And there was nothing else in existence besides you from which you might create them, God, Three in One and One in Three, and therefore you created heaven and earth out of nothing. You created a great thing and a little thing (for you are almighty and good, to make all things good)— a great heaven and a little earth. You were and nothing else was and of nothing you made heaven (i.e., the heaven of heaven) and earth, two things, one close to you, the other close to nothing, one which has only you superior to it, the other which is of all things the most low.

8   BUT THAT *heaven of heavens was for Thyself, O Lord;* but the earth which *Thou gavest to the sons of men to be* seen and felt was not like the earth which we now see and feel. It was *invisible, without form,* and there was a deep, over which there was no light; or, *darkness was* above *the deep,* that is, there was more darkness above than in the deep. This abyss of waters, which are now visible, does have even in its depths a kind of light of its own which is perceptible to the fish and living creatures which crawl on the bottom of the sea. But then all was close to nothingness, because it was still entirely formless; yet there was already something capable of receiving form. For you, Lord, made the world out of a matter which was without form, and it was from nothing that you made this formless matter, this next-to-nothing, out of which you were to create those great works which we sons of men look upon in wonder. Wonderful indeed is this corporeal heaven, this firmament set between water and water of which you said on the second day (after the creation of light on the first): *Let it be made, and it was made.* This *firmament Thou calledst heaven*—the heaven, that is, belonging to this earth and sea which you made on the third day by giving visible shape to the formless matter which you had made before any day. You had indeed also made a heaven before any day, but that was the heaven of this heaven; because *In the Beginning Thou hadst made heaven and earth.* But that earth which you made then was formless matter, because *it was invisible and without form, and darkness was upon the deep.* And of this *in-*

visible and formless earth, of this formlessness, of this
next-to-nothing you would make all those things of which
our mutable world stands in its state of flux and where its
mutability appears in the fact that the passage of time
can be felt and measured. For time is made by the changes
of things, as their forms vary and turn from one stage
to the other. And the matter of all this is that invisible
earth of which we are speaking.

9   FOR THIS REASON the Spirit, the teacher of your
servant, when relating that you *In the Beginning
created heaven and earth,* makes no mention of times and
says nothing about days. Obviously because the heaven of
heaven which you made *in the Beginning* is in some way
an intellectual creature, and, though it is in no way coeternal with you, the Trinity, nevertheless it partakes of
your eternity; in the sweet happiness of contemplating
you it finds strength to restrain its own mutability; clinging to you without any lapse from the moment of its
creation, it is outside and beyond the rolling vicissitudes
of time. That formlessness also of the *earth invisible and
without form* is not included in the number of the days
of creation. For when there is no shape and no order,
there is nothing to come into existence and pass away,
and without that condition there are certainly no days nor
any vicissitudes in the spaces of times.

10   LET TRUTH, the light of my heart, speak to me
and not my own darkness! I fell away and I was
in the dark, but even from there, even from there I loved
you. I went astray and I remembered you. I heard your
voice behind me, calling me back, and I could scarcely
hear it for all the noise made by those without your peace.
And now, look, I return thirsty and panting to your
fountain. Let no one hold me back! I shall drink of it, and
I shall live of it. Let me not be my own life! I lived evilly
of myself; I have been death to myself; I come back to
life in you. Speak to me! Teach and instruct me! I have
believed your books, and their words are secret and
mysterious indeed.

11   Already, Lord, in my inner ear I have heard your voice loud and strong telling me that you are eternal, *Who only hast immortality*, since you suffer no change in form or by motion, and your will is not altered in the course of time (for a will which is now one thing and now another is not immortal). This is clear to me in your sight, and I pray that it may become clearer and clearer and that with this truth evident to me I may continue calmly to dwell beneath the shadow of your wings.

Also, Lord, in my inner ear I have heard your voice loud and strong telling me that all natures and all substances, which are not what you are but which nevertheless exist, are created by you. Only what does not exist is not from you. Such is the movement of the will away from you, who are, toward something which has less reality; the movement is a fault and a sin and no man's sin can either harm you or disturb the order of your government in any way, great or small. This is clear to me in your sight, and I pray that it may become clearer and clearer and with this truth evident to me I may continue calmly to dwell beneath the shadow of your wings.

Also in my inner ear I have heard your voice loud and clear telling me that that creation of yours (the heaven of heavens) is not coeternal with you: you alone are its happiness and in unfailing chastity it drinks you in and never and nowhere does it exhibit its natural mutability; you are always present to it and to you with total and complete affection it holds; it has no future to expect; it has nothing to transfer from memory into the past; it is neither altered by changing circumstances nor distracted into time.

O happy creature, if such a creature there is! Happy in clinging to your blessed happiness, happy in you, its eternal inhabitant and enlightener! I can find no better name for this *heaven of heavens which is the Lord's* than your house—a house full of the contemplation of delight in you, from which there is no falling away to the contemplation of anything else, a pure mind, single in perfect concord, settled in the peace of holy spirits, the citizens of your city *in the heavenly places*—far above the heaven which we see.

From this a soul whose pilgrimage has been into a far country may understand if she now *thirsts for Thee*, if *her tears are now become her bread, while they say daily unto her, Where is thy God?* if she now *seeks of Thee one thing*, and *desireth it, that she may dwell in Thy house all the days of her life* (and what is her life, except you? And what are your days except your eternity—just as *Thy years which fail not, because Thou art ever the same);* from this, therefore, the soul that has the power may understand how far, beyond all times, you are eternal; for your house, which never went into a far country, although it is not coeternal with you, nevertheless, because it clings to you without lapse and without cessation, suffers no vicissitude of time. This is clear to me in your sight, and I pray that it may become clearer and clearer and, with this truth evident to me, I may continue calmly to dwell beneath the shadow of your wings.

Now in the changes that take place in the last and lowest creatures there is evidently a kind of formlessness. No one, I think, except a man whose empty mind is filled and disturbed with confused fantasies of his own, would maintain that, if all form were taken away so as to vanish entirely and if nothing were left but the formlessness (the medium in which things change and turn from one form to another), that this formlessness in itself could exhibit temporal variations. Obviously it could not possibly. For where there is no variety of motion, there is no time, and there can be no variety where there is no definition of form.

12   WHEN I CONSIDER these things, my God—insofar as you grant me the power, insofar as you incite me to knock, and insofar as you open to me when I do knock—I find that there are two things which you have created outside the realm of time, though neither of the two is coeternal with you. One of these is so formed that, though changeable, it is, nevertheless, unchanged and is able without any intermission of contemplation, without any interval of change, perfectly to enjoy eternity and changelessness. And the other was so formless that it

could not change from one form to another, whether of
motion or rest, and consequently was not subject to time.
But you did not allow this to remain formless because you
in the Beginning didst create heaven and earth, these two
things of which I am speaking. But *the earth was invisible
and without form, and darkness was upon the deep.* In
these words the idea of formlessness is suggested to us, an
idea which will gradually win over and convince those
who are incapable of conceiving of an utter privation of
all form which still does not amount to a reduction to
nothingness. For out of that formlessness was to be made
a second heaven and a visible and well-formed earth, the
beautiful waters and everything else which we are told
was made in the constitution of the world on the succes-
sive days of creation, and all these things are of such a
kind that, because of the ordered alterations of motion
and of form, they are subject to the vicissitudes of time.

13 This, my God, is what I feel when I hear your
Scripture saying: *In the Beginning God made
heaven and earth; and the earth was invisible and without
form, and darkness was upon the deep.* And when Scripture makes no mention of the day on which you made
these, I conclude that this is because what is meant by
"heaven" is the *heaven of heavens,* that intellectual heaven,
where it is the property of the intellect to know all things
in one act, not *in part,* not *darkly,* not *through a glass,* but
as a whole, *in manifestation, face to face;* not to know one
thing at one time and one at another, but, as has been said,
to know everything together without any vicissitude of
time. And I assume that by "earth" is meant that *earth
invisible and without form,* not subject to the vicissitude
of time in which there occurs now "this" and now "that,"
because where there is no form, there is no "this" and no
"that."

So I consider that when the Scripture says, without
making any mention of days, *In the Beginning God
created heaven and earth,* it is referring to these two, the
one formed from the beginning, the other entirely without form; the one heaven (meaning the *heaven of heaven*),

the other earth (meaning the earth *invisible and without form*). For immediately afterward comes the reference to what earth is meant, and then it is recorded that on the second day the Firmament was created and *called heaven*. We can gather from this what "heaven" it was of which the Scripture first spoke without mentioning any days.

14 How AMAZING IS the profundity of your utterances! See, they lie before us with a surface that can charm little children. But their profundity is amazing, my God, their profundity is amazing. One cannot look into them without awe and trembling—awe of greatness, trembling of love. *The enemies thereof I hate* with all my strength. I wish that you would slay them *with a two-edged sword*, so that they might cease to be its enemies. So I love to have them slain to themselves that they may live to you.

But there are others too, not critics but admirers of the Book of Genesis, who say: "The spirit of God, writing these words by means of his servant Moses, did not mean them to be understood as you say, but in another way, the way that we say." God of all of us, You are the judge. . . . To this objection of theirs my answer is as follows.

15 "YOU WILL NOT, I imagine, assert that what truth, with upraised voice, has told me in my inner ear about the true eternity of the creator is false—namely, that His substance suffers no change in time and that His will is not something separate from His substance. And, therefore, He does not will one thing at one moment and one at another; but once and at once and always He wills all things which He does will. He does not will one thing and then the same thing again; He does not will one thing and then another thing; He does not will later something which He had not willed previously, nor does He cease to will something which previously He had willed. Such a will is mutable, and nothing mutable is eternal; but our God is eternal.

"Again, would you deny this that he has told me in my inner ear—that the expectation of things to come turns into a "looking-at" them when they have come, and that this "looking-at" (or attention) turns to memory when they have passed? Now any mental experience which varies in this way is mutable; nothing mutable is eternal, but our God is eternal. I grasp these facts, I put them together, and I find that my God, the eternal God, did not in His creation exercise any new act of will and that His knowledge does not admit of anything that is transitory.

"What, then, are you going to say, you who contradict me? Are you going to maintain that these things are false?"

"No," they say.

"Well then, is this false—that every nature which has a form and all matter that is capable of receiving a form only exists from Him who is supremely good, because He supremely *is?*"

"No," they say, "we do not deny this either."

"Well then, do you deny that there is a kind of sublime creature which cleaves to the true and truly eternal God with so chaste a love that, although it is not coeternal with Him, yet it is never detached from Him nor does it flow away from Him into any variety and vicissitude of time, but rests in the true and perfect contemplation of Him alone?"

And this is because you, God, show yourself to him who loves you as much as you command, and you are sufficient to him, so that he never falls away from you nor declines toward self. This is the house of God, not of earthly mold nor of any heavenly stuff that is material; it is a spiritual house, partaking of your eternity, because it is for eternity without stain. *For Thou hast made it fast forever and ever, Thou hast given it a law which it shall not pass.* But it is not coeternal with you, for it is not without a beginning. It was created.

It is true that we do not find any time before it, for *wisdom was created before all things.* By this I do not mean the Wisdom who is altogether equal and coeternal with you, Our God, His Father—that Wisdom by Whom

all things were created and in Whom, as *the Beginning,
Thou createdst heaven and earth.* I mean the wisdom
which was created, the intellectual nature which by contemplating the light is itself light; for this too, though
created, is called wisdom. And between the wisdom that
creates and the wisdom that is created there is just the
same difference as between the light that enlightens and
the light which comes from receiving enlightenment. So
with the righteousness which justifies and the righteousness which comes from being justified. For we too are
called "your righteousness." Does not a servant of yours
say, *That we might be made the righteousness of God in
Him?*

There was, therefore, a certain created wisdom which
was created before all things, the rational and intellectual
mind of that chaste city of yours, our mother which is
above, and is free and eternal in the heavens. And what
is meant by "heavens" must be those that *praise Thee, the
heaven of heavens,* the *heaven of heavens for the Lord.*
Before this wisdom we find no time because, being created
before all things, it precedes the creation of time; yet
before it is the eternity of the creator himself; it was
created by him and from him it took its beginning—not a
temporal beginning (for there was no time) but the
beginning of its condition of existence.

Therefore, it is of you, our God, but of you in such
a way that it is clearly other than you and not the selfsame. We find not only no time before it, but also no
time in it, since it is fit always to see your face and is
never drawn away from it and, therefore, suffers no
change or variation. Nevertheless, there is in it the possibility of change, so that it could become dark and cold, if
it were not that it clings to you with such great love that
from you it receives heat and light in a perpetual noon.
O home of light, house of beauty! *I have loved thy
beauty, and the place of the habitation of the glory of my
Lord,* your builder and your owner. Let me sigh toward
you as I journey on my pilgrimage! And I ask Him who
made you to take possession of me too in you, for me
too He made. *I have gone astray like a lost sheep,* but I

hope that on the shoulders of my shepherd, your builder, I may be brought back to you.

"Now what are you going to say to me, you contradictors whom I was addressing? You believe that Moses was the holy servant of God and that his books are oracles of the holy spirit. Is not this house of God, though not coeternal with God, yet nevertheless in its own way *eternal in the heavens?* For it is no use looking there for changes of time, since you will not find them. For that which finds its happiness in always cleaving to God surpasses all extension and all the rolling space of time."

"It is true," they say.

"Then in all those things which my heart cried out to my God when inwardly it *heard the voice of His praise,* what thing in particular, I ask you, do you maintain to be false? That the matter was *without form* when, because there was no form, there was no order? But when there was no order, there could be no succession of times; yet this next-to-nothing, insofar as it was not absolutely nothing, must have been from Him from Whom everything, insofar as it has any existence at all, is."

"This too," they say, "we do not deny."

16   I WISH TO SAY a few words in your presence, my God, to those who admit the truth of all those things which your truth utters to me in my soul within. As to those who deny their truth, they may bark as much as they like and deafen themselves. I shall attempt to persuade them to be quiet and to allow your word entry into them. But if they refuse and reject my advice, I beg you, my God, *be not Thou silent to me.* Speak to me truly in my heart, for it is you alone who speak so. And I will leave the others outside, blowing onto the dust and obscuring their vision with earth, and *I will enter my chamber* and sing to you songs of love, groaning *with groanings unutterable* in my far pilgrimage, remembering Jerusalem with heart stretching out in longing for it, Jerusalem my country, Jerusalem my mother, and you the ruler of it, enlightener, father, guardian, husband, the chaste and strong delight, the solid joy and all good

things unspeakable, all, all together at once, because you are the one supreme and true good. And I shall not turn aside until from this dispersed and deformed state of mine you gather all that I am into the peace of that city, our dear mother, where are *the first fruits of my spirit* and from which my certain Knowledge is derived, and so you will conform and confirm me forever, my God, my mercy.

But with regard to those who do not maintain that all these truths are false, who honor your Holy Scripture as set forth by that holy man Moses, who, as I do, place it at the summit of authority deserving to be followed, and yet who disagree with me on certain points, my answer is as follows. And I would wish you, our God, to judge between what I confess to you and what they object to me.

17   THIS IS WHAT they say: "Though all this may be true, yet Moses was not thinking of these two creatures when, by the revelation of the spirit, he said *In the Beginning God made heaven and earth.* By 'heaven' he did not mean that spiritual or intellectual creature always contemplating the face of God, and by 'earth' he did not mean that formless matter."

I ask: "What then did he mean?" and they reply: "That great man meant what we say he meant, and it was this that he declared in those words."

"And what is that?" I ask. Then they reply as follows: "By the words 'heaven' and 'earth' he meant first to signify, in brief and comprehensive terms, the whole visible world, so that after this he could, by enumerating the days of creation, arrange in order and, as it were, piece by piece the whole of creation which it had pleased the holy spirit to express in those general terms. For the people to whom he was speaking were uncultured and carnally minded, and he naturally considered that he could only entrust them with the knowledge of those works of God which are visible."

They agree with me however that the words *earth invisible and without form and the dark deep* (from which it is subsequently shown that all these visible things which we all know were created and set in order during those "days") may quite naturally be taken to mean that formless matter of which I have been speaking.

But someone else may put forward another view and say: "The words 'heaven' and 'earth' were used first to convey the idea of this very formlessness and confusedness of matter, because out of this matter was created and perfected the visible world with all those natures which are clearly evident to us, and which we often call by the name of 'heaven and earth.'"

Or again someone else may say: "The words 'heaven' and 'earth' are quite properly used to mean nature both visible and invisible, and so the universal creation which God made in His Wisdom—that is, *In the Beginning*—is comprehended under these two words. Nevertheless, all things were made, not out of the very substance of God, but out of nothing (because they are not the same as God and in all of them there is a principle of mutability, whether they stand fast, like the eternal house of God, or whether they change, like the soul and body of man). Therefore, the common matter of all things, visible and invisible—a matter still formless, though capable of receiving form, out of which was to be made both heaven and earth (i.e., the invisible and visible creation when finally given a form)—this common matter is what is meant by the expressions *earth invisible and without form* and *darkness upon the deep*. But there is a distinction between the two. *Earth invisible and without form* refers to corporeal matter at the stage before it was differentiated by any form: *darkness upon the deep* refers to spiritual matter at the stage before any restraint was put upon its unlimited fluidity and before it received the illumination of Wisdom."

There is still another view which a man may, if he likes, put forward. It may be said: "When we read *In the Beginning God made heaven and earth*, the words 'heaven' and 'earth' do not mean the visible and invisible natures already formed and perfected; they mean the first formless starting ground of things, a matter capable of receiving form, a matter out of which something could be

made, because in it there did exist—though confused and
with no distinction of quality or form—all these things
which now, after being separated out, set in order, are
called heaven and earth, the one a spiritual, the other a
corporeal creation."

18 Now AFTER I have heard all this and thought it
over, I have no wish to *strive about words*. That
is *profitable to nothing, but the subversion of the hearers.
But the law is good to edify, if a man uses it lawfully*,
because *the end of it is charity, out of a pure heart and
good conscience, and faith unfeigned*. And our Master
knows on which *two commandments He hung all the
Law and the Prophets*.

Now, as with burning heart I confess these things to
you, my God, light of my eyes in secret, what harm does
it do me if different meanings, which are nevertheless all
true, can be gathered from these words? What harm can
it do me if my view of what Moses meant is different
from someone else's view? Certainly all of us who read
are endeavoring to find out and to grasp what the man
whom we are reading meant to say, and when we believe
that he is a man who tells the truth we dare not imagine
that he said anything which we ourselves know or believe
to be false. So while we are all trying in our reading of
the Holy Scriptures to grasp what it was that the author
of them meant to say, what harm can it do if a man
grasps hold of something which you, who are the light
of all truthful minds, show him is true, even if the author
whom he is reading did not grasp this truth—though of
course the author did express a truth, but a different
one?

19 For, Lord, it is certainly true that *Thou madest
heaven and earth*. It is true that the Beginning
is your Wisdom, in which you made all things. It is also
true that this visible world is made up of two great parts,
the heaven and the earth, which briefly comprise all
natures which are made and established. And it is true

that everything changeable must suggest to our intelligence a kind of formlessness, something by which form may be received or by which a change or mutation may take place. It is true that what clings so close to the immutable form that, though capable of change in itself, it does not change, is not subject to time. It is true that that formlessness which is next-to-nothing cannot be subject to the alterations of time. It is true that the material out of which a thing is made can, in a certain sense, already bear the name of the thing that is made from it; thus any kind of formless matter out of which heaven and earth were made can be called heaven and earth. It is true that of all things which have form, nothing is nearer to the formless than *earth* and *the deep*. It is true that not only whatever has been created and given form, but also whatever is capable of being created and given form, is made by you, *of whom are all things*. It is true that whatever is formed out of the formless, was itself first formless, then given a form.

20   Now of all these truths—which are accepted unhesitatingly by those to whom you have given the power to perceive them with the inner eye, and who believe unshakably that your servant Moses spoke in the spirit of truth—out of all these truths a man chooses just one who says: *In the Beginning God made heaven and earth* means this: "In His Word, which is coeternal with Himself, God made the intelligible and the sensible, or the spiritual and the corporeal, creation."

Another truth is chosen by the man who says: *In the Beginning God made heaven and earth* means this: "In His Word, which is coeternal with Himself, God made the formless matter of both the spiritual and corporeal creation."

Another truth is chosen by the man who says: *In the Beginning God made heaven and earth* means this: "In His Word, which is coeternal with Himself, God made the formless matter of the corporeal creation in which, still in a confused state, were the heaven and the earth which, now that they have been separated apart and given form, we see at present in the mass of the world."

Another truth is chosen by the man who says: *In the Beginning God made heaven and earth* means this: "At the very start of His work of creation God made that formless matter, which contained (though in a confused state) heaven and earth, and out of which they were formed so that now they stand out evident to the sight with all that is in them."

21 So WITH REGARD to the understanding of the words that follow. Out of all the truths already mentioned, one is chosen by the man who says: *But the earth was invisible and without form, and darkness was upon the deep* means this: "The corporeal thing which God made was as yet the formless matter of corporeal things, without order and without light."

Another truth is chosen by the man who says: *The earth was invisible and without form, and darkness was upon the deep* means this: "All that which is now called heaven and earth was still only formless and lightless matter, from which the corporeal heaven and the corporeal earth was to be made, with all things in them which are known to our corporeal senses."

Another truth is chosen by the man who says: *The earth was invisible and without form, and darkness was upon the deep* means this: "All that which is now called heaven and earth was still formless and lightless matter, from which were to be made the intelligible heaven— elsewhere called *the heaven of heaven*—and the earth— that is to say, the whole corporeal nature. Under the name of 'earth' is to be understood also this corporeal heaven. From this matter, then, was to be made the whole of creation, visible and invisible."

Another truth is chosen by the man who says: *The earth was invisible and without form, and darkness was upon the deep* means this: "Scripture did not call that formlessness by the name of 'heaven and earth.' No; that formlessness was already in existence and was called *the earth invisible and without form and darkness upon the deep*. And Moses had previously said that it was out of this that God made heaven and earth, that is the spiritual and corporeal creation."

Another truth is chosen by the man who says: *The earth was invisible and without form, and darkness was upon the deep* means this: "There was already a kind of formlessness, the material out of which, as previously stated by Scripture, God made heaven and earth—that is to say, the corporeal mass of the world, divided into two great parts, the upper and the lower, with all the known and familiar creatures in them."

22 To THESE LAST two opinions someone might make the following objection: "If you will not admit that what is meant by this formlessness of matter is, in fact, heaven and earth, then there must be something, not created by God, out of which God was able to make heaven and earth. For Scripture does not say that God made this formless matter unless we understand that it is this that is meant by the words 'heaven and earth' or only by the word 'earth,' when it is said: *In the Beginning God made heaven and earth.* Thus in the following passage, *and the earth was invisible and without form*, though Moses chose to use these words to describe the formless matter, we can only understand it to mean that which God made as written in the previous verse: *God made heaven and earth.*"

Those who hold the last two opinions, as stated above, or one or the other of them, will, when they hear this objection, reply as follows: "We do not deny that this formless matter was made by God, God from whom are all things very good; because, just as we say that what has been created and given a form is a greater good, so we admit that what has been made capable of being created and given a form is, though a lesser good, nevertheless a good. But we do say that Scripture has not recorded the fact that God made this formless matter, just as Scripture has not recorded God's creation of many other things, the Cherubim and Seraphim, for instance, and those things of which the Apostle distinctly speaks:

Thrones, Dominions, Principalities, Powers; yet clearly all these were made by God. If all things are to be understood as comprehended in the expression *He made heaven and earth*, what are we to say about the waters upon which *the Spirit of God moved?* For if they are comprised in the word 'earth,' how can this formless matter also be described by the word 'earth,' when we see that the waters are so beautiful? Or, if we do take it in this way, why is it written that out of this same formlessness the firmament was created and called heaven, but it is not written that the waters were created? For the waters are not still formless and invisible; we see them flowing in all their beauty. If you say that they received their beauty when God said: *Let the water that is under the firmament be gathered together*, thus assuming that the gathering together was in itself the forming of them, then what will you say about the *waters which be above the firmament?* They would not have deserved so honorable a position if they had been without form, yet Scripture does not record by what word they were created. We may find, then, that in Genesis there is no mention of God's having created some particular thing, though sound faith and accurate intelligence have no doubt at all that He did make it. Obviously no reasonable doctrine would go on to suggest that those waters are coeternal with God because, though we find them mentioned in the Book of Genesis, we do not find any mention of when they were created. Why, then (with truth to teach us), should we not hold that this formless matter, described by Scripture as *earth invisible and without form and the dark deep*, was created by God out of nothing, and therefore is not coeternal with Him—though the Bible story has omitted to mention when it was made?"

23   WHEN I HEAR these views and examine them so far as the weakness of my capacities (and I confess this weakness to you, God, who know it) will allow, I see that two kinds of disagreement can arise when things are reported to us in words by truthful reporters: one concerns the actual truth of the things reported; the

other concerns the meaning of the reporter. To try to find out the truth about the making of creation is one thing; it is a different thing to try to find out what Moses, that excellent minister of your faith, meant his reader or his hearer to understand by his words. As to the first inquiry, I wish to have nothing to do with those who think they know things that are really false, and in the second inquiry I will have nothing to do with those who think that Moses said things which are false. I would be with those in you, Lord, and I would take delight with those in you who feed on your truth in the largeness of charity. Together with them I would approach the words of your book and in these words try to find out your meaning through the meaning of your servant by whose pen you gave them to us.

24 But in finding the meaning there are so many truths which occur to us from these words, according to whether we understand them in one way or another. Is there any one of us who can say: "This is what Moses thought," "This is what he meant us to understand in that passage," with the same confidence as he would say: "This is true" or "That is true," whether Moses meant it or not? Consider me, my God, me, your servant, who have vowed to you the sacrifice of my confession in these words of mine and who pray to you that in your mercy I may *pay my vows unto Thee*; see how confidently I affirm that in your immutable Word you created all things, visible and invisible; could I affirm with the same confidence that Moses had just one particular meaning and no other when he wrote: *In the Beginning God made heaven and earth?* No. I can see in your truth that this is a certainty; but I cannot see equally clearly that this was in his mind as he wrote those words.

When he said *In the Beginning* he might have been thinking of the very start of creation, and when he said *heaven and earth* he might have wished us to understand by the words no already formed and perfected nature, spiritual or corporeal, but both of these inchoate and still formless. Certainly I see that whichever was his meaning, it would be true; but I do not see so clearly which he had in mind when he was writing those words. Although, whether this great man, while writing these words, saw in his mind one or other of these meanings, or some other meaning which I have not mentioned, I have no doubt that he saw what was true and that he expressed it correctly.

25 I HOPE, THEREFORE, to avoid being pestered by the kind of person who says: "Moses did not think as you say; he thought as I say." If he said: "How do you know that your interpretation of Moses' words represents what Moses thought?" that would be a question which I should take in good part, and I should probably answer it as I have written above or at rather more length, if he needed more persuading. But when he says: "Moses did not think as you say; he thought as I say," and at the same time does not deny that what each of us says is true, then, O life of the poor, my God, in whose bosom is no contradiction, I beg you to pour down into my heart some balm of mitigation to help me put up patiently with such people as this. For they are not speaking because they are divinely inspired and have seen what they say in the heart of your servant; they are speaking out of pride; they do not know what Moses thought, but they love what they think themselves, and they love their own opinion not because it is true, but because it is their own. Otherwise they would love another true opinion just as much—as I love what they say, when what they say is true—not because it is theirs but because it is true. In fact it ceases to be theirs just because it is true. If, therefore, they love it because it is true, then it is both theirs and mine; it is the common property of all lovers of truth.

But this I will not have, this I do not love, when they assert that Moses did not think as I say but did think as they say. Even if they happened to be right, nevertheless, their temerity in making the assertion comes from arrogance, not from knowledge; it is born not of vision but of swelling pride. And therefore, Lord, your judgments are terrible, because your truth is not my property nor the property of this man or that man; it belongs to all of us whom you publicly call into communion with it, warning us in most terrible terms that we must not hold it as private to ourselves lest we be deprived of it altogether. For whoever claims as his personal possession what you have given for the enjoyment of all, and wants to have as his own what belongs to everyone, is driven out from what is in common to what really is his own, that is, from a truth to a lie. For he *that speaketh a lie, speaketh it of his own.*

Listen, best of judges, God, Truth itself, listen to what I shall say to an opponent like this. Listen; for I am speaking in your presence and in the presence of my brethren who employ *the law lawfully, to the end of charity.* Listen, if you please, and see what I shall say to him. The words I address to him are fraternal and designed to make peace. I say: "If we both see that what you say is true, and we both see that what I say is true, then where, I ask, do we see this? I do not see it in you; you do not see it in me, but both of us see it in that immutable truth which is above our minds. Since, therefore, we do not disagree about the true light of our Lord God, why should we disagree about the thought that was in the head of a neighbor? For we cannot see this thought as clearly as the immutable truth is to be seen. If Moses himself appeared to us and said: 'This was what I was thinking,' we should believe what he said, but still would not actually see what was in his mind. Let us *not*, then, *be puffed up* for *one against the other, above that which is written: let us love the Lord our God with all our heart, with all our soul and with all our mind: and our neighbor as ourself.* Now we must believe that whatever Moses thought when he was writing those books, his thoughts were in accordance with those two precepts of charity; if we do not believe this, we shall be making the Lord a liar, for we shall be thinking of our fellow servant's soul in a way that is different from the way that God has taught us to think. Can you not see now how foolish it is out of all that abundance of perfectly true meanings which can be extracted from those words rashly to assert that one particular meaning was the one which Moses had chiefly in mind, and thereby in one's pernicious quarrelsomeness to offend charity herself, for whose sake he, whose words we are trying to explain, said everything that he did say?"

26 AND YET I—MY GOD, you who give height to my humility, my labor's rest, you who hear my confessions and forgive me my sins—since you tell me to love my neighbor as myself, I cannot believe that you gave less gift to your most faithful servant Moses than I would have wished and desired from you myself, if I had been born at the same time as he and had been put by you in the same position—namely, that by the service of my heart and tongue those books were to be produced which for so long after were to do good to all nations and which throughout the whole world, from such a height of authority, were to overtop the words of all the doctrines of falsehood and of pride.

Now if I had been Moses then (for we all come from the same lump and *what is man, saving that Thou art mindful of him?*), if, I say, I had been then what he was and had been given by you the task of writing the Book of Genesis, I should have wished to be granted to me such a power of expression and such stylistic abilities that those who cannot yet understand how God creates would still not reject my words as being beyond their capacity, and that those who already have understanding would find in the few words of your servant every true opinion which they had reached themselves in their own thinking, and I should wish too that if another man were to see some other true opinion by the light of truth, that that opinion also should be discoverable in these same words of mine.

27 A SPRING SHUT in a small place has a more plentiful supply of water and distributes its flow to more streams over a greater area of ground than does any single stream, however far it goes, which is derived from that spring. It is the same with the writing of him who

dispenses your word. This writing will do good to many who will preach and comment upon it, and from a narrow measure of speech it will spread and overflow into streams of liquid truth, and from these, as they wind away in lengthier stretches of language, each man may on these subjects draw what truth he can—one man one truth, one another.

Some people, for example, when they read or hear the words which we are discussing think of God as though He were a kind of man or else like some great force associated with an enormous mass, and they imagine that by some new and sudden decision He made heaven and earth outside Himself and, as it were, in some place spatially separated from Himself—heaven and earth being two great bodies, one above and one below, in which all things are contained. And when they hear *God said, Let it be made, and it was made*, they think of words with a beginning and an ending, audible in time and passing away, and they imagine that as soon as the words had passed away then what was commanded to come into existence came into existence. And there are other such notions too, all due to the fact that some people are used to thinking in material terms.

Such people are still feeble little creatures, but by this humble kind of language their weakness is protected and nourished as by a mother's breast, and so there is built up in them a healthy faith in which they have a hold for a certainty that God made all the natures which, all around them in wonderful variety, their senses look upon. And if any one of these, in a kind of proud debility, despises what may seem to him the commonness of your words and stretches out beyond the limits of the nest where you are nourishing him, then I fear that this poor creature will have a bad fall, and I pray, Lord God, that you will have pity and will not allow the passers-by to tread upon that unfledged nestling, but will send your angel to put him back in the nest so that he may live till he is able to fly.

28 BUT OTHERS NEED no longer think of your words as a nest. To them they are shady gardens of fruit, and they see the fruit hidden under the leaves, and they flutter around it in joy, and, cheerfully chirping, they peer for it and pluck it.

When such people read or hear the words which we are discussing, they see that all times past and future are swallowed up in your eternal stable permanence, and yet that there is no creature of time which is not made by you. And because your will is identical with yourself, your will suffered no change when you made all things, nor did a new will arise which was not there before. And in making all things you did not make them out of yourself in your own likeness (which is the form of all things); you created from nothing something unlike yourself and without form, yet something which was capable of receiving form in your likeness by having recourse to your unity according to the capacity ordained by you and in the measure given by you to each being in its own kind. And all things are very good, whether they stay close around you or whether, further removed in degrees of time and space, they cause or undergo their beautiful variations. These things they see, and, so far as they are able to do so here, they rejoice in the light of your truth.

And another one of these, after pondering on the words *In the Beginning God made heaven and earth*, takes "the beginning" to mean Wisdom, *because it also speaketh unto us*. Another, pondering on the same words, understands by "beginning" the actual start of the process of creation and so takes "in the beginning He made" as being equivalent to "He made first."

And of those who take *In the Beginning* to mean "In Wisdom He made heaven and earth," one believes that here the words "heaven and earth" mean the matter out of which heaven and earth were to be created; another believes that the words refer to natures already formed and distinct; another thinks that by "heaven" is meant a formed and spiritual nature, while "earth" means the formless nature of corporeal matter.

And those who understand by the words "heaven and earth" the still formless matter out of which heaven and earth were to be made, even so do not all understand the words in the same way. Some take it as meaning the matter out of which both the sensible and the intelligible creation were to proceed; others mean only the matter from which this sensible corporeal world was to come which contains in its vast embrace all natures that are visible and evident to our senses.

Nor is there agreement between those who believe that in this passage "heaven and earth" means created things already formed and set in order. Some take this to refer to both the invisible and the visible worlds, others only to the visible, in which we see the shining heaven and the dark earth and all things contained in them.

29   But if one adopts the view that *In the Beginning He made* must be equivalent to "He made first," then the only possible interpretation of "heaven and earth" is "the material of heaven and earth," that is, of the whole intelligible and corporeal creation. Any attempt to make the words mean "the universe already formed" will rightly provoke the question: "If God made this first, what did He make afterward?" One will not find anything coming after everything, and, whether one likes it or not, one will be faced with the question: "How could this be 'first,' if there was nothing afterward?"

But to say that God made matter first formless and then formed is not absurd so long as one is capable of distinguishing between priority in eternity, priority in time, priority in choice, priority in origin (in eternity, as God is before all things; in time, as the flower is before the fruit; in choice, as the fruit is before the flower; in origin, as the sound is before the tune).

Of these four which I have mentioned, the first and last are extremely difficult, the middle two very easy to understand. For rarely, Lord, do we have the insight, and hard it is for us to see your eternity creating in its changelessness things that change, and thus prior to them. Again not many people are acute enough in understanding as to be able to see without difficulty how it is that the sound is prior to the tune: the reason being that a tune is a sound

that has been given form, and, though a thing that has not
been formed can at least exist, a thing that does not exist
cannot be given a form. Thus the matter is prior to the
thing which is made from it—not prior because it makes
the thing (it is rather the case that it is made than that it
makes), and not prior in any temporal sense; for we do not
first of all utter formless sounds without a tune and then
later on shape them and fit them together into the form
of a song, as we do in the case of the wood or silver out
of which we are making a box or vessel. Such materials,
certainly, are prior in time to the forms of the things
which are made out of them. But it is not so in the case
of a tune. When the tune is sung, the sound of it is heard;
we do not first have an unformed sound and later a sound
that is shaped into a song. Each sound, just as it is made,
passes away, and you can find nothing that you can call
back again and shape by art, and thus the tune has its
being in the sound and the sound of the tune is the matter
of the tune. And this matter receives a form so that it may
become a tune. And therefore, as I said, the matter of the
sound is prior to the form of the tune—not prior in the
sense of having the power to make it, for sound is not
the composer of tunes, it is merely supplied by the body
to the mind of the singer for him to use in making a song;
nor is it prior in time, for it is uttered simultaneously
with the tune; nor is it prior in choice, for a sound is not
better than a tune, since a tune is not only a sound, but a
beautiful sound. But it is prior in origin, because a tune is
not given form in order to become a sound, whereas a
sound is given form in order to become a tune.

From this example those who have the ability may
understand that the matter of things was first made and
called "heaven and earth," because heaven and earth were
made out of it. But this matter was not made first in time,
because the forms of things give rise to time, but this
matter was without form; only when time itself was in
existence could it be observed in time. Yet in speaking of
this formless matter we have to speak of it as though it
were first in time, while it is inferior in value (since what
is formed is clearly better than what is formless) and it is
preceded by the eternity of the creator, so that from

nothing there might be the material out of which something was to be made.

30   IN THIS DIVERSITY of true opinions, let Truth herself bring forth concord. And our God have mercy upon us, that we may *use the law lawfully, the end of the commandment, pure charity*.

So if anyone asks me which of these meanings was in the mind of your servant Moses, I should not be speaking in the language of my Confessions, if I did not confess to you: "I do not know." But I do know that all these opinions are true, except for those carnal ones, about which I said what I thought. Yet those little ones of high promise who understand the Scripture in this carnal sense are kept safe from fear by the words of your book, words so lofty in humility, so copious in brevity.

And let all of us who, as I confess, see the truth and speak the truth that is in these words, love one another, and let us all together love you, our God, the fountain of truth, if what we thirst for is truth itself and not vanity, and let us so honor that servant of yours, the dispenser of this Scripture, a man full of your spirit, as to believe that when, by your revelation, he wrote these things, his mind was bent toward that meaning in them which is the best meaning, both for the light of truth which it sheds, and for the practical good which it does.

31   SO WHEN SOMEONE SAYS: "Moses meant what I think," and someone else says: "No, he meant what I think," would it not be more reverent to say: "Why not as you both think, if what each of you thinks is true?" And if in these words someone should see a third or a fourth truth, or indeed any other truth at all, why should we not believe that all these truths were seen by Moses, through whom the one God tempered the Holy Scriptures to the minds of many, so that their minds should see different things, though all true things. Certainly for my own part (and I say this fearlessly from my heart), if I were to write anything that could have this height of

authority, I should prefer to write in such a way that my words could convey any truth that anyone could grasp on such matters, rather than to set down one true meaning so clearly as to exclude all other meanings which, not being false, could not offend me. And so, my God, I will not be so rash as to believe that Moses did not deserve as much at your hands. When he was writing these words he was entirely aware in his thought of all the truth that we have been able to find there, and also of all the truth which we have not been able to find, or not yet, though it still remains there to be found.

32   FINALLY, LORD, you who are God and not flesh and blood, even if one who was a mere man did not see everything, it is certain that everything which you yourself in those words intended to reveal to future readers must have been evident to *Thy good Spirit*, who shall *lead me into the land of uprightness*. This is so, even if Moses, through whom the words were said, perhaps was thinking of only one out of the many true meanings which are to be found in them. And if this was the case, then let us grant that the meaning which was in his mind was the highest and loftiest of all. And Lord, we ask you to show us either that meaning or any other true meaning that you please; so that, whether you make clear to us the same thing as that which you made clear to your servant, or whether you show us something else arising from the same words, we may still be fed by you, not mocked by error.

See, Lord my God, how much I have written on these few words! Really, how much! What strength of ours, what length of time would be enough to comment in this way on all your Scriptures!

Allow me, then, to speak more briefly to you in my confessions on these words, and to choose one meaning which, by your inspiration, I shall see to be true, certain, and good, even though many other meanings may occur to me, since many others are possible. For I wish my confession to be made in this faith—that, if I have said what your own minister meant himself, that is right and that is best and for that I ought to try; but if I have failed to achieve this, I shall nevertheless say what your Truth has been pleased to say to me by his words, that Truth which also said what it willed to Moses.

Book XIII

1   I CALL UPON YOU, my God, my mercy, who made
me and did not forget me when I had forgotten
you. I call you into my soul which you are making ready
to receive you by the longing which you yourself inspire.
Do not forsake me now that I call upon you; for before
I could call you at all, you were ahead of me; by all
sorts of voices and in all kinds of ways over and over
again you pressed yourself on my attention, so that I
might hear you from far away and be converted and
might call upon you who were calling me.

For you, Lord, have wiped away all those acts of mine
which deserved punishment; from my hands which sinned
against you you did not exact the price due, and in everything I did that deserved well, you were ahead of me, so
that you might give the due reward to the work of your
own hands, the hands that made me. Because before I
could be, you were; nor was I such as to deserve the gift of
being. Yet, see, I am and I am because of your goodness
which went before—before all that you have made me and
before all out of which you made it. For you had no need
of me, nor am I anything so good as to be of help to you,
my Lord and my God. It is not that I should serve you in
case you grew tired in your work, nor that without my
service your power would be less. You are not like land
which requires cultivation if it is not to be barren; it is
not in that way that you need my worship. No, I worship
you and I serve you so that it may be well with me in rela-

tion to you, from whom it comes that I exist as someone capable of well-being.

2   FROM THE FULLNESS of your goodness every created thing has its being, so that a good—which cannot benefit you in any way, which, not being of your substance, cannot be equal to you—might still be, because it could come into existence from you. For what did *heaven and earth which Thou madest in the Beginning* deserve of you? Let the two natures, spiritual and corporeal, which you made *in your Wisdom* say how they deserved it of you that they should depend on that Wisdom even in their inchoate and unformed state, whether in the spiritual or in the corporeal order (the spiritual, though *without form*, being superior to the corporeal, even if formed, and the corporeal in its formlessness being superior to absolute nothingness), a state which tended toward the chaotic in an increasing distance from your likeness. How did they deserve so to depend upon your Word, still formless and remaining so unless they were recalled by the same Word to your unity, and given form and made by you, the supreme good, altogether very good? How did they deserve it of you that they should even be *without form*, since they could not even have been this without you?

How had corporeal matter deserved it of you that it should exist even in that invisible and formless state, since even in that state it could not have existed unless you made it? Since it did not exist, it could not have deserved to exist.

And how had that original beginning of your spiritual creation deserved to have even that dark, watery existence, like the deep, and unlike you? An existence that by the same Word was to be turned toward the Word by which it was created and, receiving light from it, should become light, not in equality with you, but nevertheless conformed to a form that is equal to you. For as in a body to be is not the same thing as to be beautiful (otherwise there would be no ugliness), so in a created spirit to live is not the same thing as to live wisely; otherwise such a spirit would be changelessly wise forever. But *good it is* for it always to *hold fast to Thee*, lest it should lose by turning away from you the light which it gained by turning toward you, and should fall back again into the life that is like the dark deep. For we too who in our souls are a spiritual creation, when turned away from you, our light, have been in this life *sometimes darkness*, and we still labor among the remains of our obscurity, until in your only Son we become *Thy righteousness, like the mountains of God*. For we have been *Thy judgments, which are like the great deep*.

3   AT THE BEGINNING of the creation you said: *Let there be light, and there was light.* I think I have good reason to take these words as referring to the spiritual creation, for there was already a life of a sort for you to illuminate. But just as it had no claim upon you to be of a kind capable of illumination, so, when it did exist, it had no claim actually to be illuminated. Its formless state could not please you unless it became light, and became light not simply by existing but by beholding the light shining upon it and by cleaving to it; so that it owed entirely to your grace both its life and the happiness of that life, being turned, by a change for the better, toward that which can suffer no change either for the better or the worse—toward you, who alone exist in simplicity, to whom it is not one thing to live and another to live happily, because you are your own happiness.

4   YOU ARE YOURSELF your own good; what, then, could have been lacking to that good even if these created things had never existed at all, or if they had remained without form? These things you made not because of any want, but out of the fullness of your goodness, setting bounds to them, giving them form, though it was not as if your joy was increased by them. To your perfection their imperfection is displeasing; perfected by you they will please you, but not in the sense that you were imperfect and needed for your own perfection that

they should be made perfect. For your good spirit was *borne over the waters*, not borne up by them, as though He rested on them. When one says that your spirit rests on people, it means that He causes them to rest in Him. But your incorruptible and immutable will, itself sufficient to itself, was *borne upon* the life which you had created, a life to which living is not the same thing as living happily, because there was still life even in its wavering watery darkness. But it remains for it to turn to Him by whom it was made and more and more to live by the fountain of life, and in His light to see the light, and to be perfected and illuminated and blessed.

5   SEE NOW, there appears to me *in a glass darkly* the Trinity, which is you, my God, since you, Father, *in the Beginning created heaven and earth*—in the beginning of our Wisdom, which is your Wisdom, born of you, equal to you and coeternal, that is, in your Son. I have said much of the *heaven of heavens* and of the *earth invisible and without form* and of the dark *deep*, dark in respect to the flux and the disorder of its spiritual formlessness, until it became converted to Him from whom it received its humble degree of life and by His illumination became a life of beauty, and was the heaven of that other heaven which was later created *between water and water*. And now under the name of God I understood the Father, who made these things, and under the name of the Beginning I understood the Son, in whom He made these things, and believing, as I did, my God to be a Trinity, I searched in His holy writings and, see, I found your Spirit *moving over the waters*. There it is, the Trinity, my God, Father, Son, and Holy Ghost, Creator of all creation.

6   BUT WHAT WAS the reason, O Light that speaks the truth, I lift my heart to you; let it not teach me vanities; dispel its darkness and tell me, I beg you by our mother Charity, I beg you, tell me what was the reason why it was only after the mention of heaven and

of *the earth invisible and without form and darkness upon the deep* that finally your Scripture made mention of your Spirit. Was it because it was right that your Spirit should be introduced in the phrase "borne above," and this phrase could not have been used unless there had previously been a mention of that above which your Spirit was to be understood as being borne? For the Spirit was not "borne above" the Father or the Son, nor could He rightly be said to be "borne above" nothing. It was necessary, therefore, that that over which He was borne should first be mentioned and that only then should come the mention of the Spirit who could not be described otherwise than as being "borne above." But why was it necessary that He could only be introduced to us in the phrase "borne above"?

7   I SHOULD LIKE everyone who can to follow in his understanding your Apostle when he says: *Because Thy love is shed abroad in our hearts by the Holy Ghost, which is given unto us,* and when *concerning spiritual gifts* he teaches and *showeth unto us a more excellent way* of charity, and when *he bows his knee, unto Thee for us,* that we may *know the supereminent knowledge of the love of Christ.* So from the beginning was the Spirit *borne* supereminent *above the waters.*

To whom can I tell it, and how can I tell of the weight of concupiscence dragging us toward that steep abyss, and of how charity raises us up by your Spirit which was *borne above the waters?* To whom shall I tell it? How shall I tell it? For it is not in space that we sink down and are raised up again. The experience is very like this, but at the same time quite unlike. There are affections, there are loves, there is the uncleanness of our spirit flowing away downward in love of care and distraction, and there is your sanctity raising us upward in the love of freedom from care, so that to you we may lift up our hearts, where your Spirit is *borne above the waters,* and come to that supereminent peace, when our soul shall have passed through *the waters that are without substance.*

8 THE ANGEL FELL, the soul of man fell, and they showed us the abyss in that deep darkness, the abyss for the whole spiritual creation, if from the beginning you had not said *Let there be light* and light was made and every obedient intelligence of your Heavenly City cleaved to you and rested in your Spirit which is borne unchangeably over all things mutable. Otherwise even the *heaven of heaven* would have been in itself a dark deep; but *now it is light in the Lord*.

For even in that miserable restlessness of spirits who fall away from you and discover their own darkness, bared of the garment of your light, you show us clearly enough how noble a thing is the rational creature which you have made, which, for its peace and happiness, can be contented with nothing less than you, and so cannot be contented with itself. For you, our God, will *lighten our darkness;* from you arises our *garment of light,* and then *shall our darkness be as the noonday*.

Give yourself to me, my God, and give yourself back to me. See, I love, and if my love is too little, I would love more. I cannot measure it so as to know how much my love falls short of what is enough for my life to run to your embraces and never be turned away until it is *hidden in the hidden place of Thy presence*. This is all I know, that apart from you it is ill with me, not only without, but within myself, and all my abundance, which is not my God, is poverty.

9 BUT WAS NOT either the Father or the Son also *borne above the waters?* If one is thinking in terms of a body in space, then it would not be true to say this even of the Holy Spirit. But if our meaning is the unchangeable supereminence of divinity over all things mutable, then both Father and Son and Holy Spirit were *borne above the waters*.

Why then are these words used only of your Spirit? Why only in His case is there mention of a place where He was (though it is not a place), in His case only of whom it was said that He is your gift? In your gift we rest; there we enjoy you. Our rest is our place. Love lifts us up to it, and your good spirit raises our lowness *from the gates of death*. In your *good pleasure is our peace*. A body tends to go of its own weight to its own place, not necessarily downward toward the bottom, but to its own place. Fire tends to rise upward; a stone falls downward. Things are moved by their own weights and go toward their proper places. If you put oil underneath water it will rise above the level of the water; if you pour water on top of oil, it will sink below the oil; things are moved by their own weights and go to their proper places. When at all out of their place, they become restless; put them back in order and they will be at rest. My weight is my love; wherever I am carried, it is my love that carries me there. By your gift we are set on fire and are carried upward; we are red hot and we go. We *ascend Thy ways that be in our heart* and sing a *song of degrees*. We are red hot with your fire, your good fire, and we go; for we are going upward toward *the peace of Jerusalem;* for *gladdened was I in those who said unto me, We will go up to the house of the Lord*. It is there that your good pleasure will have us settled, so that we may desire nothing else but to remain there forever.

10   HAPPY THE CREATURE which knows no other state! Yet even this creature would have been different, had it not been that by your gift, *borne above* all things mutable, it was raised up as soon as it was created and became light immediately by that summons of yours, *Let there be light*. With regard to us there is a distinction of time when it is said: *We were darkness and shall be made light;* but with regard to that creation it is only said what it would have been if it had not received light, and the reason why the passage is so phrased as to suggest that it was previously in a state of flux and darkness is to make clear the cause why it was made to be something different, that is the cause by which it was turned toward the light that is unfailing and itself became light. Let him, who can, understand this. Let him ask guidance

from you and not trouble me. It is not I who *enlighten every man that cometh into this world.*

11   Who can understand the almighty Trinity? Yet we all speak of it, if it really is the Trinity of which we speak. Rare is the soul which in what it says of the Trinity knows what it is saying. And men struggle and contend, and no one without peace sees that vision.

I should like men to consider three aspects of their own selves. These three are something very different from the Trinity; I only make the suggestion as a mental exercise which will allow people to find out and to feel how far distant they are from it. The three things I mean are existence, knowledge, and will. For I am, and I know, and I will. I am a being that knows and wills. I know that I am, and I know that I will. I will to be and I will to know. Now he who is capable of doing so will see how there is in these three an inseparable life—one life, one mind, one essence—and how, finally, how inseparable a distinction there is between them, yet nevertheless there is a distinction. Every man has this fact in front of him. Let him look into his own self and see and tell me what he sees. But when he has discovered something in these and has stated it, he must not go on to suppose that he has discovered that immutable which is above all these things, that which exists immutably, knows immutably, and wills immutably. But whether because of these three there is in God also a Trinity, or whether all three are in each Person so that each Person has three aspects, or whether both views are correct and in some unimaginable way, in simplicity and in multiplicity, It itself, though unbounded, is within Itself and bound to Itself, by which it exists and is known to itself and is sufficient to itself, unchangeably the Selfsame in the plentiful magnitude of its unity—who can easily grasp this in his mind? Who can in any way tell of it? Who could in any way venture to make a pronouncement upon it?

12 GO ON WITH your confession, my faith. Say to
your Lord: *Holy, Holy, Holy, O Lord my God*,
in your name we have been baptized, *Father, Son, and
Holy Ghost*; in your name we baptize, *Father, Son, and
Holy Ghost*, because among us too God made in His
Christ *a heaven and an earth*, namely the spiritual and the
carnal members of His Church. And our "earth" before
it received the form of doctrine was *invisible and without
form*, and we were clothed in the darkness of ignorance.
For *Thou chastenedst man for iniquity*, and *Thy judgments were like the great deep unto him*. But because
your Spirit was borne above the waters, your mercy did
not forsake our misery and you said: *Let there be light,
Repent ye for the kingdom of heaven is at hand. Repent
ye; let there be light*. And because our soul was *troubled
within us*, we remembered Thee, O Lord, *from the land
of Jordan, and that mountain*, equal to you, but *little
for our sakes*, and our darkness was displeasing to us and
we turned to you *and there was light*. And, see, we were
sometimes darkness, but now light in the Lord.

13 BUT UP TO NOW it is still *by faith and not by sight,
for by hope we are saved; but hope that is seen is
not hope*. Still *deep calls to deep*, but now *in the voice of
Thy waterspouts*. Still even he who says: *I could not
speak unto you as unto spiritual, but as unto carnal*, does
not yet *think himself to have apprehended*, and *forgetteth
those things which are behind* and *reacheth forth to those
which are before*, and *groaneth being burdened*, and *his
soul thirsteth after the living God, as the hart after the
waterbrooks*, and says: *When shall I come?* desiring to be
clothed upon with his house which is from heaven, and
calleth upon this *lower deep*, saying, *Be not conformed to
this world, but be ye transformed by the renewing of
your mind*. And, *be not children in understanding, but in
malice be children that in understanding ye may be perfect*, and, *O foolish Galatians, who hath bewitched you?*
But now he is not speaking in his own voice; he is speaking in yours who sent *the Spirit from above*, through Him
who ascended upon high and *set open the floodgates of*

His gifts, that the force of His *streams might make glad the city of God.* For that city the friend of the bridegroom sighs who has now the *first fruits of the Spirit laid up with Him, yet still groaning within himself, waiting for the adoption, to wit, the redemption of his body.* For that city he sighs, for he is a member of *the Bride;* he is jealous for it, because he is a friend of the Bridegroom; he is jealous for it, not for himself, because it is *in the voice of Thy waterspouts,* not in his own voice, that he calls to that other deep of which he is jealous and fears lest *as the serpent beguiled Eve through his subtlety, so their minds should be corrupted from the purity that is in* our Bridegroom, your only Son. And what a light of beauty is that, when we shall *see Him as He is, and those tears be passed away, which have been my meat day and night, whilst they daily say unto me, Where is now thy God?*

14 AND I TOO SAY "My God, where is He?" See where you are. In you I breathe a little when *I pour out my soul by myself in the voice of joy and praise,* the sound of *him that keeps holy-day.* And still my soul is sad, because it slips back again and becomes *a deep,* or rather it realizes that it is still *a deep.* And my faith speaks to it, my faith which you have kindled to be a light before my feet in the night, *and says: Why art thou sad, O my soul, and why dost thou trouble me? Hope in the Lord; His word is a lanthorn unto thy feet:* hope and endure until the night, which is the mother of sinners, passes; until the wrath of the Lord passes, for we too were children of wrath, we *were sometimes darkness,* and we bear about with us relics of this darkness in our body, *dead because of sin, until the day break and the shadows fly away. Hope thou in the Lord; in the morning I shall stand in Thy presence, and contemplate Thee: I shall forever confess unto Thee. In the morning I shall stand in Thy presence, and shall see the health of my countenance, my God, Who also shall quicken our mortal bodies, by the Spirit that dwelleth in us,* because in mercy He has been *borne over* the flowing darkness of our inner

deep. And as in our pilgrimage we have received *an earnest* that we should *now* be *light*, while we are still *saved by hope*, and *are* the *children of light and the children of the day*, *not the children of the night, nor of the darkness*, which yet *sometimes we were. Betwixt* whom and us, in what is still the uncertainty of human knowledge, *Thou* alone *dividest, Thou* who *provest* our *hearts* and *callest the light, day, and the darkness, night*. For who except you discerns us? *And what have we that we have not received of Thee? out of the same lump vessels unto honor, from which others* too are made *unto dishonor*.

15 OR WHO EXCEPT YOU, our God, made for us a firmament of authority over us in your divine Scripture? For *heaven shall be folded up like a scroll*, and now it is stretched over us like a skin. For your divine Scripture is of all the more sublime authority because those mortals, through whom you gave it to us, have died their deaths. And you know, Lord, you know how you *clothed men with skins* when by their sin they became mortal. And so you have *like a skin stretched out the firmament* of your book, that is, your words which so well agree together and which, through the agency of mortal men, you have placed above us. By their death that solid firmament of authority in your words delivered by them was extended sublimely over all things that are below it; which, while they still lived here, was not so sublimely extended. For you had not yet *stretched out the heaven like a skin*, you had not yet spread abroad in every direction the glory of their deaths.

Lord, let us *look upon the heavens, the work of Thy fingers*. Clear away from our eyes the mist with which you have covered them. *There is Thy testimony, which giveth wisdom unto the little ones*. My God, *perfect Thy praise out of the mouth of babes and sucklings*. For we know no other books so destructive of pride, so destructive of *the enemy and the defender* who resists reconciliation with you by defending his own sins. I do not know, Lord, I do not know any writings so pure, so apt to persuade me to confess, to bow my neck to your yoke and take service with you for nothing. Good Father, let me understand them; grant this to me who am placed below them; for it was for us who are placed below that you established them so firmly.

There are, I believe, above this firmament other waters which are immortal and separated from all earthly corruption. Let them praise your name, let them praise you, those supercelestial peoples, your angels, who have no need to look up at this firmament, no need of reading to understand your word. For they always see your face, and there they read without syllables that are spoken in time what is willed by your eternal will. They read; they choose; they love; their reading is perpetual and what they read never passes away; for by choosing and by loving they read the very unchangeableness of your counsel. Their book is never closed, nor is *their scroll folded up*, for you yourself are their book and you are forever; because you have set them above this firmament which you established over the infirmity of the lower peoples so that they might look up at it and learn your mercy as it tells of you in times, you who made time. For *Thy mercy, O Lord, is in the heavens, and Thy truth reacheth unto the clouds*. The clouds pass away, but the heaven remains; the preachers of your word pass from this life into another life, but your Scripture is stretched out over the peoples until the end of time. *Heaven and earth shall pass away, but Thy words shall not pass away*. Because *the scroll shall be folded up*, and *the grass* over which it was spread *shall with the goodliness of it pass away*, but *Thy word remaineth forever*, which now appears to us not *as it is* but *under the dark image* of the clouds and *through the glass* of the heaven; because although we too are the well-beloved of your Son, it has *not yet appeared what we shall be. He looketh through the lattice of our flesh*, and He caressed us and set us on fire, and *we run after His odors. But when He shall appear, then shall we be like Him, for we shall see Him as He is.* It will be ours, Lord, to see Him *as He is*, though it is not for us yet.

16 FOR ALTOGETHER "as you are" is known to you alone, who are unchangeably, and know unchangeably, and will unchangeably, and your essence knows and wills unchangeably, and your knowledge is and wills unchangeably, and your will is and knows unchangeably. Nor does it seem right in your eyes that just as the unchangeable light knows itself, so it should be known by the changeable being that receives that light. And so *my soul is like a land where no water is*, since, just as it cannot by itself give light to itself, so it cannot by itself satisfy itself. For so *is the fountain of life with Thee* as *in Thy light we shall see light*.

17 WHO *gathered* the embittered *together into one* society? For they all have the same end, a temporal and earthly felicity, and for this they do everything that they do, however much they may waver here and there in the innumerable variety of their anxieties. Who except you, Lord, said: *Let the waters be gathered together into one place, and let the dry land appear, which thirsteth after Thee?* For *the sea also is Thine, and Thou hast made it, and Thy hands prepared the dry land.* And what is meant by "sea" here is the *gathering together of the waters*, not the bitterness of men's wills. For you also restrain the wicked desires of the soul, and you set up bounds, how far the waters shall be allowed to go, so that their waves may break upon themselves, and so you make it a sea by the order of your power which is above all things.

But as to the souls which *thirst after Thee* and which *appear* before Thee (souls which are separated from the society of the sea by other bounds) you water them from a secret and sweet spring, so that *the earth may bring forth her fruit*. And she brings forth her fruit, and at your command, the command of her Lord God, our soul blossoms with works of mercy *according to their kind, loving our neighbor* in the relief of his bodily necessities, *having seed in itself according to its likeness*, since from our own weakness we feel compassion for others and are ready to help those in want, helping them as we ourselves would

wish to be helped if we were in the same need, and not
only in easy matters (like *the herb bearing seed*), but with
help and protection given with all our strength (like *the
tree yielding fruit*)—the sort of kindness as is shown, for
example, in rescuing a man who suffers injustice from the
grip of a powerful oppressor, or in giving him the shelter
of our protection by the strong force of a just judgment.

18 So, Lord, so let it spring up, as you already make
it spring up, as you give cheerfulness and ability,
so *let truth spring out of the earth, and righteousness look
down from heaven* and *let there be lights in the firmament.*
Let *us break our bread to the hungry* and *bring the* home-
less *poor to our house.* Let us *clothe the naked, and despise
not those of our own flesh.* And when these fruits have
sprung from the earth, see that it is good, and let our temporary *light break forth,* and let us proceed from this
lower harvest of action toward the delights of contemplation and, obtaining the word of life above, let us appear
like lights in the world, clinging to the firmament of your
Scripture. For there you instruct us so that we may distinguish between the intelligible and the sensible or between souls given either to the intelligible or to the
sensible, as *betwixt day and night.* So that now it is not
you alone in the secrecy of your judgment, as before the
firmament was made, who *divide between the light and
the darkness;* but, now that your grace is made manifest
throughout the world, your spiritual children also, set
and ranked in the same firmament, may *give light upon
the earth, and divide betwixt the day and the night, and
be for signs of times,* that *old things are passed away,
and, behold, all things are become new,* and that *our
salvation is nearer than when we believed,* and that *the
night is far spent, and the day is at hand,* and that *Thou
wilt crown Thy year with blessing, sending* the *laborers*
of Thy *goodness* into Thy *harvest,* in the sowing of which
others have labored, sending also into another field, whose
harvest shall be *in the end.* So you grant the prayers to
him who asks and *Thou blessest the years of the just; but
Thou art the same* and in *Thy years* which *fail not* you

prepare a granary for our passing years. For in your eternal place you bestow upon the earth heavenly blessings in their proper seasons. *For to one is given by the Spirit the word of wisdom*, as it were *the greater light* (for those who are delighted with the light of perspicuous truth) as *for the rule of the day. To another the word of knowledge by the same Spirit*, as it were *the lesser light; to another faith; to another the gift of healing; to another the working of miracles; to another prophecy; to another discerning of spirits; to another divers kinds of tongues*. And all these like stars—for *all these worketh the one and selfsame spirit, dividing to every man his own as He will*, and causing stars to appear *manifestly, to profit withal*.

But *the word of knowledge*, in which are contained *all Sacraments*, which vary in their *seasons* as it were *the moon*, and the other *gifts* which are mentioned and reckoned up in their order as it were *stars* so far differ from that bright light of wisdom in which the abovementioned *day* rejoices that they are only *for the rule* of the night. For they are necessary to those to whom that most prudent servant of yours *could not speak unto as unto spiritual, but as unto carnal*, he who speaketh wisdom among those that are perfect.

But the natural man who is as it were *a babe in Christ* and must be *fed on milk* until he gains strength for *solid meat* and has an eye strong enough to look steadily at the sun must not have a night that is without light but must be content with the light of *the moon* and of *the stars*.

So you instruct us, our God all-wise, in your Book, that Firmament; so that in wonderful contemplation we may discern all things, though still *in signs, and in times, and in days and in years*.

19   BUT FIRST, *wash you, be clean; put away evil* from your souls, and *from before mine eyes*, that the *dry land may appear. Learn to do good, judge the fatherless, plead for the widow*, that *the earth may bring forth the green herb for meat, and the tree bearing fruit*, and *come, let us reason together, saith the Lord*, that there may be *lights in the firmament of the heaven, and they* *may shine upon the earth.* That *rich man* asked the *good master what he should do to attain eternal life.* Let the *good master* tell him (that good master whom he thought to be no more than man; but He is good because He is God); let Him tell him, *if he would enter into life,* he must *keep the commandments;* he must put away from him the bitterness of *malice and wickedness; not kill, not commit adultery, not steal, not bear false witness;* that *the dry land may appear, and bring forth the honoring of father and mother, and the love of our neighbor. All these,* he says, *have I kept.* Why then are there so many thorns, if the earth is fruitful? Go, root out those rough thickets of avarice; *sell that thou hast,* and be filled with fruit, by *giving to the poor, and thou shalt have treasure in heaven,* and *follow* the Lord *if thou wilt be perfect,* in the company of those among whom *He speaketh wisdom*—He who knows what to distribute *to the day* and what *to the night,* so that you too may know it, and for you too there may be *lights in the firmament of heaven.* But they cannot be unless your *heart* is there; and your *heart* will not be there unless your *treasure* is there also, as you have heard from the *good master.* But that barren earth *was grieved,* and *the thorns choked the word.*

But you, *chosen generation,* you *weak things of the world,* who have *forsaken all* to follow the Lord, go after Him, beautiful feet, *shine in the firmament,* that *the heavens* may *declare His glory,* as you *divide between the light* of the perfect (though not yet as perfect as the angels) and *the darkness* of the little ones (who are still not without hope). Shine over all the earth, and let *the day,* all bright with *the sun, utter unto day* speech *of wisdom,* and *night,* shining with the moon, *show unto night the word of knowledge.* The moon and the stars shine by night, but the night does not obscure them; instead they themselves lighten it so far as it may be. For see, it is as if when God said: *Let there be lights in the firmament of heaven;* there *came suddenly a sound from heaven, as it had been the rushing of a mighty wind, and there appeared cloven tongues like as of fire, and it sat upon each of them.* And there were *made lights in the firmament of heaven,* having the *word of life.* Run, run everywhere, holy fires, fires of

beauty. For you are *the light of the world* and you are
not *put under a bushel*. He to whom you have clung has
been raised up and he has raised you up. Run to and fro
and be known to all nations.

20 LET THE SEA also conceive and bring forth your
works, *let the waters bring forth the creeping
creatures having life*. For you, *separating the precious
from the vile*, are made the mouth of God, by which He
said: *Let the waters bring forth*, not *the living creature*
which the *earth brings forth*, but *the creeping creatures
having life and the fowls that fly above the earth*. For
your sacraments, God, by the ministry of your holy ones
have crept through the midst of the waves of the temptations of this world to hallow the gentiles in your name
by your baptism.

Meanwhile great miracles were done, as it were *great
whales*, and there were the voices of your messengers *flying above the earth, in the open firmament* of your Book,
which was placed above them in authority as something
under which they must fly wherever they went. For
*there is no speech nor language where their voice is not
heard:* since *their sound is gone through all the earth, and
their words to the end of the world*, because you, Lord,
by blessing them have multiplied them.

Can I be speaking untruly or mixing things up or failing
to distinguish between the clear knowledge of these things
in the firmament of heaven and the corporeal works in
the wavy sea and *under the firmament of heaven?* Certainly there are things of which our knowledge is solid and
definite with no increase by generation, as it were lights
of wisdom and knowledge; but these same things have
many different corporeal operations; one thing grows
from another and they are multiplied by your blessing,
God; for you have made allowances for our mortal senses
which soon cloy, and have so arranged matters that in
the understanding of our mind one thing may be represented and expressed in many different ways through
bodily motions. These things the waters have brought
forth, but still in your word; they have been brought

forth by the needs of people estranged from the eternity
of your truth, but still brought forth in your Gospel; for
they were cast out by those very waters whose diseased
bitterness was the cause why they were sent forth in your
word.

All things of your making are beautiful; and, see, you
who made all things are yourself inexpressibly more
beautiful. If Adam had not fallen away from you, there
would never have flowed from his loins the brackishness
of that sea which is the human race, so deeply curious, so
stormily tossing, so restlessly flowing here and there, and
then there would have been no need for the dispensers
of your word to work *in many waters,* declaring in corporeal and sensible forms mysterious doings and sayings.
For this is the sense in which I now take those *creeping
and flying creatures;* people are trained and initiated to
accept the authority of corporeal sacraments, but they
would not get beyond this point unless their souls became
spiritually alive on another level and after the word of
admission looked forward to perfection.

21   So in your word it is not the depth of the sea,
      but the earth separated from the bitterness of the
waters which brings forth, not *the creeping creatures having life,* but *the living soul.* And this soul no longer has
need of baptism, as the heathen do and as it did itself when
it was covered with the waters (for there is no other *entrance into the kingdom of heaven,* since you appointed
this as the entrance); nor does it seek after wonders and
miracles to create faith; it is not of the kind which *unless it
sees signs and wonders, it will not believe;* for now the
faithful earth is separated from the waters that were bitter
with infidelity and *tongues are for a sign, not to them that
believe, but to them that believe not.* Nor does the earth
which *Thou hast founded upon the waters* have any need
of that *flying kind* which *the waters brought forth* at your
word. Send your word into the earth by your messengers.
For we speak of their labors, but it is you who are working in them so that they may work out a *living soul* in it.
The earth brings it forth, because the earth is the cause

334 THE CONFESSIONS OF ST. AUGUSTINE

that they work this in the soul, just as the sea was the cause that they worked upon the *creeping things having life* and the *fowls that fly under the firmament of heaven.* These the earth does not need, though it feeds upon that Fish which was taken out of the deep, upon that *table* which *Thou hast prepared in the presence* of those who believe. For He was taken from the deep so that He might feed the dry land, and the *fowl,* though bred in the sea, is nevertheless *multiplied upon the earth.* For it was man's infidelity which was the cause of the first preaching of the Evangelists, but the faithful too are exhorted and blessed by them every day in all sorts of ways. But *the living soul* takes its beginning from the earth, because only the faithful find profit in restraining themselves from the love of this world, so that their soul may live for you, a soul which was *dead while it lived in pleasures,* death-dealing pleasures, Lord; for you are the life-giving pleasure of the pure heart.

Now then let your ministers do their work on *the earth,* not as they did in the waters of infidelity by means of preaching and speaking with miracles and sacraments and mystic words—things which, through fear of such mysterious signs, attract the attention of ignorance, which is the mother of wonder. All this is a means of entrance to the faith for those sons of Adam who have forgotten you and, while *they hide themselves from Thy face,* have become a *dark deep.* But let your ministers now do their work as on the *dry land* which is separated from the whirlpools of the deep; let them be a pattern to the faithful by living among them and stirring them up to imitation. For in this way men hear not so as just to hear, but so as to do. *Seek the Lord, and your soul shall live,* so that the *earth* may *bring forth the living soul. Be not conformed to the world.* Restrain yourselves from it. The soul's life is in avoiding those things which are death to seek. Restrain yourselves from the monstrous savagery of pride, the sluggish voluptuousness of luxury, and the *false name of knowledge,* so that the wild beasts may be tamed, the cattle brought under the yoke, and the snakes made harmless. For these are an allegory for the movements of the mind. The arrogance of pride, the pleasure of lust, and the poison of curiosity are movements of a soul that is dead—not dead in the sense that it is motionless, but dead by *forsaking the fountain of life* and so engrossed in this transitory world and *conformed to it.*

But the Word, O God, is the fountain of life eternal and it does not pass away. Therefore, in your word that departure of the soul is checked, when it is said to us *Be not conformed unto this world;* so that *the earth* may in *the fountain of life bring forth a living soul*—in your word (delivered by the Evangelists) a soul that has become continent by imitating those who imitate your Christ. For this is what is meant by *after his kind,* since a man imitates the one who is his friend. *Be ye,* he says, *as I am, for I also am as ye are.*

So in *the living soul* there shall be *good beasts,* tamed in their behavior. For you have commanded, *Go on with thy business in meekness, so thou shalt be beloved by all men.* The cattle shall be good, for *neither if they eat, shall they overabound, nor, if they eat not, have any lack.* And the snakes shall be good, not dangerous and harmful but wise and full of caution, only searching into this temporal nature so far as is enough that *eternity may be clearly seen, being understood by the things that are made.* For these animals obey reason when they are checked from their death-bringing courses and live and become good.

22 For, see, Lord, our God, our Creator, when our affections, in which we were dying by evil living, have been restrained from the *love of the world* and we have begun to be by good living a *living soul,* and the word has been fulfilled which you spoke by your apostle, *Be not conformed to this world,* then there will follow next what you added directly afterward. *But be ye transformed by the renewing of your mind.* And now this does not mean *after your kind,* as in the cases of imitating one's neighbor who went before one or of following the example in life of some better man. For you did not say: "Let man be made *after his kind.*" What you said was: *Let us make man after our own image and similitude,* that we *might prove what* Thy *will is.* And, therefore, that

great dispenser of your word who *begat* children *by the gospel*, not wanting to have them always as *babes* whom he must *feed with milk* and *cherish as a nurse* said: *Be ye transformed by the renewing of your mind, that ye may prove what is that good and acceptable and perfect will of God*. And so instead of saying: "Let man be made" you say: *Let us make man*. And instead of saying: "according to his kind" you say: *after our image and likeness*. For where man is *renewed in his mind* and sees and understands your truth he is in no need of another man to direct him in the sense of following *after his kind;* instead, with you to direct him, *he proveth what is that good, that acceptable and perfect will of Thine*, and, now that he has the capacity for it, you teach him to see the Trinity of the Unity and the Unity of the Trinity. So to the phrase in the plural, *Let us make man*, there is added in the singular *And God made man*, and after the phrase in the plural *After our likeness* there is added in the singular *After the image of God*. So man is *renewed in the knowledge of God, after the image of Him that created him*, and, having become spiritual, *he judgeth all things* (all things that are to be judged) yet *himself is judged of no man.*

23 By "*he judgeth all things*" is meant that he has dominion *over the fish of the sea, and over the fowls of the air*, and *over all cattle* and wild *beasts, and over all the earth, and over every creeping thing that creepeth upon the earth*. This he does by the understanding of his mind by which he *perceiveth the things of the Spirit of God*, whereas otherwise *man, being placed in honor, had no understanding, and is compared unto the brute beasts, and is become like unto them*. Therefore, our God, in your Church, according to your grace which you have given it (*for we are Thy workmanship created unto good works*), not only those who are in spiritual authority but also those who are spiritually subordinate judge spiritually; for in this way *you made male and female* in your spiritual grace, where according to bodily sex *there is neither male nor female* just as there is *neither Jew nor Greek, neither bond nor free*. So spiritual peo-

ple, whether those in authority or those who are subjected to that authority, judge spiritually. They do not
indeed judge of that spiritual knowledge *which shines in
the firmament* (for they ought not to make judgment on
such sublime authority at that); nor do they judge of your
Book, even if certain passages are obscure, because we
submit our intellects to that book and we regard it as
certain that even what is closed to our gaze is still rightly
and truly said. For so man, though he is now *spiritual and
renewed in the knowledge of God after His image that
created him* ought to be a *doer of the law*, not *a judge*.
Nor does he take it upon himself to judge which men are
spiritual and which carnal; these, our God, are known to
your eyes and have not yet shown themselves to us by
their works, so that *by their fruits we might know them;*
but you, Lord, know them already, and you have *divided*
and *called* them in secret even before the firmament was
made. Nor, even though spiritual, does he judge of the
unquiet and restless people of this world, *for what hath
he to do, to judge them that are without*, when he does
not know which of them will come into the sweetness
of your grace and which will remain in the perpetual bitterness of ungodliness?

So man, whom you have made after your own image,
did not receive *dominion* over *the lights of heaven*, nor
over the secret heaven itself, nor over *the day and the
night* which you called into being before the foundation
of the heaven, nor over *the gathering together of the
waters*, which is *the sea*. He received *dominion over the
fishes of the sea, and the fowls of the air, and over all
cattle, and over all the earth, and over all creeping things
which creep upon the earth*. For he judges, approving
what he finds good and condemning what he finds evil,
and he exercises this judgment whether in the celebration
of those Sacraments by which are initiated those whom
your mercy searches out *in many waters;* or in that ceremony symbolized by the "Fish" which is taken out of the
deep and which the good "earth" feeds upon; or in dealing with the significations and expression of words (which
are under the authority of your book, as it were flying
beneath the firmament) in interpreting, exposition, teach-

ing, discussion, in praising you and in praying to you—signs proceeding from the mouth and sounding out aloud so that the people may answer: Amen. And the reason why these words have to be pronounced physically with the voice is *the deep* of this world and the blindness of the flesh because of which it is not possible to see thoughts, so that they have to be uttered audibly in our ears. So, although the *flying fowls are multiplied upon the earth*, their origin is nevertheless in the waters.

The spiritual man also judges by approving what he finds good and condemning what he finds bad in the actions and way of life of the faithful, in their almsgiving (which is like *the earth bringing forth fruit*), and he judges of the *living soul*, *living* by the taming of the affections, in chastity, in fastings, in holy meditations; also of those things which are perceived by the bodily senses. On all these things he is now said *to judge*, and in these things too he has the power to correct.

24   BUT HERE IS another mystery. What can it mean? See, Lord, you bless men so that they may *increase and multiply and replenish the earth*. Surely you are hinting here that there is something for us to understand, that we must ask ourselves why it was that you did not in the same way bless the light, which *thou calledst day*, nor *the firmament of heaven*, nor *the lights*, nor *the stars*, nor *the earth*, nor *the sea*. I would say, O God who created us after your image, I would say that you had wished to bestow this blessing peculiarly on men, if it were not for the fact that you had not in the same way blessed the fishes, and the whales, that they *should increase and multiply and replenish the waters of the sea*, and also that *the fowls should be multiplied upon the earth*. Again I would say that this blessing belonged properly to those creatures who are bred of their own kind, if it were not for the fact that I find the same blessing given to trees and plants and beasts of the earth. But now neither to the plants, nor the trees, nor the beasts, nor the snakes is it said *Increase and multiply*;

although all these, as well as fish, birds, and men, increase and continue their kind by generation.

What am I to say then, truth, my light? That there is nothing here of importance? That the words are meaningless? Certainly not, Father of piety. Certainly a servant of your word must not say this. And if I do not understand what you mean by that phrase, then I hope that better people, that is, more intelligent people than I, will make a better use of it, according as you have given to each man his measure of understanding. And I hope that my confession will be pleasing in your sight when, Lord, I confess that I believe you did not speak thus for no good reason, and I shall say what is suggested to me by the reading of this phrase. For what I think it means is true, nor do I see what should stop me from understanding in this way the figurative expressions in your books. For I know that what is understood by the mind in a single way can be represented corporeally in a number of ways, and also that what is understood by the mind in a number of ways may have only one corporeal expression. Consider, for instance, the single idea of the love of God and of our neighbor. This is corporeally expressed in numbers of sacraments, in innumerable languages and, in each language, by countless varieties of speech. So do the offspring of *the waters increase and multiply*. And now I invite my readers to consider something which Scripture expresses and which the voice utters in only one way: *In the beginning God made heaven and earth*. Cannot this be understood in a number of ways, and not erroneously, but in different senses, each of which is true? So do the offspring of man *increase and multiply*.

So, if we think of the natures of things in their proper sense and not allegorically, the phrase *Increase and multiply* applies correctly to all things born of seed. But if we regard the words as having been set down figuratively (which is what I think Scripture meant here, since it would not without some good reason ascribe this benediction only to the offspring of aquatic creatures and of men), then we shall find "multitudes" in creatures both spiritual and corporeal (as in *heaven* and *earth*); in souls both righteous and unrighteous (as in *light* and *dark-*

ness); in the sacred writers who have been ministers of the law to us (as in *the firmament* which is established *between the waters and the waters*); in the society of peoples still in the bitterness of infidelity (as in *the sea*); in the zeal of holy souls (as in *the dry land*); in the works of mercy done in this life (as in *the herbs bearing seed and the trees bearing fruit*); in the *spiritual gifts set forth for edification* (as in the *lights of heaven*), and in the affections which have been reformed to temperance (as in the *living soul*). In all these cases we find "multitudes," "abundances," "increases." But only in signs corporeally pronounced and in things intellectually conceived do we find that kind of growth and increase where one idea can be expressed in a number of different ways and where one mode of expression can be understood in a number of different ways.

I take it that what is represented by the generation of aquatic creatures is the corporeally pronounced signs, which are necessary because of our deep immersion in the flesh, and what is represented by the generation of man is the things intellectually conceived, because of the fertility of reason.

And for this reason we believe, Lord, that you said to these two kinds *Increase and multiply*. For I take it that in this blessing you have granted us the faculty and the power both to express in many ways what we have grasped intellectually in only one way, and to understand in many ways what we find obscurely expressed in only one way. So *the waters of the sea* are *replenished*, waters whose movement indicates the variety of different significations, and so too *the earth* is *replenished* with human increase, and its *dryness* appears in its eagerness, and it is ruled by reason.

25 LORD, MY GOD, I wish also to say what the next phrase of your Scripture puts into my mind. I shall speak without fear; for, with you inspiring me, I shall speak the truth which from these words you have willed me to say. For by no other inspiration except yours do I believe that I speak truth, since you are *the Truth, and*

every man a liar. Therefore *he that speaketh a lie, speaketh of his own.* So in order that I may speak truth, I must speak not "of my own" but "of yours."

See now, you have given us *for food every herb bearing seed that is upon all the earth, and every tree, in which is the fruit of a tree yielding seed.* And this not only to us, but also *to all the fowls of the air, and to the beasts of the earth, and to all creeping things.* But you did not give these things to *the fishes* and to *the great whales.*

Now we have said that these *fruits of the earth mean,* in an allegorical way, the works of mercy which are produced for the necessities of this life by the *fruitful earth.* Such an "earth" was the devout *Onesiphorus,* unto whose *house Thou gavest mercy,* because he often refreshed your servant Paul, and *was not ashamed of his chain.* The same was done by *the brethren,* and the same sort of fruit was borne by those who *out of Macedonia supplied what was lacking* to him. But how Paul grieves for some "trees" which failed to give him the fruit that was due! He says: *At my first answer no man stood by me, but all men forsook me. May it not be laid to their charge.* For these fruits are due from us to those who, from their understanding of the divine mysteries, minister the spiritual doctrine to us. They are due to them as men; yes, and they are also due to them as to *the living soul,* since they offer themselves to us as patterns for imitation in all kinds of continence. And they are due to them as to *flying creatures,* because of their blessings which are *multiplied upon the earth,* because *their sound went out into all lands.*

26 THOSE WHO FIND JOY in this food are fed by it, and those *whose God is their belly* find no joy in it. And also in those who give these fruits, the fruit is not in what they give, but in the spirit in which it is given. And so in the case of Paul who *served God and not his own belly,* I see clearly whence comes his joy; I see it and I greatly rejoice with him. For he *had received from the Philippians* what they sent to him *by Epaphroditus.* But still I see the reason for his joy. He feeds upon what he

finds his joy in, for, speaking in truth, he says: *I rejoiced greatly in the Lord, that now at the last your care of me hath flourished again, wherein ye were also careful but ye had grown weary.* These Philippians, as we see, after a long period of weariness had become as it were parched and dried up for the bearing of *the fruit* of a good work, and Paul rejoices for them because *they flourished again,* not for himself because they supplied his needs. For he proceeds as follows: *I speak not in respect of want, for I have learned in whatsoever state I am, therewith to be content. I know both how to be abased, and I know how to abound; everywhere and in all things I am instructed both to be full, and to be hungry; both to abound and to suffer need—I can do all things through Him which strengtheneth me.*

In what then do you rejoice, great Paul? In what do you rejoice? On what do you feed, you *man renewed in the knowledge* of God; *after the image of Him that created Thee,* you *living soul* of such continence, tongue like *the flying fowls,* speaking mysteries? (For to such creatures is this food due.) On what do you feed? Joy. Hear what follows: *notwithstanding, ye have well done, that ye did communicate with my affliction.* It is in this that he rejoices and it is upon this that he feeds—that they had acted well, not that his own wants had been relieved. He says to you: *Thou hast enlarged me when I was in distress;* for he knows how *to abound and to suffer want in Thee Who strengthenest him.* He goes on to say: *For ye Philippians also know that in the beginning of the Gospel, when I departed from Macedonia, no Church communicated with me as concerning giving and receiving, but ye only. For even in Thessalonica ye sent once and again unto my necessity.* He now rejoices because they have returned to these good works, and he is glad that they have flourished again, as when a field becomes fertile once more.

Was he thinking of his own necessities when he said: *Ye sent unto my necessities?* Was that the reason for his joy? Certainly not. But how do we know? Because he says immediately afterward: *not because I desire a gift, but I desire fruit.* I have learned from you, my God, to distinguish between a *gift* and *fruit*. A *gift* is the actual thing that is given to meet these necessities of ours, such as money, food, drink, clothes, shelter, help; but the *fruit* is the good and right will of the giver. For the good Master did not say only: *He that receiveth a prophet;* he added: *in the name of a prophet.* He did not say only: *He that receiveth a righteous man;* he added: *in the name of a righteous man.* And indeed the one shall *receive the reward of a prophet* and the other *the reward of a righteous man.* Nor did he say only: *He that shall give to drink a cup of cold water to one of my little ones;* he added: *in the name of a disciple,* and went on to add: *Verily I say unto you, he shall not lose his reward.*

The *gift* is to receive a prophet, to receive a righteous man, to give a cup of cold water to a disciple; but the *fruit* is to do this in the name of a prophet, in the name of a righteous man, in the name of a disciple. It was with *fruit* that Elijah was fed by the widow who knew that she was giving food to one who was a man of God and gave him food just for that reason; but he was fed by the raven with a *gift*, and it was not the inner man of Elijah that was fed by the raven, but the outer man, which might have died for lack of that food.

27 So, LORD, I will say what is true in your sight. We suppose that what is meant by the *fishes* and *whales* are the ignorant and the infidels who have to be won over and initiated by sacraments of initiation and the wonders of miracles. And when these men give bodily refreshment to your children or help them in any way that is useful to this present life, they do not know why they ought to do as they are doing nor what is the real direction of their actions. Thus neither do they really feed these children of yours, nor are your children really fed by them, because they are not acting out of a holy and right will and your children do not rejoice in their *gifts,* since they do not yet see the *fruit.* For it is certain that the soul feeds on that in which it finds joy. And that is why the *fishes* and *whales* are not fed on that food which is only brought forth by the earth after it was

separated and divided from the bitterness of the waves of the sea.

28   AND *Thou, O God, sawest everything that Thou hadst made, and, behold it was very good.* We also see these things and indeed they are very good. With regard to each particular order of things, after you had said "Let them be made," you saw each of them in turn *that it was good.* I have counted that there are seven times when it is written: *Thou sawest that that which Thou madest was good,* and then, the eighth time, we find: *Thou sawest everything that Thou hadst made* and, behold, it was not only *good,* but *very good,* being now considered altogether. For taken individually they were only good, but taken all together as a whole, they are both good and very good. The same truth is expressed by all beautiful bodies. A body made up itself of members which are all beautiful is very much more beautiful than the individual members out of whose well-ordered harmony the whole is made up, even though all those members taken separately are beautiful.

29   AND I LOOKED closely to see whether it was seven or eight times that you saw that your works were good when they pleased you. And in your seeing I found no time by means of which I could understand what was meant by "how often" you saw what you had made. And I said: "Lord, is not this Scripture of yours true, for you are true and you who are Truth have spoken it? Why then do you tell me that in your seeing there is no time, yet your Scripture tells me that with regard to what you made each day, *Thou sawest that it was good,* and when I counted I found how often?" In answer to this you say to me, for you are my God and you speak out loud into the inner ear of your servant, breaking through my deafness and crying out: "O man, what my Scripture says, I say. But my Scripture speaks in terms of time, and time does not affect my Word, because my Word stands together with me in an equal eternity. So the things which

you see by my spirit, I see; just as the things which you say by my spirit, I say. And thus, although you see these things in time, I do not see them in time; just as, although you speak in terms of time, I do not speak in terms of time."

30 AND I HEARD YOU, Lord my God, and I sucked a drop of sweetness from your truth and I understood. Because there are some people who find your works displeasing and who say that you made many of them under the compulsion of necessity—the fabric of the heavens, for instance, and the harmonious order of the stars. They say that you did not make them out of what was yours, but that they were created elsewhere and from some other source, and that you merely brought them together and fixed them and set them in place, and that you did this at the time when you had conquered your enemies and built up the ramparts of the world so that these enemies might be held down by that fortification and never rebel against you again. And they say that other things were neither made by you nor even put together by you—for example, all flesh, and very small living creatures and all things which are rooted in the earth—and that these things were brought into existence and given form in the lowest levels of the world by a mind hostile to you, a nature different from you, not created by you and contrary to you. Those who hold these views are mad; they do not see your works by your spirit, nor do they recognize you in them.

31 BUT WHEN WE SEE these things by your spirit, it is you who see in us. Therefore, when we see that they are good, you see that they are good, and when things please us for your sake, it is you in them who please us, and when things please us by your spirit, they please you in us. *For what man knoweth the things of a man, save the spirit of a man, which is in him? Even so the things of God knoweth no one but the Spirit of God. Now we (he says) have received not the spirit of this*

*world, but the Spirit which is of God, that we might
know the things that are freely given to us of God.*

And here I am moved to say: "Certainly *the things of
God knoweth no one but the Spirit of God:* how then
do we also *know the things that are given us of God?*"
And the answer is given to me: "Because in the case of
those things which we know by His Spirit, even so *no
one knoweth them but the Spirit of God.* For just as it
was rightly said to those who were to speak by the Spirit
of God *it is not ye that speak,* so it is rightly said to those
that know through the Spirit of God: "It is not you who
know." And it is just as right to say to those who see in
the Spirit of God: "It is not you who see." Therefore,
whatever a man sees in the Spirit of God as good, it is
not he but God who *sees that it is good.*

It is one thing to think that what is good is bad, like
the men mentioned above, and it is another thing for a
man to see that what is good is good in the way of those
who are pleased by your creation because it is good, but
who still do not find their pleasure in your presence in
your creation, so that they prefer to enjoy the creation
itself rather than you. And it is another thing again when
a man sees that something is good, but it is God in him
who sees this, so that God should be loved in the thing
made by Him. And God could not be loved in this way
except through the Spirit which He has given. *Because
the love of God is shed abroad in our hearts by the Holy
Ghost, which is given unto us;* by whom we see that
whatever in any degree is, is good; for it is from Him
who is not in degree, but Is what He Is.

32   I THANK YOU, LORD! We see *heaven and earth*—
whether it be the upper and lower parts of the
corporeal world or the spiritual and corporeal creation—
and for the adorning of these two—whether they constitute the whole mass of the world or the whole total of
creation—we see *light* made and *divided from the darkness.* We see *the firmament of heaven,* by which may be
meant either that primary body of the world between the
upper, or spiritual, waters and the lower, or corporeal,

waters, or else (since this is also called heaven) the space of air through which the birds of heaven go wandering, *betwixt those waters* which rise above them in vapors to fall again in clear nights as dew, and those heavier *waters* which flow upon the earth. We see the face of the *waters gathered together* in the fields of *the sea;* and *the dry land,* both void, and formed so as to be visible and set in shape, the mother of plants and trees. We see the *lights* shining from above, *the sun* sufficient for *the day, the moon and the stars* to cheer *the night,* and time marked and signified by all of these. We see on all sides of us a moist element teeming with fishes, animals, and birds; because by the evaporation of the water the air acquires the density which supports birds in flight. We see the face of the earth decked out with land animals, and *man, created after Thy image and likeness* with dominion over all irrational creatures simply because of that *image and likeness,* that is, because of the power of reason and understanding. And just as in man's soul there is one part which rules by taking thought and another part which is subject to obedience, so for man, also corporeally, a woman was created to have a nature equal indeed to his in mind and rational intelligence, but to be in sex subjected to the masculine sex, in the same way as the appetite which leads to action is subjected to the skill, mentally derived, of acting rightly. We see these things, and they are individually *good* and all together *very good.*

33 LET YOUR WORKS praise you that we may love you, and let us love you that your works may praise you. For they have a beginning and an end in time, a rising and a setting, growth and decay, form and privation. So they have their succession of morning and evening, in part secretly, in part evident. For they were made of nothing, by you, not of you; not of some matter not made by you or previously in existence, but from matter which was concreated, that is created by you simultaneously with the things made of it, because without any interval of time you gave form to its state that was *without form.* For the matter of heaven and earth is a different

thing from the form of heaven and earth, and while you
made the matter out of absolutely nothing, you made the
form of the world out of the formless matter; but, nevertheless, you made them both simultaneously so that form
should follow matter with no intervening space of time.

34 WE HAVE ALSO CONSIDERED what you wished to be
allegorically intimated by the particular order in
which you made these things or had their creation described. And we have seen that things are individually
good and all together *very good*, in your Word, in your
Only-begotten, both *heaven and earth*, the head and body
of the Church, in predestination before all times, without
morning and evening. Then you began to work out in
time what you had predestined, so that you might reveal
what was hidden and bring order into our disorder; for
our sins were over us and we had gone away from you,
into the *dark deep*, and your good *Spirit was borne* above
us to help us *in due season*. And you *justified the ungodly*
and *divided* them from the wicked, and you established
the authority of your Book between those *above* who
were to be docile to you, and those *under*, who were to
be subject to them. And you *gathered together* the society of the unbelievers *into one* membership, so that the
zeal of the faithful might appear, and they might *bring
forth* for you works of mercy, distributing even to the
poor their earthly riches so that they might obtain heavenly riches.

And after this you kindled *lights in the firmament*, your
saints holding the word of life and shining in sublime
authority raised up by spiritual gifts. And then for the
initiation of unbelievers, and as a blessing also to believers, you brought out of corporeal matter the sacraments and visible miracles and the sounds of words according to the firmament of your book. Next you formed
the *living soul* of the faithful through affections set in
order by the strong force of continence. And then you
took the mind, subjected to you only and needing to imitate no human authority, and you renewed it after your
image and likeness, and you subjected rational action to

the excellency of the intellect, as the woman to the man, and to all offices of your ministry necessary for the perfection of the faithful in this life you willed that these same faithful should bestow gifts for the temporal uses of your ministers, gifts which would bear fruit in the future for the givers.

All these things we see and they are *very good*, because you see them in us—you who have given us the Spirit by which to see them and in them to love you.

35   Lord God, give us peace—for you have granted us all things—the peace of quiet, the peace of the Sabbath which has no evening. For indeed this most beautiful order of things that are *very good* will finish its course and pass away, since in it there *was morning and evening*.

36   But the seventh day is without evening. The sun does not set on it, because you sanctified it to last forever. For after all your works which were *very good, you rested on the seventh day*, although you made all these works in an unbroken rest. So may the voice of your book tell us in advance that we too, after our works (which are *very good* only for the reason that you have given them to us), may rest in you in the Sabbath of eternal life.

37   Then too you will rest in us just as now you work in us, and so that rest will be your rest in us just as now these works are your works in us. But you, Lord, are always at work and always at rest. You do not see in time nor move in time nor rest in time. Yet you make the things which we see in time, and time itself and the rest which comes from time.

38   We see the things you have made, because they are, and they are, because you see them. Outwardly we see that they are; inwardly we see that they are

good. But you saw them made when you saw that they were to be made. And we at a later time, after our heart had conceived by your Spirit, were moved to do well; but previously we were moved to do evil, forsaking you. But you, the one, the good God, have never ceased to do well. And we too have some *good works*, of your gift, but not eternal; *after them* we hope for *rest* in your great *hallowing*. But you, the Good which is in need of no other good, are always at rest, because you are your own rest.

How can one man teach another man to understand this? What angel will teach an angel? What angel will teach a man? This must be *asked* of you, *sought* in you, *knocked* for at you. So, so shall it be *received*, so shall it be *found*, so shall it be *opened*. Amen.

Recommended Readings

Bourke, V. J. *Augustine's Quest of Wisdom*. Milwaukee: Bruce Publishing Company, 1945.

Courcelle, P. *Recherches sur les Confessions de saint Augustin*. Paris: De Boccard, 1950.

Flood, J. M. *The Mind and Heart of Augustine*. Fresno, California: Academy Guild Press, 1960.

Foran, E. A. *The Augustinians*. London: Burns, Oates & Washbourne, Ltd., 1938. (Contains Possidius' *Biography* in English.)

Gilson, E. H. Tr. by L. E. M. Lynch. *The Christian Philosophy of St. Augustine*. New York: Random House, Inc., 1960.

Le Blond, J. M. *Les Conversions de saint Augustin*. Paris: Aubier, 1950.

Marrou, H. I. *St. Augustine and His Influence Through the Ages*. Tr. by Patrick Heburne-Scott; texts by Edmund Hill. New York: Harper & Brothers, 1957; London: Longmans, Green & Co., Ltd., 1957.

O'Meara, J. J. *The Young Augustine: The Growth of St. Augustine's Mind up to His Conversion*. London: Longmans, Green & Co., Ltd., 1954.

Pope, H. *St. Augustine of Hippo*. Westminster, Maryland: Newman Press, 1949; London: Sands & Company, Ltd., 1937.

Portalié, E. Tr. by Ralph J. Bastian. *A Guide to the Thought of Saint Augustine*. Chicago: Henry Regnery Co., 1960; London: Burns, Oates & Washbourne, Ltd., 1960.

Saint Augustine. Essays by D'Arcy, Blondel, Dawson, Gilson, Maritain, Martindale, Przywara, Reeves, Roland-Gosselin, and Watkin. New York: Meridian Books, Inc., 1957.

Van Der Meer, F. *Augustine the Bishop: The Life and Work of a Father of the Church*. Tr. by Brian Battershaw and G. R. Lamb. New York and London: Sheed & Ward, Inc., 1962.

The MENTOR Philosophers

A distinguished series of six volumes presenting in historical order the basic warnings of the outstanding philosophers of the Western world—from the Middle Ages to the present time.

☐ **THE AGE OF BELIEF: THE MEDIEVAL PHILOSOPHERS** edited by Anne Fremantle. Basic writings of St. Augustine, Boethius, Abelard, St. Bernard, St. Thomas Aquinas, Duns Scotus, William of Ockham and others.
(#MW1258—$1.50)

☐ **THE AGE OF ADVENTURE: THE RENAISSANCE PHILOSOPHERS edited by Giorgio de Santillana.** Da Vinci, More, Machiavelli, Michelangelo, Erasmus, Copernicus, Montaigne, Kepler, Galileo, Bruno. (#ME1342—$1.75)

☐ **THE AGE OF REASON: THE 17TH CENTURY PHILOSOPHERS edited by Stuart Hampshire.** Bacon, Pascal, Hobbes, Galileo, Descartes, Spinoza, Leibniz.
(#MW1428—$1.50)

☐ **THE AGE OF ENLIGHTENMENT: THE 18TH CENTURY PHILOSOPHERS edited by Isaiah Berlin.** Locke, Berkeley, Voltaire, Hume, Reid, Condillac, Hamann.
(#MY1213—$1.25)

☐ **THE AGE OF IDEOLOGY: THE 19TH CENTURY PHILOSOPHERS edited by Henry D. Aiken.** Kant, Fichte, Hegel, Schopenhauer, Comte, Mill, Spencer, Marx, Nietzsche, Kierkegaard. (#MY1019—$1.25)

☐ **THE AGE OF ANALYSIS: 20TH CENTURY PHILOSOPHERS edited by Morton White.** Peirce, Whitehead, James, Dewey, Bertrand Russell, Wittgenstein, Croce, Bergson, Sartre, Santayana and others.
(#MW1179—$1.50)